FIGHTING SPRAWL AND CITY HALL

FIGHTING SPRAWL

The University of Arizona Press

Tucson

AND CITY HALL

Resistance
to Urban Growth
in the Southwest

MICHAEL F. LOGAN

The University of Arizona Press
© 1995 by the Arizona Board of Regents
All rights reserved.

⊗ This book is printed on acid-free, archival-quality paper.
Manufactured in the United States of America

00   99   98   97   96   95   6   5   4   3   2   1

Library of Congress Cataloging-in-Publication Data
Logan, Michael F., 1950–
    Fighting sprawl and City Hall : resistance to urban growth
in the Southwest / Michael F. Logan.
       p.   cm.
    Includes bibliographical references and index.
    ISBN 0-8165-1512-3 (acid-free paper).
    —ISBN 0-8165-1553-0 (pbk. acid-free paper)
    1. Cities and towns—Growth.   2. Opposition (Political
science)   3. Tucson (Ariz.)—Politics and government.
4. Albuquerque (N.M.)—Politics and government.   I. Title
HT371.L64   1995
307.1′716′09791778—dc20   95-5590
                               CIP

British Cataloguing-in-Publication Data
A catalogue record for this book is available from the British
Library.

To Virgie Walker Logan, 1923–1993

CONTENTS

ILLUSTRATIONS

FIGURES

TABLES

ACKNOWLEDGMENTS

I am very cognizant of the debt I owe to those who have helped shape this book. Dr. Juan R. Garcia has been my kind and helpful guide throughout graduate school. The fact that I have come this far academically is due in no small regard to his interest and assistance. I am also especially grateful to Dr. Katherine Morrissey and Dr. Oscar Martinez for their critiques and guidance. Revisions suggested by them have improved this book immeasurably. My deep appreciation also goes to Joanne O'Hare and Alexis Noebels for their suggestions and corrections. Thank you for the literary glue and polish. If errors remain in fact or form, it is through no one's fault but my own.

I also wish to thank my family and friends—you know who you are—for the unconditional understanding that has flowed so generously in my direction over these last several years. I will never be able to repay the countless kindnesses you all have shown me.

FIGHTING SPRAWL AND CITY HALL

INTRODUCTION

■ ■ ■ ■ ■ ■ ■ ■ ■ ■ ■ ■ ■ ■

The Other Half of the Story

On September 6, 1993, *Time* magazine featured the cover story "Boom Time in the Rockies." *Time's* reporters described this latest boom in the West as predicated upon "more jobs and fewer hassles," qualities supposedly endemic to the mountainous West. The fundamental, perhaps inevitable, conundrum associated with growth in western cities appeared in this retelling of the boom story: development degrades the environment and "lifestyle" that instigated the boom in the first place. When people come in droves, they ruin the place.[1]

Time's article appropriately introduces this book because it discusses the West as an urban society closely related to its natural environment. The relationship between western cities and nature has always been self-conscious, a result, no doubt, of the variously daunting and awe-inspiring "nature" of the mountainous West. The mountain views, sunsets, and wide-open spaces are real and can cause residents as well as tourists to gawk and coo in wonderment, but water shortages and perspiration are also qualities of the "real" environment. Although the meanings and valuations given to these natural surroundings have shifted over time, the region's depiction by residents, visitors, boosters, environmentalists, and the media has remained generally naturalistic, which contributes to a misleading myth. The West is, to some degree, defined by its cities, but in the public consciousness, the region appears as much pastoral and natural as urban. What then constitutes "the West"?

Historians periodically offer regional definitions, but debate continues on the precise formulation of "the West." Frederick Jackson Turner described the region in terms of the process of settlement on the frontier. This process definition had the advantage of freeing western history from rigid constraints of time and place but added little to the definition of an identifiable western region. Turner's West migrated along with the frontier, until the frontier "closed" in the 1890s. And yet the West persisted as a recognizable region. Even the frontier persisted, mostly in a cultural context, as a viable model for describing the process of development.[2]

Walter Prescott Webb formulated a geographic and environmental definition of the region. In *The Great Plains*, Webb described the West as the arid region beyond the ninety-eighth meridian. Donald Worster characterized the region in similar terms, focusing on the scarcity of water. Criticism of this geographic and environmental definition comes mostly from within the region. Fractious subregions, moist and green, clamor for equal attention.[3]

Historians have also defined the West as a cultural phenomenon explained in part by shared experiences. Native American and Hispanic traditions, legacies of ranching and mining, federal tutelage—all have added to the self-conscious perceptions that define western culture. Of course, these perceptions may spring from experiences more mythological than historical, but any cultural definition of the region must accommodate these perceptions as real enough today. Westerners think of themselves as unique because of their culture, defined, for instance, by an individualism bred from a closeness to nature; Barry Goldwater believed this to be true and historically factual, and he shaped his political ideology accordingly.[4]

My depiction of the urban Southwest draws on all of these definitions of the broader region. "Urban" refers to an ongoing process of western urbanization, including waves of migration such as Turner might have recognized. Geographically, the Southwest is the southwest corner of the continental United States, including Arizona, New Mexico, and portions of Colorado, Texas, California, Nevada, and Utah.[5] Topographically and environmentally, "the Southwest" refers to the visually startling and somewhat arid basin and range country of Arizona and New Mexico. Cul-

TABLE 1 Population by Decade of Albuquerque and Tucson

	Albuquerque	Tucson
1900	6,238	7,531
1910	11,020	13,193
1920	15,157	20,292
1930	26,570	32,506
1940	35,449	35,752
1950	96,815	45,454
1960	201,189	212,892
1970	243,751	262,433

SOURCE: Census of the Population, 1960[a]

[a] Census statistics often mislead. Tucson's population was accurately counted (within the inherent inaccuracies of census surveys) until suburbanization in the 1940s and 1950s caused about 70,000 fringe residents to be left out. Conversely, Albuquerque's population was consistently undercounted until the 1940s, when Old Town and other satellite communities were brought into the city limits through annexation. Prior to the 1940s, "Greater Albuquerque" contained more residents than the census counted. For example, the *Albuquerque Journal* counted the population of "Greater Albuquerque" as 54,268 in 1930 (numbers derived from city directories) when the census counted the population as 26,570 ("A Market Study of New Mexico").

turally, the process of urbanization in the Southwest following World War II was shaped by the natural environment and the self-conscious perceptions of environment and culture held by established as well as newly arrived Westerners.

The urbanization of Tucson, Arizona, and Albuquerque, New Mexico, proceeded along remarkably similar paths. Of course, each city possessed certain unique characteristics that shaped their development, but they also fall neatly into a regional identity. Both cities began as agricultural settlements on the banks of flowing rivers in the midst of arid regions that were first the domain of Native Americans, and then of the colonizing Spanish. Anglo presence in both locales increased dramatically with the arrival of the railroad in the 1880s: the Santa Fe in Albuquerque in 1880, the Southern Pacific in Tucson in 1881. Both cities acquired their respective state universities in the late 1880s. Tourism and the health-care industry (including sanatoriums for tuberculosis patients) became central to boosters' development plans in the early 1900s. Federal expenditures fueled local booms in both Albuquerque and Tucson during and following World War II. Kirtland Air Force Base and Sandia Laboratories provided an economic influence in Albuquerque just as Davis Monthan Air Force Base and the Hughes Aircraft Company influenced Tucson's development. Topographically inviting terrain to the east of the original settlements also dictated the direction of early suburbanization.

Western historians of late have taken a decidedly nonmythological view of the development of western cities and their relationship with nature. One of the deflated myths is the boosterish idea of triumph over nature. Rather than declaring western development a victory by stalwart Anglo pioneers over intractable nature, historians now paint their accomplishments as a "legacy of conquest." Westerners, as described by the new western history, never saw a boom they didn't like. To these rapacious city builders, the central problem with development in the West was its cyclical nature, dependent on natural resources that rose and fell in value. Bernard DeVoto, an early deflator of western mythology, described the West as an economic colony, subject to booms that inevitably went bust. The imperial power in this schema was, of course, the East, a view reiterated in western history by Earl Pomeroy. Gerald Nash took the next historiographical step by describing the boom following World War II as reshaping the West's relationship with the rest of the country. The period of colonial dependence ended, and the West became the "pacesetting" region for the nation. The West assumed leadership, for example, in the rising environmental awareness that made growth in western cities so problematic.[6]

The new western history places environmentalism in conflict with the notion of progress. The push by boosters for unlimited urban development in the West equates with their broader faith in progress (which according to new western historians is outmoded in this postmodern age of limited possibilities). Earlier examples of a preservationist environmental critique or resistance to headlong urban expansion were doomed if they appeared amidst the pre–Earth Day consensus in favor of development. Most historians of the urban West ignore this early resistance, but those few who do mention opposition to urbanization prior to the rise of environmentalism describe it as visionary, eccentric, or spiritually John Muir–ish. However, serious resistance to urban growth arose at the beginning of the post–World War II boom and persisted throughout the 1950s and 1960s. Even new western historians truncate their studies of urbanization in the West by assuming that serious opposition to growth only appeared with the rise of environmentalism in the late 1960s.[7] The assumed consensus behind development invades even conscientious efforts by historians to expand the analysis of the West's urbanization.[8]

Historians of Tucson and Albuquerque fit into these general historiographical trends, emphasizing opposition to growth in the 1970s. Although Don Bufkin, C. L. Sonnichsen, Howard Rabinowitz, Robert Turner Wood, Marc Simmons, and V. B. Price have all acknowledged opposition to urban development, they generally classify it as significant only late in the game. Bufkin and Sonnichsen describe the urbanization of Tucson in consensus terms, with development meeting only minor resistance in the late 1950s.[9] Both historians place opposition to urbanization as a footnote to the larger story of incredible expansion.

In Albuquerque's case, Rabinowitz describes resistance in more serious terms as suburban residents resisted both annexations and efforts to consolidate city and county governments. Yet even though Rabinowitz recognizes the multifaceted critique of "growth," his study still focused on amazing census statistics and an evolving concern over the future of the city based on heightened environmental and cultural awareness in the 1960s: "As elsewhere . . . the late 1960s brought an increased awareness of the weaknesses of uncontrolled growth. Calls for limited growth came from environmentally conscious migrants and longtime residents who claimed urban sprawl, pollution, and destruction of old landmarks were undermining the quality of life."[10]

The term "growth" serves Rabinowitz and other scholars as a handy label for the various manifestations of urbanization that gave rise to a cultural critique of a degrading lifestyle and environment: land development on the suburban fringe resulting in a simultaneous increase in population and dispersal into low-density development; increasing government centralization and regulation, both at the city and county level; and expansion and diversification of the economic base of the community.

The image of a gradually developing opposition to urbanization appears clearly in V. B. Price's *A City at the End of the World*. Price defines

Albuquerque's uniqueness in environmental terms, both natural (the river, mesas, and mountains) and cultural (Indian and Spanish/Mexican). Underpinning this environmental perspective was the author's assumption that his analysis was new, reflective of a post–Earth Day sensitivity toward the natural and cultural environment:

> In the early 1960s, Albuquerque's leaders were unconcerned that its unique character was being threatened by uncontrolled growth. By the early 1970s, however, environmentalists, historic preservationists, and others interested in quality-of-life issues had risen to public prominence. Albuquerque found itself embroiled in what would prove to be a more-than-twenty-year struggle to conserve its New Mexican identity while continuing to benefit from the prosperity of its growth.[11]

Price's analysis assumes that the political leadership necessarily reflected the community itself. In fact, Albuquerque's expansion, both of geographic size and governmental reach, encountered vociferous resistance in the 1940s and 1950s. Although Robert Turner Wood referred to this resistance periodically, his analysis of the city's "transformation" required him to ignore the persistence of contentiousness within the community. Wood required a change in community ethos to suit his thesis of an evolving "orientation toward groups, [and] the relaxation of authority on all levels" in the 1970s.[12] Marc Simmons also described an evolving sensitivity to growth issues appearing in the 1970s: "Then slowly but forcefully a new sentiment began to be felt. . . . Albuquerqueans themselves had at last taken a hand, and they pressured the business community and government managers to move in new, more thoughtful directions."[13] Rabinowitz provided the most rigorous analysis of the resistance to Albuquerque's expansion, including early annexation protests, but he also described it as developing significance later rather than sooner. A more accurate rendering of Albuquerque's growth must accommodate persistent and vociferous resistance throughout the urbanization process.

As this study demonstrates, urbanization in Tucson and Albuquerque proceeded in the face of constant opposition, which first arose in conservative and libertarian political critiques and in ethnic resistance to urban renewal plans for barrio areas. Perhaps it is also safe to argue that a loosely defined environmentalism appeared in these early forms of opposition as residents fought to preserve their lifestyle (including political idealism) and their native culture. A preservationism at once conservative and activist describes this resistance.

Although not phrased within an urban context, Richard White placed such conflict at the center of the new western history: "There are many possible relationships between us and the land, and such meanings are contested. Despite multiple use, land cannot be simultaneously range, parking lots, and wilderness; discovering which perceptions and which uses of land prevail, and why, has become much of the subject matter of environmental history and the New Western History." [14]

Explanations of why and how one set of perceptions prevailed in shaping the urban West should also be part of the new western history. Tucson and Albuquerque formed in an environment of contested urbanization during the post–World War II boom. One side prevailed, but not without a fight. The contentiousness created winners and losers, and the side that prevailed in the conflict over urbanization described the contest. Boosters, planners, and politicians generally characterized their opponents as nuisances, and historians often adopted this denigrating view. Although evidence of resistance abounds, it must be culled from a historical record that is largely unsympathetic.

The two parts of this study deal with Tucson and Albuquerque, respectively. Both cities witnessed multifaceted opposition to the urbanization that took place during the post–World War II boom. The introductory section of each part gives a general overview of the origins, topography, and development of each city prior to World War II. Regional similarities appeared at the outset.

Before analyzing the resistance to growth in Tucson and Albuquerque, I describe the booster and governmental efforts in each city to promote development (chapters 1 and 6). The booster-government partnerships in the two cities varied in their degree of effectiveness and cohesiveness.

After mapping the familiar booster terrain, I begin the survey of resistance to urbanization. Chapters 2 and 7 describe the "political" resistance in Tucson and Albuquerque. Annexations and zoning reforms drew concerted opposition from mostly Anglo, middle-class residents in both cities, primarily through standard forms of political protest: referendum elections, petition drives, and complaints lodged at city council meetings.

Chapters 3 and 8 shift the focus to a broadly defined "ethnic" resistance in each city. Hispanic residents opposed efforts to redevelop barrio areas, which federal and local bureaucrats, in their zeal for urban renewal, labeled as "blighted." Before the bulldozers arrived, Tucson and Albuquerque Hispanic residents protested the destruction of their neighborhoods and succeeded in modifying renewal plans to accommodate their concerns.

Chapters 4 and 9 chronicle the increasing environmental awareness that most historians identify as the root of "slow-growth" movements. The environmental critique became explicit late in the process of urbanization, serving eventually as a focal point for otherwise disparate forms of resistance. The preservationist motivation for the opposition to urbanization appeared clearly within the environmental framework. Once the environmental critique made its way into the lexicon of political possibilities, historians began to notice the resistance to urban growth.

The final chapters in each part (chapters 5 and 10) summarize the recent resistance to development. Opposition became more visible in the 1970s and 1980s, but rarely with a recognition of the deep roots of the controversy.

An adequate description of the modern urban West requires a recognition of environmental perceptions explicitly directed toward nature and native cultures. Urban and environmental history intersect in this book. The goal is to achieve a broader understanding of western, and American, urbanization.

PART 1

TUCSON

Tucson's prosperity at the turn of the century depended on the
Southern Pacific Railroad line, the state's agricultural college (now
the University of Arizona) established in 1891, and mining and
ranching interests in southern Arizona.[1] The town's early development was dominated by climactic and topographical factors. The
original town (two square miles incorporated in 1877) remained
on the site of the Spanish presidio near the Santa Cruz River, and
the town stayed generally river-bound for its first thirty years.[2] The
river, flowing year-round until the early 1900s, provided a ready
supply of water and power and some refuge from the blistering
summer heat.[3] The population grew steadily but unremarkably
through the first half of the twentieth century with an average
population increase by decade of 36.5 percent.[4]

Mountains just west and north—and also twenty and thirty
miles distant to the east and south—dictated the direction of expansion. Tucson began expanding generally eastward with its
first small annexation in 1905.[5] Improved transportation added

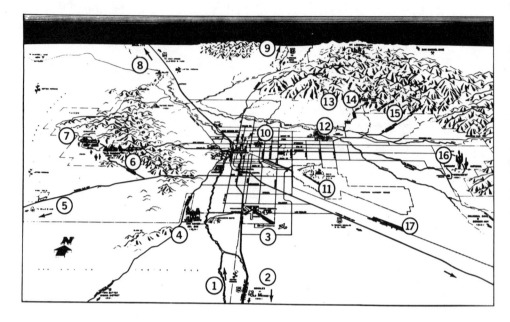

FIG. 1 The Tucson Valley. Originally river bound, Tucson sprawled to the east over inviting desert terrain. This 1965 rendering of the Tucson valley depicts sparse development in the Catalina foothills to the north of the city, and vacant land near the Saguaro National Monument to the east. (Source: "The Pueblo Center Redevelopment Project," University of Arizona Library Special Collections)

1. Santa Cruz River
2. To Mexico, via Nogales
3. Tucson International Airport
4. San Xavier Mission, on the Tohono O'odham Reservation
5. To Ajo
6. Old Tucson movie set and theme park
7. Arizona-Sonora Desert Museum
8. To Phoenix, via Casa Grande
9. To Phoenix, via Florence
10. University of Arizona
11. Davis Monthan Air Force Base
12. Old Fort Lowell Park
13. Flying V Ranch
14. Sabino Canyon
15. Santa Catalina Mountains, via Mount Lemmon Highway
16. Saguaro National Monument
17. Southern Pacific Railroad
18. To El Paso, Texas, via Benson

tourism to Tucson's economic base, and belief in the curative power of Tucson's dry desert air attracted tuberculosis and asthma patients and an allied health industry.[6] The Depression of the 1930s slowed growth, but federal expenditures during World War II expanded it again. With the war, Davis Monthan Air Force Base grew in importance to Tucson's economy. The addition in 1950 of a Hughes Aircraft plant further tied Tucson's prosperity to federal and military/industrial spending.[7] In short, Tucson was well situated for a boom in the post–World War II years.

Tucson residents both supported and opposed the boom. Boosterism occupies familiar historiographical ground (most notably trod by Daniel Boorstin), but the resistance to growth is largely unexplored terrain. Although Boorstin describes the booster as representative of the American character in the developing West,[8] more recent studies see boosters as part of a broader "growth machine," "growth network," or "growth coalition." The advantage of these newer models of pro-growth alliances is that they provide a more thorough and inclusive picture of the traditional booster edifice. For example, Harvey Molotch's model of the "growth machine" includes politicians, planners, developers, neighborhood associations, and individual citizens.[9]

Resistance to urban growth has also come under more recent scrutiny by sociologists, urban geographers, and political scientists, but these studies tend to focus on the post–Great Society proliferation of neighborhood activism.[10] Revisions of the booster paradigm and definitions of neighborhood resistance in the 1970s tend to leave Boorstin's basic polarity in place for the 1940s and 1950s: those in favor of growth versus those opposed to growth, with the opposition marginalized out of the historical record.

As mentioned previously, both Bufkin and Sonnichsen largely neglect the early resistance, or characterize it as eccentric. Such interpretations support Boorstin's characterization of a cooperative community ethos in which conflict is anomalous until some pressure point is reached—in Tucson's case, in the mid- to late 1960s. But resistance to growth accompanied boosterism in Tucson from the outset. The early level of conflict did not match the boisterous battles of the 1960s and 1970s but was certainly sufficient to challenge the "cooperative" or "consensus" view of the 1950s as a period of mute acquiescence to growth.

An alternative definition of a community ethos founded on conflict rather than cooperation corrects the previous oversimplification, but in fact neither model is singularly appropriate for Tucson in the 1950s. The dichotomous representation of residents as either for or against growth misses the nuances and shifting opinions within the community. For although antigrowth partisans targeted Tucson's expanding population, burgeoning city boundaries, and swelling government, only in the most general sense did they oppose "growth." Studying the resistance to urbanization quickly uncovers the ambiguity of the term. For example, the statement "developers at times opposed growth" is a non sequitur only as long as "growth" remains monolithically defined. In fact, developers opposed the expansion of government's regulatory reach in Tucson. Thus the simple dichotomy that pits pro-growth forces against antigrowth forces breaks down almost immediately. The resistance to urbanization was as multifaceted as the process of urbanization itself.

Even if reflecting something less than complete consensus within the community, boosterism nonetheless provides comforting cultural landmarks. Tucson's Chamber of Commerce looms as the most recognizable cultural landmark, and a local variation on the booster theme was "the Sunshine Climate Club." Explicating the resistance to growth will offer a fresh view of the cultural landscape, but placing the resistance within the proper context first requires a description of more-familiar ground.

Although the partnership between business and government in Tucson has been traditionally characterized as promoting growth with single-minded determination, such single-mindedness is evident only in the realm of the fundamental assumption that prosperity, both civic and personal, depended upon continuing urban growth. Beneath this fundamental assumption, fractures appear.

1 THE PRO-GROWTH PARTNERSHIP

"The Optimistic Assumption"

Although Tucson's boosters may have appeared monolithically united behind promotions of growth, organizationally they maintained three separate promotional identities targeting tourists, prospective residents, and businessmen. The effort to attract tourists, for example, sometimes conflicted with the effort to attract corporations.

Stephen Elkin describes the "privatist" urban regime in terms of its close working relationship between business interests and local government to promote growth. Elkin's succeeding model, the "pluralist regime," describes a more complex political milieu including "land-use coalitions" and "functional bureaucracies."[1] During Tucson's apparent "privatist" stage, the working relationship between boosters and the city government appeared monolithic, but even though the city's booster-government partnership sometimes functioned effectively, at other times it functioned haphazardly—or not at all.

As early as 1904, Tucson businessmen were pushing for unbridled growth through the Chamber of Commerce.[2] Unfortunately, turn-of-the-century boosters rarely bothered to define what sort of growth they had in mind. Blissfully self-assured, the boosters grounded their politics in an assumption as fundamental as the earth itself: cities must expand to prosper. To boosters, this was common sense, and anyone arguing against this view was considered eccentric, weird, silly, or demented. The boosters' own economic prosperity provided the bedrock for this assumption, and in a personal sense, businessmen whose prosperity required legions of new residents or hordes of tourists were correct in their analysis. But not all businessmen required thousands of new residents to ensure their own success. Even within the Chamber of Commerce, that icon of traditional boosterism, divisions appeared among businessmen whose prosperity required different approaches to urbanization. At the level of political rhetoric, however, resistance to growth remained marginalized, to say the least. Not unexpectedly, the political hyperbole that labeled antigrowth forces peculiar made its way into the historical record.

The eccentric label came from boosters such as William R. Mathews, editor of the *Arizona Daily Star*.[3] The ideological power exerted by Mathews reflected, in general, the stance of the Tucson Chamber of Commerce, which was founded in 1896 by five "energetic" businessmen and later attracted dozens and eventually thousands of members.[4] The growth-is-good assumption linked individuals of varied interests and pursuits, whether real-estate developers profiting from the expanses of open land, or manufacturers profiting from the supply of inexpensive Hispanic labor.

Politicians, doctors, lawyers, teachers, and retail merchants also shared the assumption. These proponents of growth shared the same sense of optimism and faith in capitalism that had marked Boorstin's nineteenth-century boosters. Sinclair Lewis created the character of Babbitt to represent the more settled but no less acquisitive booster of the twentieth century: the quintessential real-estate man. In fact, the waspish, middle-class Babbitt is a sort of Chamber of Commerce archetype. This updated image of the booster lends itself easily to a simplistic dichotomy: pro-growth versus antigrowth. At times, even contemporary studies of pro-growth coalitions ignore the variations within the "class" of boosters.[5]

From its founding, the chamber sought to exploit Tucson's position as a regional center for mining, ranching, and trading with Mexico. Hispanic businessmen played a key role in this developing commerce, although Anglo businessmen dominated the commercial life of the city. As Thomas Sheridan described in *Los Tucsonenses*, Mexican businessmen enjoyed a relatively benign business environment in Tucson and established enterprises that "transcended ethnic boundaries."[6] Prosperous Hispanic merchants and entrepreneurs belonged to the Chamber of Commerce and also formed *mutualistas*, or mutual-aid societies, which fostered economic development and social solidarity within the ethnic community.[7]

Despite Tucson's development as a commercial center for the region, business declined in the early 1920s as part of the post–World War I downturn.[8] In 1922, fifteen businessmen gathered to discuss their declining prospects. At this point a fracture appeared in the booster edifice, not on the basis of the underlying assumption that motivated the businessmen, but on the means through which prosperity could best be achieved. The fifteen self-styled visionaries who "realized that Tucson really had something to shout about" formed the Sunshine Climate Club as a branch of the Chamber of Commerce.[9] With a disparaging tone, the new club's brochure described the other members of the Chamber of Commerce as stick-in-the-mud types who

> had lived in the city so long that they could see nothing attractive about the interesting Mexican quarter, the several Indian villages, the beautiful San Xavier Mission, the giant cactus forests, the rugged mountains, western ranch life, the proximity of Mexico with its big game hunting and excellent deep sea fishing, and last but not least, the glorious sun that makes it possible to play golf in shirt sleeves on Christmas Day.[10]

The Sunshine Climate Club shifted the focus toward tourism and the commodification of bits of nature and exotic "other" worlds. During the 1920s, Tucson and other western cities emphasized tourism, "a new kind of western ranching," as characterized by historian Robert Athearn.[11] Despite ambivalence about the visitors, enterprising Westerners sought to provide "wild, magnificent scenery, excitement, adventure, a bit of rusticity, and an occasional whiff of imagined danger. In other words, the chance to escape, briefly to be sure, the dailiness of their [Easterners'] lives."[12] Whereas earlier entrepreneurs had "mined the miners," twentieth-century entrepreneurs like the Sunshine Climate Club endeavored to mine the tourists. Railroad and motor tours deposited sojourners at scenic points throughout the West, and by the early 1920s, this "most recent gold rush" had spread to almost every western city.[13]

The Sunshine Climate Club operated under the organizational umbrella of the Chamber of Commerce but focused on this different aspect of development, occasionally arguing over budgets, resources, and methods of promotion. They remained linked by their optimism, but unanimity among boosters rarely materialized. Capitalism, after all, trumpets individual achievement. Shrinking economic prospects during the Depression of the 1930s brought calls for concerted and unified action, while at the same time businessmen and residents scrambled to preserve their individual interests.

The "Bank Holiday" in 1933 disrupted the normal business routine even though the currency shortage in Tucson was alleviated through issues of scrip and warrants, and the use of the barter system.[14] The banking crisis, in fact, led to opportunities for enterprising businesses such as Albert Steinfeld & Company, a retail merchant who gained many new customers by accepting checks and scrip, and opening new charge accounts. Conversely, many businesses refused to accept promissory warrants issued by the state even after the banks, which would redeem the warrants, had reopened. This policy left out scores of local University of Arizona employees who suffered from businessmen's suspicion of the fiscal integrity of the state government.[15] In short, businessmen responded differently to the economic crisis depending on how they defined their individual self-interests.

Another indication of dissent within the pro-development community was the Sabino Canyon dam proposal. At a public meeting in 1936, "citizens and government officials testified unanimously in favor of the project." The boosters' rhetorical unanimity convinced the federal government to support the plan to build a dam in Sabino Canyon near Tucson if city and county governments agreed to share in the cost of the project. But when the Army Corps of Engineers placed Pima County's contribution at $500,000, support for the dam melted like snow in the desert. The city and county governments offered to provide only $600 toward the project. One of the casualties of the fracas was the manager of the Chamber of Commerce, Al Coudron. A lifelong resident, Coudron resigned and left town in a huff when the chamber's board failed to back the dam.[16]

Other disagreements arose as the city began aggressively annexing surrounding areas after World War II. Although never challenging the underlying assumption that expansion was desirable, some developers questioned the timing and pace of expansion. (Developer resistance to annexations will be discussed more fully in chapter 2.)

The organizational separation of the Tucson Chamber of Commerce and the Sunshine Climate Club indicates an awareness among Tucson boosters of variations within a context of shared fundamental goals. Businessmen aimed promotional brochures at different audiences in the effort to lure tourists, residents, and businesses to Tucson, with the messages sometimes running afoul of each other. In promotions aimed at vacationers, Tucson's charms were described as "here," intricately entwined within the community, yet in promotions aimed at prospective residents, they were also described as "there," perhaps nearby but distinctly segregated. Barrio culture provides the clearest example of this dichotomous approach: barrios appeared in tourist promotions as integral to the Old Pueblo image, but they are distinctly segregated in promotions directed toward Anglo, middle-class prospective residents.[17]

Although boosters banked on Tucson's particular brand of quaintness— a multicultural heritage suitable for tourists' explorations—they also chafed at the notion that the city was somehow provincial. In Tucson, the quaintness was to be sold as readily accessible but not unduly intrusive. Thus Tucson offered sophisticated accommodations and modern conveniences so that the Old Pueblo could remain conveniently at hand yet comfortably remote. Campaigns aimed at tourists advertised Tucson's climate, Old West traditions (maintained in thirty-four nearby dude ranches),[18] and a cultural heritage found in the Hispanic barrios, Indian villages, and western ghost towns. Tourists were sold the western playground image, and happy visitors rode horseback for fun, not out of necessity. The degree to which urban development degraded this image, perhaps inevitably, led to another sort of resistance to growth based on preserving Tucson's environment, both natural and cultural (to be discussed in chapter 4).

Campaigns aimed at prospective residents painted a different image of Tucson. The Chamber of Commerce, for example, did its best to present the city in a sophisticated, metropolitan light. "Facts for Prospective Residents of Tucson," published in 1956, listed favorable tax rates and general information on the city's population, banks, parks, museums, and schools.[19] The pamphlet estimated the city's population at 205,000 and described the "urban area" of the city as extending a whopping seven miles "from the downtown post office."[20]

The valorizing tone remained in "The Answers to All Your Questions about Tucson, Arizona," issued in a series beginning in 1962 and extending into the 1970s. The overall presentation was slicker, with information more adroitly managed and directed toward specific types of prospective residents, from married-with-children to retirees.[21]

Provincial or sophisticated? Playground or community? Tucson businessmen accommodated diverging aims, seeking ultimately to characterize the city as all of the above. A neat cleavage failed to materialize between the Chamber of Commerce's promotion of Tucson as a place to live and the Sunshine Climate Club's promotion of the city as a place to vacation. Reasons to live in Tucson were often the same as reasons to visit: the climate, cultural heritage, and Old West traditions. But promotions aimed at prospective residents mentioned Tucson's small-town qualities— a slower pace of life, a relaxed work environment, and leisure opportunities—as often as they mentioned metropolitan sophistication. Thus, promotional efforts appear monolithic only to the degree that growth is defined monolithically. The boosters defined it as such, united by their fundamental assumption that growth is good.

A third type of promotion with its own organizational identity appeared in 1952, when the Industrial Development Department was formed specifically to recruit businesses to Tucson.[22] The Pima County Board of Supervisors assisted the Chamber of Commerce in this effort by providing an industrial engineer to recruit "new and diversified industries that fit into the characteristics of our community and provide service for those industries that [already] have been established."[23] Tucson's effort matched, somewhat belatedly, the systematic efforts by other southwestern cities to foster industrial development during and after World War II.[24]

In 1954 the Chamber of Commerce began issuing a series of pamphlets geared toward businessmen titled "Facts and Figures: A General Survey of Tucson and Pima County, Arizona."[25] The first edition described the city as an "urban area" extending "about 15 miles north-and-south and 10 miles east-and-west." The favorite slogan of the Industrial Development brochures was "Come to Tucson, for Industry and a Way of Life." The 1954 brochure described the "way of life" as "informal and always friendly." It also presented statistics of interest to businessmen contemplating a move to Tucson, and described cultural/environmental aspects favorable to business, claiming, for example, that "firms that have established plants in Tucson report their employees are happy here. There is less absenteeism due to sickness."[26]

The healthful "way of life" advertised by the Chamber of Commerce relied on nature, albeit in a 1950s context. The favorite logo, shared by the three promotional organizations, portrayed a trademark saguaro cactus framing the scene of a city dominated by mountains. The 1950s viewer probably accepted the atomic symbol in the industrial logo as a shorthand representation of progress and technology. At least that was the hope of the Chamber of Commerce.

Prospective employers heard appeals based on metropolitan sophistication and small-town friendliness. Information on housing and tax rates assured employers that workers could find decent, affordable housing with modest tax burdens, resulting in lower costs of living, which, presumably, would justify paying lower wages. Employers also heard references to a cultural segregation in Tucson based, once again, on the western playground image: "Ranch living has become almost standard with Tucson executives who still are within easy driving distance of all the city's commercial and industrial areas."[27] A photograph in the brochure shows happy, healthy adults enjoying outdoor activities "ten minutes from downtown."[28]

The three wings of the Chamber of Commerce appealed to different audiences—the Sunshine Climate Club to tourists, the Industrial Development Department to businesses and businessmen, and the Chamber of Commerce itself to prospective residents—but the promotional efforts blended together as advertising copy and slogans were modified to suit each particular audience. The various manifestations of the Chamber of Commerce's logo illustrate the difficulty of speaking of business and growth in singular terms.

The "diversified interests" logo (fig. 2) is a good example of the mixed message sometimes unwittingly conveyed in the Chamber of Commerce's promotions. The logo summarizes Tucson's reliance on "climate, cattle, cotton, and copper" with images of a brightly shining sun, grazing cattle, plowed fields, and a copper smelter sharing the scene. The messianic male figure in the foreground could be a tourist, rancher, developer, or engi-

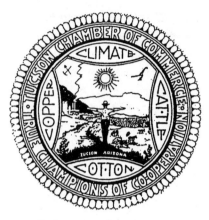

FIG. 2 "A City of Diversified Interests." In 1950, Tucson's Chamber of Commerce added a fourth "C"—climate—to the traditional triumvirate that dominated Arizona's economy: cattle, cotton, and copper. The uneasy mix of these appeals appears in a Chamber of Commerce brochure depicting a bright sun shining merrily through the sulfur dioxide plume emitting from the copper smelter to the left. (Source: University of Arizona Library Special Collections)

neer. Perhaps the greatest ambiguity, however, arises from the juxtaposition of the sun and the sulfur dioxide plume spewing forth from the smelter.

In 1954 the Chamber of Commerce launched an effort to attract high-technology business to Tucson by trumpeting the close working relationship between the Chamber of Commerce and local government.[29] "Tomorrow is Today in Tucson" appeared with the atomic symbol logo surrounding downtown Tucson.[30] Western hospitality was given a new twist as the Chamber of Commerce advertised the government-business partnership in Tucson: "Recently, a nationally-known scientific research company came to Tucson; found an ideal location with a building already up. Problem: one of rezoning to allow them to move in. Within *weeks*, residents of the area in cooperation with the city and county officials and the Chamber of Commerce had rezoned the area and provided additional new zoning for other areas of similar nature. Result: Tucson is a city actually *zoned* for scientific research."[31]

City of Tucson internal memorandums provide support for the Chamber of Commerce's claim of helpfulness. In 1954 the city attorney advised officials to be "liberal" in their inspections of construction sites so that "construction costs will not be unnecessarily increased."[32]

Chamber of Commerce members expressed pride in their leadership position within the community. The Old Pueblo Club, founded in 1907 as "a gentlemen's club for social purposes," fairly chortled over the political and financial prominence of its members in the community.[33] The link between the club and the Chamber of Commerce was acknowledged in 1955: "The Old Pueblo Club might as well have been called the Old Pueblo Sunshine Climate Club . . . because OPC members held all the important positions."[34] The interchange of membership was, in fact, routine and appeared in self-congratulatory announcements phrased as rhetorical slaps-on-the-back. The good-ole-boy network appeared most clearly in a reference to William F. Kimball, a former president of the Old Pueblo Club who had been elected Arizona senate majority leader. The jocular tone of the account expresses self-confidence bordering on hubris:

> Kimball, as majority leader, was the most powerful politician in the state, with the possible exception of the governor. But that was only a "possible

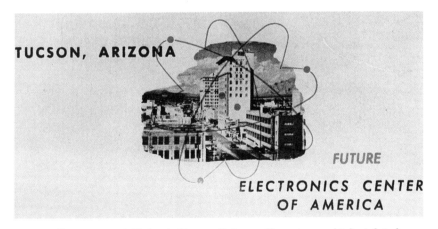

FIG. 3 "Tomorrow Is Today in Tucson." In an effort to attract high-tech industry to Tucson in 1954, the Chamber of Commerce produced a brochure with a pictorial representation of the city's hopefully nuclear (that is, central) position in the industry. In hindsight, the image has a different, sinister connotation: an irradiated downtown. In 1979, the city closed an atomic manufacturer after tritium emissions were detected in nearby swimming pools. (Source: University of Arizona Library Special Collections)

exception" in those days. Much "law" was made at the Flame Restaurant at night. Much "law" was made at the 20-Grand Bar during the days. Much "law" was made on the eighth floor of the Adams Hotel at any time, day or night. The eighth floor was the headquarters of the Phelps-Dodge Mining Company's lobbyists. Some "law," but not much, was made on the floor of the House and Senate which seemed only to approve the "law" made elsewhere.[35]

Developers who served on zoning commissions, on planning boards, and as city managers provide a more visible interconnection between the booster organizations and local government. In 1961, for example, the *O.P. Chronicle* announced S. Lenwood Schorr's appointment as assistant Tucson city manager.[36] Schorr had been a member of the Pima County Planning and Zoning Commission and also a developer in the Tucson Mountain foothills. He was hired to help formulate the city's urban renewal plan. Although to some this might appear to be a case of a fox hired to guard the chicken coop, concerns over potential conflicts of interest—developers regulating development—never materialized during Schorr's tenure. Rather, the city manager cited Schorr's experience as a developer as providing the "expertise" necessary for successful urban planning.[37]

In 1970, one of Tucson's newspapers summarized the twentieth-century link between business and government in a laudatory article that brings nineteenth-century boosters to mind:

> A look at the real estate business in Tucson not only reveals the growth of the city; it also mirrors a segment of the business community that is fairly typical of the courageous, pioneering and at times a bit unmanageable people who have settled this area. . . . Real estate men traditionally have served on zoning committees, as members of school and church organizations, on civic promotion boards; in short, real estate people are where the action is.[38]

The article echoed Boorstin's characterization of developers as community leaders, "gregarious individuals" possessed of boundless "community spirit." The article also described the "filling in" of Tucson's wide-open spaces as happily inevitable.[39] The reporter apparently shared the fundamental assumption of the developers and boosters that the health of the city required ever-expanding growth: in size, in prosperity, in sophistication.

The effort to plan for Tucson's growth—or as later opponents to the city's expansion would claim, the effort to encourage growth—was well established by the 1950s. The planning effort began in 1930 with the city's first zoning ordinance. In 1932 "concerned citizens" formulated the Tucson Regional Plan. In 1941 the city established a nine-member planning and zoning commission, which was followed in 1943 by a joint county-city planning department. In 1949 the state legislature passed legislation allowing countywide zoning.[40] The federal government encouraged cities' planning efforts by providing federal financing through the 1949 Housing Act, which became known as "the planner's full-employment act" because it mandated that grants go only to cities with "a redevelopment strategy that conformed to a comprehensive plan for the entire locality."[41]

Thus, the growth bureaucracy was generally in place when the city's expansion took place. At times, however, planning efforts encountered opposition from developers who resented proposed land-use constraints. Likewise, government officials lost their enthusiasm for plans perceived as too expensive or controversial. The regional plan developed by Ladislas Segoe in the early 1940s exemplifies this ambivalence toward planned growth. (The plan was completed and presented to the city council in 1945.)[42]

Segoe was a pioneer in urban planning and a nationally recognized planning consultant based in Cincinnati.[43] In 1940 the "concerned citizens" who in 1938 had formulated Tucson's first "regional plan" hired Segoe to professionally appraise Tucson's development.[44] The regional plan that Segoe developed sought to rationalize Tucson's urban growth by regulating both development and developers. The plan explicitly criticized Tucson's developers: "In spite of the state platting laws designed to ensure the continuity of streets . . . there are clear indications that the owners of large holdings considered their subdivisions as self-contained developments rather than parts of the larger community with which the layout of these subdivisions should be coordinated."[45]

In contrast to the optimistic assumption of boosters, planning professionals such as Segoe offered a tempered vision of growth as occasionally inevitable but not always beneficial. As such, planners sometimes found themselves outside the government-business partnership promoted so assiduously by the Chamber of Commerce. Planners became "hired guns" (or an example of a quasi-independent "functional bureaucracy," in Stephen Elkin's "pluralistic" model), and their plans were implemented, compromised, or discarded according to the latest electoral whim.[46]

The gaps and fissures within Tucson's booster structure and the flaws within the business-government partnership indicate a less than monolithic force pushing development. Nonetheless, businessmen wielded considerable influence in the city government. After barrio homeowners thwarted developers' efforts to buy up property in neighborhoods south of downtown, the developers successfully lobbied government agencies to declare the areas "blighted," which facilitated condemnation proceedings and eligibility for federal funds.[47] Although such "urban renewal" efforts seem to indicate that the partnership between government (both local and federal) and developers was fully functional, renewal plans often met with vociferous resistance that caused the plans to be modified, truncated, or scrapped altogether. (Urban redevelopment will be discussed in detail in chapter 3.)

In general, city and county governments enthusiastically supported growth despite the occasional reluctance of urban planners. In 1953, City Attorney Harry L. Buchanan submitted a pro-growth legal opinion to Tucson's city manager, J. Luther Davis (who as Buchanan's former assistant had written several pro-growth legal opinions himself).[48] Resistance to annexation was the subject of Buchanan's 1953 opinion:

> Every annexation is a potential lawsuit and many need only an unlitigated point upon which to hang their hats for a so-called test case, which has the effect of delaying the objective we are seeking even if we should prevail. . . . I recognize the present annexation laws are cumbersome, but only the Legislature can correct them, which we have tried to get its members to do, so far without success. Therefore we must do the best with what they have given us.[49]

Of course, annexation laws were "cumbersome" only to those seeking unlimited power to annex. The city attorney thus defined resistance to growth as legally obstructionist, and a pernicious nuisance that the misguided legislature failed to recognize. The following year, Buchanan submitted a legal opinion to the city council explicitly stating the fundamental assumption about growth: "Is annexation of the fringe areas a matter that may be deemed expedient or necessary for the promotion and protection of the health, comfort, safety, life, welfare and property of the inhabitants of the city? Yes." [50]

Why should the city attorney address the issue of annexation in terms of life and, presumably, death? The fundamental assumption appears in the attorney's statement, less optimistic in the face of opposition to growth, but no less certain of its rectitude: Growth was essential not just for prosperity but for the city's very survival.

Tucson's mayor in 1955, Fred Emery, expressed the assumption as succinctly as anyone: "In its role as the heart of a metropolitan area, the city of Tucson itself has acquired new strength and stature. The Businesses of our community will gain by this, and as they gain, all of us will gain." [51]

In Emery's concept of a healthy city, "Business" (the mayor's capitalization) and government were linked. In terms of the optimistic assumption, the mayor was correct to link the two, but this conflation required a monolithic view of both "business" and "growth." However, as Tucson's expansion continued and as promotional efforts proliferated, conflicting goals began to surface. A booster's self-interest sometimes forced him to oppose "growth"—not in terms of the fundamental assumption that said growth is good but in terms of individual assessments of profit margin. Thus political resistance to specific manifestations of growth began to surface among those with the power and opportunity to resist.

For the most part, though, Tucson boosters, city government, and even the planners continued to argue for "progress." The pro-growth partisans shared a weltanschauung that defined history as steadily, although at times fitfully, marching forward. Linear and dynamic assumptions defined their perspective, along with a dichotomous ordering of "nature." They defined the cosmos in terms of progressive civilization versus static, unproductive nature. Some boosters considered nature (defined as flat, easily bulldozed desert) as wasted unless plowed, platted, or paved. Other boosters came to realize that even flat, easily bulldozed desert had its uses—for example, you could put a fence around it and make tourists pay for the pleasure of walking through it. But even this use remained within the assumed virtue of individual progress because boosters made the capitalist assumption that individual profits created community prosperity. Consequently, businessmen could describe their individual interests in terms of the common good.

The communalism of boosters lasted until the individual interests of businessmen dictated otherwise. Variations in promotional efforts indicated an awareness among boosters that private interests diverged within a context of shared general goals. Planners also shared a faith in "progress," but their faith was tempered by a concern for rational development, which sometimes ran afoul of booster profits. Politicians trumpeted "progress" most consistently. Consensus among boosters, planners, and politicians varied in completeness, but opponents were defined as universally beyond the pale. How could anyone argue against progress? It is, perhaps, surprising then that the political resistance to growth in Tucson that surfaced in the early 1950s appeared among those who shared the boosters' Whiggish faith in progress.

2 POLITICAL RESISTANCE

■ ■ ■ ■ ■ ■ ■ ■ ■ ■ ■ ■ ■ ■ ■

"The Laws Serve the Majority"

Political resistance to growth first appeared among white, middle-class suburban residents of Tucson in the 1950s. Criticism of the city's expansion became so vociferous that at one point Tucson's mayor, seeking to deflect criticism with humor, wore a suit of armor to a public hearing on annexation. The resistance never succeeded in stopping the city's expansion, but it did succeed in obstructing growth by forcing the city and county governments to maneuver around the resistance. The pro-growth forces in Tucson never lost their majority status during the 1950s, but resistance to growth remained part of the community ethos.

The ambiguity in the language surrounding urbanization—usually including an oversimplified definition of growth—defined the resistance in many cases. Developers resisted the expansion of government when it appeared to be obtrusive and a hindrance to their projects. In this sense, a political conservatism bordering on libertarianism surfaced among those who would never question the underlying assumption that growth was good. After all, increasing profits for individual developers translated into community prosperity through the immediate impact of construction

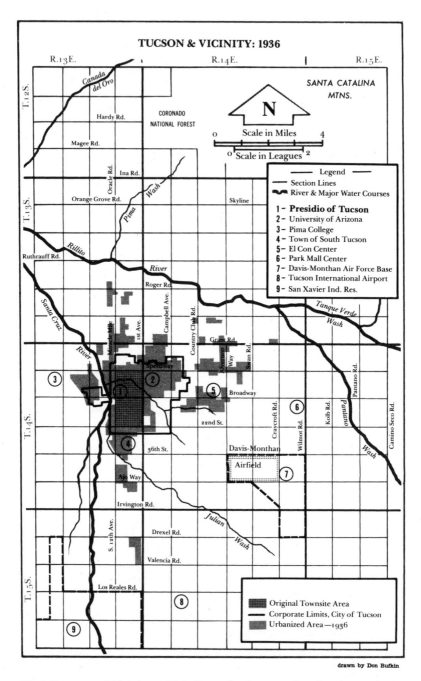

FIG. 4 Tucson and Vicinity: 1936. Vacant land remained within the city limits, but the less expensive land beyond the city limits lured developers to the east, resulting in suburban sprawl over the desert floor, already evident in 1936. (Source: Bufkin, *Journal of Arizona History* 22 : 80)

jobs and the more sustained influence of expanding service industries and an increasing tax base—or at least so the developers claimed.

Expanding government bureaucracy, regulatory agencies, and neighborhood activism, however, were viewed with suspicion by these same developers. The spread of Tucson over the valley floor also engendered a broader resistance based on environmental and cultural perceptions (to be discussed in chapter 4), but the early resistance to growth arose among individuals or small groups of individuals with personal interests and private concerns expressed in economic and political terms. The first to resist were residents with access to political power who felt no qualms in asking the political system to redress their grievances.

Tucson's physical expansion proceeded over a bumpy road during the 1950s. The growth bureaucracy was generally in place but found itself serving primarily as a forum for rancorous debate among developers, politicians, homeowners, bureaucrats, horse owners, and retirees.

Mirroring the general Sunbelt shift of population after World War II, Tucson's population increased 368.4 percent during the 1950s, and the area within the city limits increased almost eightfold, from 9.5 to 70.9 square miles.[1] Workers, both blue collar and white collar, and their families followed defense industry and manufacturing jobs to the Sunbelt, and retirees arrived in search of an amenity-filled lifestyle. These two groups of new residents possessed potentially competing worldviews: one acquisitive, expansion-minded, and seeking better prospects, and the other conservative, stasis-minded, and seeking a stable lifestyle.[2]

Tucson's expansion in size and population can be more clearly understood by examining figures 4, 5, and 6. As the 1936, 1950, and 1960 maps indicate, Tucson's city limits tended to lag behind actual development in the urban area. The 1936 map shows relatively few developed areas beyond the city limits and, indeed, several undeveloped areas within the city limits. By 1950, however, the situation was completely reversed, with approximately twice as many residents of the metropolitan area living outside the city limits. The county residents (primarily white and middle class) are listed as the "fringe population" in table 2.[3] The 1960 map and table 2 show that Tucson's population increase of 167,438 over the previous decade (from 45,454 in 1950 to 212,892 in 1960) consisted of many former fringe residents as well as a large number of new residents.

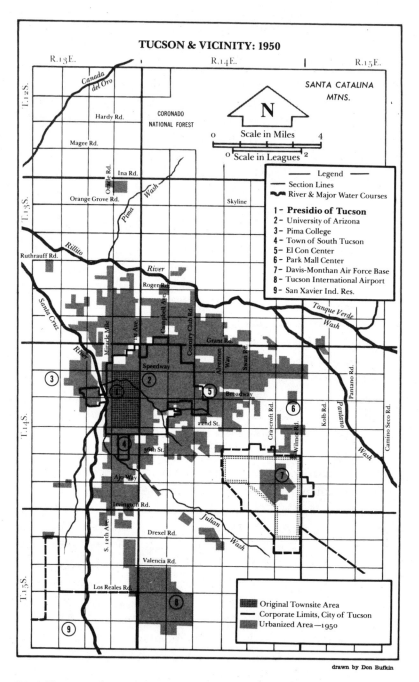

FIG. 5 Tucson and Vicinity: 1950. In 1950, some areas within the expanded city limits remained undeveloped, but the majority of new residents had settled outside the city's boundary. The spread of urbanization beyond the city limits set the stage in Tucson for resistance to city annexation efforts throughout the 1950s. (Source: Bufkin, *Journal of Arizona History* 22:85)

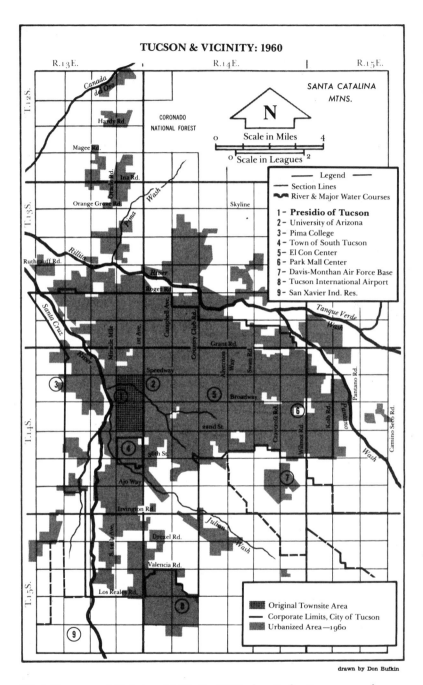

TUCSON & VICINITY: 1960

R.13E.   R.14E.   R.15E.

SANTA CATALINA
MTNS.

N

CORONADO
NATIONAL FOREST

Scale in Miles

Scale in Leagues

Legend

——— Section Lines
River & Major Water Courses

1 – Presidio of Tucson
2 – University of Arizona
3 – Pima College
4 – Town of South Tucson
5 – El Con Center
6 – Park Mall Center
7 – Davis-Monthan Air Force Base
8 – Tucson International Airport
9 – San Xavier Ind. Res.

Original Townsite Area
——— Corporate Limits, City of Tucson
Urbanized Area—1960

drawn by Don Bufkin

FIG. 6 Tucson and Vicinity: 1960. By 1960, the city limits more nearly conformed to the extent of urbanization in the Tucson valley. City leaders and planners had found that annexing undeveloped, uninhabited land was the surest way to avoid controversy. (Source: Bufkin, *Journal of Arizona History* 22 : 89)

TABLE 2 Tucson Population, 1950-1960

	1950	1960	Change
City Population	45,454	212,892	+ 368%
Fringe Population	77,310	21,590	− 72%
Total Population	122,764	234,482	+ 91%

This recognition of the fringe element as part of the population increase is significant for its effect on the debate in Tucson over growth in the 1950s and 1960s. As generally characterized by scholars in the 1960s, the "urban crisis" in the United States resulted from overcrowded and decaying urban cores, but in Tucson the crisis resulted from sprawling growth and the fringe problem of the suburbs. Land-rich western cities such as Tucson tended to spread out rather than build up during the 1950s. Tucson's efforts to "fill in" vacant areas within the city boundaries ran afoul of cheaper land and building costs beyond the incorporated area, leading to low-density, sprawling development.

Terms such as "fringe problem" and "new residents" must be used carefully, however. "New residents" might be expected to cause a mounting tension among established residents, especially if racial, ethnic, or class differences arose between the new and established residents.[4] But in Tucson, many of the "new residents" added to the city's population by 1960 were suburban residents who at the time of the previous census lived outside the city limits. Likewise, the "fringe problem" in the 1950s, as discussed by later-day urban historians, might be misinterpreted as a new problem, perhaps unsuspected or in some way newly urgent. But the phenomena of fringe growth and population decentralization were neither new nor surprising to Tucson urban planners in the 1950s. Contemporary professional journals debated solutions to the problem of decentralization, and Tucson planners and politicians drew on these sources to defend their reliance on annexation. Supporters defended the policy as not only "common sense" but also professionally "rational," which placed opponents of annexation further into the rhetorical realm of the weird.[5]

The spread of the city to the east during the 1940s and 1950s pro-

ceeded unencumbered by topographical barriers, and the population center of the city moved steadily eastward, sometimes rivaling the advance
of the city limits. The City's planners, the Board of Realtors, and the
Chamber of Commerce all worked actively to encourage Tucson's growth.
Motivations included the general desire for profit by the developers and a
genuine concern for orderly progress on the part of city bureaucrats and
politicians.[6] The desire to annex was accompanied by city-sponsored efforts to upgrade the utility and transportation infrastructure.[7] City finances also stood to gain from annexations, because the city's share of
state tax revenue was based on its official population.[8]

Nevertheless, a sizable, vocal, persistent minority opposed the city's
expansion throughout the 1950s. These residents—individualistic, libertarian, and mostly unorganized[9]—opposed annexations, zoning ordinances, and changes in city and county plans. More than simply a no-
growth reaction, the resistance targeted both the physical size of the city
and the increasingly arbitrary nature of the city government. This resistance to Tucson's expansion originated in private interests that crossed
party lines. The record of virtually every city council meeting during the
1950s, whether controlled by Democrats or Republicans, contains some
reference to rezoning requests, neighborhood plan revisions, or inquiries
into the possibility of expanded city services, with each request for action
accompanied by the commensurate protest demanding a halt.

This debate over the desired nature of the community and its government included thousands of fringe residents who already possessed keenly
felt interests and strong opinions. Among the most noticeable of their
opinions—expressed in letters to the editor, petitions to city government,
legal suits, and referendum elections—was a distrust of governmental
authority, which motivated a wide range of complaint, protest, and resistance by "individualists." A 1951 study of annexation in Tucson described the concerns of fringe residents: "Just as fringe residents usually
play the dominant role in initiating annexation movements, so they usually are in the forefront of opposition to specific annexation proposals
because of their fear of increased taxes, city zoning and building regulations (though some desire the latter), and of losing their identity."[10]

This identity was based primarily on the amenities of suburban life:
single-family detached homes, better schools, open space, and freedom
from governmental authority. "Some individualists will go a long way to

avoid the more adequate and therefore more severe city police protection. The police patrol car, while a symbol of protection to some, is an object of suspicion and annoyance to others." [11]

The fragmented, contentious, and individualistic opposition often targeted zoning and plan revisions. In April 1953, after the city council revoked several building permits in recently annexed areas, Sidney Szerlip, president of the real estate board, cautioned the city council that "if we continue [this] way, we realtors will have to warn our clients that they can't depend upon zoning in areas about to come into the city." [12] In another vein, Mrs. Margaret McClain protested the construction of a city playground in her recently annexed neighborhood. McClain argued that the presence of children violated deed restrictions and that young people caused vandalism. [13] The ownership of livestock, mostly horses, became another issue as fringe areas fell under the purview of city regulations, and "grandfather clause" protection for existing property uses generally failed to assuage the emotional concerns of the horse owners. [14]

Certainly the president of the real estate board was not expressing a desire for a no-growth community; rather, he sought the clarification of apparently arbitrary zoning decisions. On the other hand, horse owners, and perhaps McClain, may have been comfortable voicing a desire for no growth. Clearly a divergence existed within the community resistance between those who sought to limit the physical growth of the city and those who sought to limit the centralization of the city's government. Realtors sometimes found themselves in the awkward position of opposing government actions that were designed by city planners to foster rapid, far-reaching development. Two of Tucson's quintessential developers, Roy Drachman and Evo DeConcini, found themselves at different times opposing annexations of their undeveloped land, both arguing that such premature annexations would actually hinder development. [15]

By far the most visible early opposition movement, including both no-growth and antigovernment forces, arose during the countywide zoning fight of 1952–53. Thousands of residents opposed the proposed countywide zoning ordinance, and Lesley Allen, a local attorney, emerged as the nominal leader. They mounted petition drives and court fights, and campaigned in a referendum election against the combined forces of city and county government, leaders of the business community, both city newspapers, and the League of Women Voters. But it is not surprising that opponents of countywide zoning were eventually swamped in the referendum election; the pro-growth forces in the city and county never lost their power in the 1950s. Nevertheless, the extent and intensity of the resistance during the countywide zoning fight belies any "consensus" depiction of Tucson's growth in the early 1950s.

Prior to 1949, Arizona counties lacked the statutory authority to enact countywide zoning ordinances, but the state legislature granted that authority in June 1949, and Pima County (Tucson was the county seat) was the first to enact a countywide zoning ordinance.[16] Drafts of the ordinance percolated through the county's planning and zoning bureaucracy, and public hearings began in 1951. Opposition to the proposed ordinance sprang up immediately.

Supporters of the countywide ordinance (city and county government, planners, the Chamber of Commerce) described the proposal as necessary to ensure orderly growth and responsible development. Opponents "roundly attacked" the ordinance and offered their own local-option alternative.[17] Local-option zoning, if enacted, would establish a system allowing property owners in areas as small as 160 acres to enact their own building and land-use regulations. Countywide supporters portrayed the local-option alternative as tantamount to no zoning at all or, possibly worse, a chaotic hodgepodge of conflicting zoning. Local-option supporters protested the arbitrary extension of government regulation into the uses of private property in the county and expressed concern over the effect of suburban development on land prices outside the city limits. Land prices in fringe areas increased as development proceeded into fringe areas, causing tax assessments to increase—a development that threatened fixed-income residents. These residents, according to local-option supporters, were being forced to sell their property, admittedly for a tidy profit but without the opportunity to move onto an equivalent parcel of land near the city.[18]

Whereas supporters of the countywide proposal generally had a firm organizational identity—backed by the city and county government, the Board of Realtors, and the League of Women Voters—supporters of the local-option alternative were individual property owners, loosely confederated in the League for Zoning by Local-Option Only. Attorney Lesley

Allen, chairman of the group, expressed the league's view that the countywide ordinance was being "crammed down the public's throat," and that the matter should be submitted to the public for a final decision.[19] Initial resistance to the countywide proposal took the form of protest at the forty-two public hearings held by the planning commission. The board of supervisors considered the countywide ordinance on February 25, 1952, but after a tumultuous meeting, the board postponed the vote for thirty days. Because tempers and opinions remained unsettled, the supervisors did not adopt the ordinance until August 6, 1952.[20]

In the meantime, league members had circulated petitions and gathered more than 8,000 signatures to force a referendum election offering the local-option alternative. Supporters of the countywide ordinance attempted to cancel the referendum in a court suit, arguing that the league had gathered insufficient valid signatures. A seven-day trial in district court followed in which 147 witnesses testified either for or against the referendum. Finally, four days before the scheduled election, the court validated 5,384 signatures, a sufficient number to force the election.[21]

As the court maneuvering proceeded, supporters of the countywide ordinance mounted a campaign to assure that, should the election come about, local-option zoning would be defeated. One month before the election, scheduled for February 10, 1953, the League of Women Voters announced its intention to oppose the local-option ordinance.[22] The league set up booths in the lobbies of banks, distributed leaflets, and scheduled pro-countywide speakers for its regular meetings. One week before the election, the *Arizona Daily Star* ran front-page banner editorials opposing the proposed ordinance. Two days before the election, the newspaper printed sample ballots on the front page with a "no" vote on local-option prominently displayed. Countywide zoning defeated the local-option alternative 4,872 to 2,176.[23]

Given the organizational sophistication and general weight of support for the countywide ordinance, the defeat of the local-option alternative was not surprising. That such an effort to defeat local-option was deemed necessary indicates that urban planners and promoters in the city and county were aware of the depth of antigrowth and antigovernment sentiment within the community. Election returns from the fringe areas surrounding the city limits showed that the local-option alternative received majority support in six precincts, and healthy minority support in eleven others.[24] For example, the Flowing Wells precinct, composed mostly of middle-class fringe residents to the north of the city, approved the local-option alternative. The neighboring Amphitheater precinct narrowly defeated it. The degree to which this local-option support indicated no-growth or antigovernment sentiment is unknown,[25] but neither possibility could have been comforting to expansionist politicians and bureaucrats.

Annexation protests in the 1950s presented city leaders with a similar scenario. Residents protested the first four annexations in 1953 at the city council meeting enacting each annexation. In all, residents protested six of the first eight annexations. Beyond these protests of specific annexation plans, the very process of annexation virtually assured that many new city residents would feel ambivalent, since annexation laws only required the approval of the owners of 51 percent of the assessed valuation in the area.[26] The owners of 49 percent of the assessed valuation, perhaps a majority of the population in the area, could find themselves annexed despite their active opposition.

Small annexations involving few property owners were most likely to avoid protests. Four individuals owned the ten-acre parcel that became the Bunnell addition in 1952, but no protest materialized because all four approved the annexation. Three other special cases involved no protest. These were a "railroad corridor" annexed in March 1955 to display a Southern Pacific Railroad locomotive donated to the city, an annexation requested by the Sisters of St. Mary's Hospital in 1956, and the South Fourth Avenue addition in March 1957, which facilitated a street re-alignment.[27]

The first annexation in 1953 was more typical. The North Campbell addition, to the northeast, entered the city with the approval of 60 to 65 percent of the property owners (accounting for 51.5 percent of the assessed valuation). Morris F. Baughman, a pro-annexation resident of the area, explained to the city council that the approval of 60 to 65 percent of the property owners was necessary because several large property owners in the area opposed the annexation. Once the owners of 51 percent of the property valuation approved, opposition to the annexation became futile. In this scenario the solicitation and coordination of support for annexation became critical. The city council commended Baughman and R. R. Guthrie, the city's right-of-way agent, for their work in coordinating the annexation.[28] In later years the city appropriated funds for the hiring and training of persons to circulate annexation petitions, and Guthrie became even more involved in the solicitation of annexations.

Opponents of the annexation, however, criticized the city's agents for making false promises to lure residents into signing annexation petitions. Guthrie and Baughman, using documentation provided by the city and published in pro-annexation editorials in the *Arizona Daily Star*, maintained that property taxes would actually decrease by six dollars per year in the annexed area. Agents also promised "free" garbage collection and regular police protection. Residents of the targeted area, including retired dentist Nathan O. Lynn, feared that property taxes would actually increase thousands of dollars. They also questioned the ability of the city to extend city services to thousands of new residents when city services were already strained to the breaking point. In fact, both sides hedged the truth somewhat in the controversy: taxes did increase with annexation, but not to the extent predicted by Lynn. City services were delivered despite the strain, but not as quickly as promised, and not at the expected level.[29]

As the city expanded to the east in 1953, annexation protests generally involved requests by property owners to be removed or excluded from an area to be annexed. Property owners expressed concern not only over higher tax rates but also the city's more rigorous building restrictions. The uncertainty of zoning regulations and the impact of annexation on utility costs and service delivery also factored into opposition.[30] As the city's role in soliciting annexations became more obvious, court challenges arose. Lynn filed the first legal suit in July 1953, charging that the city had made false statements to residents to induce them to sign annexation petitions. Lynn also claimed that the city's valuation figures were fraudulent. His court challenge failed, but echoes of Lynn's charges reappeared in later annexation protests.[31]

In October 1953, Gordon Canning protested the inclusion of his Ocotillo Park subdivision in the Desert Highland addition. Canning's lawyer submitted an anti-annexation petition to the city council, questioning the valuation figures on the city's petitions. Canning's protest also failed, and yet the message to the city seemed clear: resistance would greet any sizable annexation.[32]

The Country Club Manor addition later that year engendered protest from a different angle. Property owner John V. Crosby protested the annexation because of the lack of firm boundaries. The city maintained that the final boundaries of annexed areas could be changed after the annexation petition signatures had been gathered, thus extending or limiting the area to be annexed. Crosby's lawyer argued that only the property of those who had signed the petitions should be annexed. Crosby's protest also failed.[33]

The city accomplished only one annexation in 1954, and that came after the city took drastic action to assure its physical expansion. Using the emergency clause of its "home rule charter power," in November the city council passed Ordinance 1532, providing for the establishment of its own standards for the annexation of "contiguous areas." The ordinance was necessary from the council's point of view because of recent changes by the Arizona legislature in state annexation laws. The amendments required cities to include the "personal property" of utility companies when tabulating property valuations in areas to be annexed, and also increased the number of instances in which cities were required to purchase utility companies (mostly private water companies) outright. The legislature went out of its way to protect the interests of privately owned "municipal water companies" in 1954 and 1955.[34] According to City Manager J. Luther Davis (the former assistant city attorney), the legislature's action made it impossible for Tucson to comply with the state law "as it is now written."[35]

The city attacked the new annexation law on two fronts. First, Tucson, under the auspices of the Arizona Municipal League, sought changes in the new annexation law, especially modification of the so-called tin-pipe bill that required the outright purchase of utilities. Second, the city argued that the county assessor and the State Tax Commission "have not the force or funds" to provide the city with personal property valuations for the utilities. The city council passed the ordinance excluding the personal property of public utilities but still requiring the signatures of the owners of half the real and personal property within the area to be annexed. The Parkside annexation, enacted immediately after the passage of Ordinance 1532, was completed only after the personal property of the Mountain States Telephone and Telegraph Company was removed from consideration.[36]

Ordinance 1532 significantly eased the process of annexation for the city, not only by eliminating the personal property of utilities but also by allowing the city to establish its own standards for annexation. Of course, to opponents of annexation, the ordinance simply reaffirmed the image of the city's government as arbitrary and obtrusive.

The southside annexation in 1956 illustrated the fully developed use of Ordinance 1532. On April 26, Mayor Don Hummel (a pro-growth Democrat who in 1955 had replaced Fred Emery, a pro-growth Republican, as mayor) called a special meeting of the city council to announce the annexation of 1,600 acres of industrial property on the south side of Tucson. No previous public announcement about annexation plans in the area had been made. Mayor Hummel stated, "The Council prefers to announce its programs in advance, but we departed from this policy because of the importance to Tucson's future."

The threat to Tucson's future was the City of South Tucson's expansion program to the east. Businessmen had formed South Tucson as a separate municipality in 1936 to avoid annexation by the City of Tucson. In 1956 the City of South Tucson had announced its own expansion program to the east, which Mayor Hummel described as so troublesome, "the effect of this would be to put the town of South Tucson between (the city of Tucson) and all of the industrial sites . . . that are available in the area. . . . It was important that we not allow the southward expansion (of the City of Tucson) to be interrupted." The legality of the annexation was based, Hummel said, on the "personal assurances" of the city's right-of-way agent, R. R. Guthrie.[37]

Such reassurances, it can be imagined, did not assuage the concerns of antigrowth and antigovernment forces in Tucson. South Tucson residents, in the meantime, accused the city of "hijacking" the area and annexing "with a gun."[38] The City of Tucson's attorney Harold Neubauer defended the annexation as legal and binding, but he apologized to southside residents for the surprise move: "The city has not used such methods previously and does not intend to do so in the future."[39] Ultimately the annexation faced only rhetorical opposition. South Tucson leaders recognized that the prospective legal challenge would be long and expensive, and beyond their means.[40]

Fewer in number but much larger in scope, annexations in the last half of the decade began to resemble eminent domain proceedings, irrespective of Neubauer's assurances. The southside example was repeated. Affidavits by R. R. Guthrie replaced petitions, and valuation percentages disappeared from the public record. The single annexation in 1957 (the South Fourth Avenue street realignment) appeared on the public record as "presented and read for the first time . . . declared passed and adopted and signed by the Mayor."[41] Residents Bob and Mary Barber and Rose Costano protested the 445-acre Freedom Homes annexation in 1958 and requested removal of their forty acres from the annexation. Ignoring the protest, the city adopted the annexation with the same cut-and-dried procedure.[42]

The large annexations completed in 1955–1956 created a new problem for city planners: the size of the additions proved to be "a bit indigestible."[43] The needs of the new additions strained city services, and the city required some time to catch up. Another factor in the 1957–1958 lull in annexations was the clearly understood resistance to annexation of northside neighborhoods, which on the basis of development, population, and topography would be the next logical area to be annexed. Bitter protest had accompanied the Winterhaven annexation, north of the city, in 1956. It was during the Winterhaven controversy that Mayor Hummel wore a suit of armor—tongue-in-cheek—to an annexation meeting in an effort to deflect the criticism of angry residents. But the mayor's sense of humor was sorely tested as angry residents—the "vociferous majority" of 400 in attendance—accused the city of attempting a "tax grab."[44]

The wrenching Winterhaven annexation foreshadowed the battle over the nearby, northside Amphitheater and Flowing Wells neighborhoods. The city's continued effort to expand northward dominated newspaper headlines and radio talk shows in 1959, in a manner similar to the countywide versus local-option fight of 1952–1953.[45] The mayor and council even acknowledged the resistance in their announcement of the Amphitheater annexation plan: "There will be many rumors adverse to annexation circulated by those opposed to it."[46]

Opposition was inevitable given the strong sense of community identity in the Amphitheater area. A separate water system serviced the area, and E. L. Wetmore had formed the Amphitheater School District in 1893, when the nearest Tucson school was six miles distant over open desert and farm land. The presence of a Tucson Gas and Electric plant provided ample tax revenues for the area's schools.[47]

The resistance to annexation involved lawsuits on both sides, charges of fraud, and a countermove by the Amphitheater, Flowing Wells, and

Freehaven neighborhoods to incorporate as separate, independent communities. The presence of the Tucson Gas and Electric plant further complicated the city's efforts. The city finally accomplished the annexation in a manner reminiscent of the southside addition three years earlier. The *Arizona Daily Star* noted: "Moving with feverish haste, the Council took in the huge area (over 20 square miles) immediately after the County Board of Supervisors denied three petitions seeking incorporation elections that would have delayed annexation by nearly two years [beyond the next census]. The Council, poised for the possible denial by the Supervisors, went into session only seconds after the incorporation moves were denied."[48]

The council issued a prepared statement explaining its hurried action, once again speaking of a threat to Tucson's future.[49] Meanwhile, the former fringe residents continued to resist. The familiar pattern of legal suits followed, along with a petition to the city council signed by "about fifty persons." Mayor Hummel viewed the court challenge as particularly obstructionist since it interfered with the city's ability to float the bonds that would be necessary to finance improvements in the annexed area: "This is no fault whatsoever of the Mayor and Council or of anyone in the City but must be laid directly at the door of the people who have challenged the legality of the City annexation."[50]

Hummel criticized opponents of annexation for their lack of civic-mindedness, accusing them of allowing their own self-interest to interfere with their loyalty to the city. Despite his repeated efforts to engender more community spirit—i.e., pro-annexation spirit—opposition persisted. At least in one case, however, Hummel came to understand the resistance. Tucson businessman Paul Robinson had supported the city's expansion through 1959 but then had voiced opposition to the next annexation in 1960. Hummel initially presumed that Robinson's opposition was motivated by crass self-interest, since Robinson owned a water company in the area to be annexed. Not so, as Hummel later realized:

After a full discussion of our differences, it was revealed that Mr. Robinson's opposition was based not on the ownership of a water company, but on Tucson's recent increase in water rates. He felt that city officials must have known that the water rates would have to be increased prior to the annexation of 1959 and that the failure to acknowledge this necessity for an increase was a breach of faith. . . . Unfortunately, in our haste to complete annexation within the April 1 deadline, we did not take time to sit down and discuss these matters with Mr. Robinson and others similarly situated. As the City spokesman, I must take the major responsibility for the misunderstanding.[51]

Hummel's apology to Robinson came after the Amphitheater opponents' legal challenge had failed. The city's successful annexation of the area brought 70,000 fringe residents into the city, some of them unwillingly.[52] Although difficult to quantify, a mark of the continued independence of the area is the persistence of Amphitheater and Flowing Wells in maintaining their own school districts and water systems. According to annexation coordinator Ray Leon, the area still buzzed with animosity toward Tucson's city government into the 1980s.[53]

In 1960 the city accomplished the last of its great annexations—twenty-five square miles to the southwest, abutting the San Xavier Indian Reservation. This area was sparsely populated, but still resistance appeared (Paul Robinson, for example). Hummel overcame the resistance so efficiently that even pro-growth Republicans approved of the Democratic mayor's performance. As one noted in a letter to the mayor, "It is hard to understand why people want to fight this annexation, but under your term you have done an excellent job."[54] After the southwest annexation, the city reverted to its previous pattern of many small annexations.[55]

Opposition to the expansion of Tucson continued throughout the 1960s and 1970s and continues to this day (see chapter 5). Although tactical sophistication evolved to new heights in the 1980s, the resistance itself was nothing new.

Clearly, during the 1950s the majority view in Tucson supported urban expansion, but this majority should not be characterized monolithically, ignoring the significant minority in the community that opposed both expanding urbanization and the government that supported it. Likewise, the resisting minority itself should not be categorized in oversimplistic terms as knee-jerk protestors or harmless community cranks. The debate over expansion in Tucson, carried out in the language of petition drives and annexation protests, was a contentious struggle over the desired nature of the community. That debate continues today.

The 1950s seem to suffer a lingering classification—at least in urban studies—as a period of consensus and cooperation beyond that recognized by the participants in urbanization. A statement by J. Luther Davis—city manager, former assistant city attorney, pro-growth partisan—illustrates the awareness of diverse opinions and the dilemma such diversity presented for local government: "The majority of the people in Arizona obviously live in the urban areas, that is, the city and the areas surrounding the city. Phoenix and Tucson have found that the residents in the surrounding areas, on the whole, want annexation, but that others appear to be opposed to annexation. The question is then presented: Are the laws designed for and do they serve the majority of the people of Arizona?"[56]

As annexations proceeded during the 1950s, laws clearly supported the majority will, but minority opposition was always present. Although annexation protests to the east and north involved white, middle-class suburban residents, the boosters projected onto the protesters a "minority" identity akin to that of ethnic residents more typically described as politically powerless. Politicians and boosters, united by faith in the virtues of growth, expressed a confident paternalism toward these recalcitrant residents, and then efficiently countered their resistance. Perhaps surprisingly, opposition originating in barrio neighborhoods proved more difficult to overcome.

3 ETHNIC RESISTANCE

■   ■   ■   ■   ■   ■   ■   ■   ■   ■   ■   ■   ■   ■

"The Wrong Side of the Tracks"

The first successful opposition to Tucson's expansion appeared in South Tucson in the late 1930s and in the southside barrio neighborhoods in the 1950s and 1960s. The early annexation resistance in South Tucson was more political in nature and occurred in areas with a majority of Hispanic residents—but generally without Hispanic participation. The later resistance was both politically and ethnically motivated. Political conservatives opposed the federal aspects of urban renewal. Hispanic residents opposed urban renewal plans that targeted their neighborhoods for destruction.

The purpose of setting this resistance apart from that previously mentioned is to describe events transpiring within the traditionally Hispanic part of Tucson, even if those events played themselves out in a "political" manner similar to that in middle class, Anglo suburbs to the north and east. The opposition to annexation in South Tucson began as a predominantly Anglo story, reflecting the usual patterns of political involvement in the 1930s. Eventually, however, Hispanic voices grew more numerous and certain, reflecting contemporary patterns of increased Hispanic political participation in the 1960s.

Easily recognizable within Tucson are the industrial and commercial regions, the old downtown, ethnic neighborhoods, and the inevitable bedroom developments, each region replete with its own particular sense of community identity. Variations occur along socioeconomic lines, from the haunts of the unemployed poor to the foothills homes of the rich. Since the 1950s, South Tucson has defined ethnic and class divisions for Tucsonans, who know the area for its good Mexican food, dog racing—and poverty. At times, boosters found the cultural variations pleasing: Tucson's affectionate sobriquet, trumpeting its Indo-Hispanic heritage, is "Old Pueblo." By 1950, eighteen Tucson businesses, by no means restricted to the south side, had "Old Pueblo" in their companies' names.[1] The poverty of the barrios no doubt detracted from Tucsonans' appreciation for the city's happily casual lifestyle, but given the geographic enclavement of living patterns, residents were conveniently able to ignore the less palatable aspects of the Old Pueblo: "dirt, disease, and delinquency," as described by Mayor Hummel in 1957.[2]

Tucsonans also recognize other regions within the city. "The foothills" most often refers to the residential area at the base of the Santa Catalina Mountains north of the city. However, the Rincon and Tucson Mountains to the west and east also have foothills residential developments. Why, then, should only one set of foothills be recognized as a definable community within the larger metropolitan entity? The answer lies in definitions of both physical and cultural environment (including "lifestyle," to be discussed in chapter 4). Definitions of class and ethnicity apply to South Tucson, but in the same sense as the foothills, at times inappropriately. How can Tucson market its Indo-Hispanic past and refer to itself affectionately as the Old Pueblo while still considering South Tucson to embody, culturally, the wrong side of the tracks?

Tucsonans pride themselves on the harmonious mixture of cultures in their history. As Thomas Sheridan described in Los Tucsonenses, Mexican Americans in Tucson, as in other southwestern cities, were subjected to segregation and economic manipulation by Anglos, but they suffered from fewer political and cultural disabilities. Although no Hispanic was elected mayor after the 1870s, and few Hispanics appeared in governmental service, social conditions remained relatively benign, especially when compared with communities in Texas and California.[3] Hispanics with wealth and property could escape the barrio neighborhoods if they chose to, and they were accorded status within the business community. As Sheridan explains: "Members of the Mexican elite could live where they chose, and several of these families like the Ronstadts and the Jacomes became part of the city's business and political power structure."[4] Nonetheless, the dominant Anglo culture limited the general Hispanic population's opportunities for acquiring wealth and property by confining them to lower-paying, blue-collar occupations. The geographic segregation of the barrios also maintained the distance between the general Hispanic population and the dominant Anglo culture.

Whether or not scholars agree with Sheridan's depiction of Tucson exceptionalism, it is clear that residents would like to believe in it. Tucsonans gather annually for a celebration of the city's cultural diversity at "Tucson Meet Yourself," an outdoor fair of ethnic food and music. On the surface at least, Tucson's self-image is one of tolerance.

The "Old Pueblo" nickname symbolizes Tucson's Indian and Hispanic cultural heritage. The specific region within the city most Old Pueblo—like is the area surrounding downtown, in the vicinity of the original townsite, and the barrio areas to the south and west. Tucson also harbors a legally separate municipality within its borders: the City of South Tucson, approximately one-square-mile situated slightly to the south of downtown, and completely surrounded by the city of Tucson. Ethnic resistance to urbanization in Tucson involved both regional entities: one political (the City of South Tucson), the other cultural (the barrios).

The expected political powerlessness that so often accompanies economic hardship failed to materialize in South Tucson and the barrios. The first successful political resistance to Tucson's growth occurred in South Tucson. The first successful neighborhood resistance also occurred in the south, and it was not in a middle-class, affluent, suburban development resisting annexation, but in a barrio neighborhood resisting urban redevelopment. After Tucson's city government labeled the barrios "blighted," the so-called blighted resisted, preserving their neighborhoods and in the process shaping the final renewal plan. .

The City of South Tucson incorporated in 1936 when the City of Tucson attempted to annex the area. Southside businessmen and residents feared the higher taxes and more stringent building codes that would

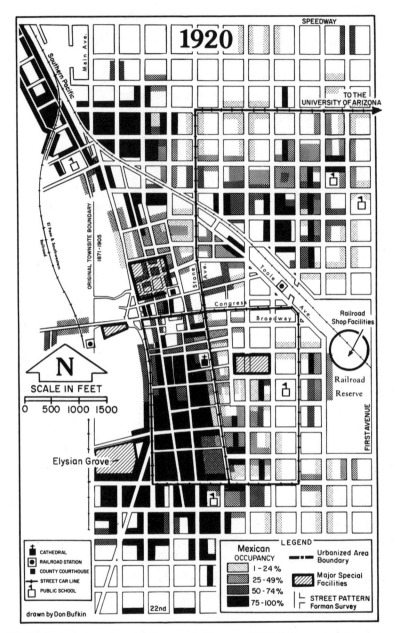

FIG. 7 Mexican American Settlement in Tucson, 1920. The geographic segregation of Hispanics in Tucson increased as suburban development spread to the east, but as Tom Sheridan describes, segregated living patterns in Tucson were never rigid. Note, for example, the Hispanic neighborhoods north and east of the railroad tracks. (Source: Sheridan, *Los Tucsonenses*, p. 187)

accompany annexation, and they moved to forestall the annexation by incorporating as a separate municipality.[5] The incorporation vote by residents of the area passed 52 to 35. The 87 total votes were cast from a population of approximately 1,000, including about 380 property tax payers. At this time, South Tucson's ethnic composition was mixed, but the organizers of the incorporation movement were almost exclusively Anglo.[6] Hispanics remained the majority in South Tucson (see figures 7 and 8), but in the 1930s, many Mexican American residents maintained a cautious distance from electoral politics.[7]

South Tucson's first mayor was Jewish businessman Sam Knipnis, one of the disenchanted, "feisty" residents who felt the area could be operated efficiently "without the increase in taxes which annexation by the city would have caused." The *Arizona Daily Star* opposed the incorporation drive, painting the South Tucson partisans as pie-in-the-sky optimists who thought they could run a modern city "by voluntary or free services" offered by residents. Organizers calculated that maintaining the county's tax rate would bring the new city $3,500 to $5,500 in revenue, which would be ample financing for city services.[8]

Legal wrangling immediately occupied the fledgling city. The City of Tucson provided water to South Tucson, requiring the former county residents, now South Tucson residents, to "meet city building, plumbing and electrical requirements and to pay the customary (fees) for permits and inspections." Once again, South Tucson organizers, mostly Anglo businessmen, challenged what they perceived to be an obtrusive policy by the City of Tucson. South Tucson's city council petitioned the Arizona Corporation Commission to supervise the sale of water by the City of Tucson, claiming that the fees and inspections required by the city were an infringement on South Tucson's sovereignty. In return, the City of Tucson threatened to turn off South Tucson's water supply in 120 days.[9]

Faced with Tucson's ultimatum, a group of South Tucson residents led by businessman G. J. McElroy started a disincorporation movement.[10] If they were successful, these South Tucson dissidents planned either to remain in the county or to seek annexation into the City of Tucson. To McElroy, maintaining South Tucson as a separate municipality was akin, politically, to cutting off your nose to spite your face.[11]

South Tucson's administration, in the meantime, made plans to develop their own water supply, announcing that "no alarm" was felt. The

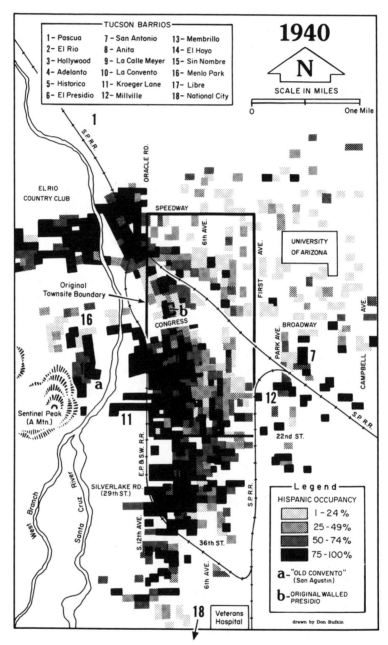

FIG. 8 Mexican American Settlement in Tucson, 1940. Hispanic settlement patterns remained centered on downtown in 1940, spreading from Congress Street south and north along Sixth Avenue and the railroad tracks. Note the El Rio Country Club to the northwest. (Source: Sheridan, *Los Tucsonenses*, p. 238)

Arizona Daily Star reported the range of sentiment in South Tucson, some of which was mildly militant and occasionally reflective of the familiar racism of the day: "As one put it, 'We are now free of Tucson's strings.' Another said, 'We are not worried at all. This is just a political squabble and reminds me of the Japs and Chinese. Instead of acting like children, both sides should get together.' " South Tucson's city council displayed its militancy by voting to tax Tucson's sale of water to southside residents. As the *Arizona Daily Star* reported, not quite tongue-in-cheek, "The South Tucson license collector will get you if you don't watch out. . . . every Tucson business and other enterprise, which so much as pokes a foot across the border into its limits, is a possibility for collecting licenses." [12]

The South Tucson dissidents who favored disincorporation presented the Pima County Board of Supervisors with petitions signed by 258 people, representing approximately two-thirds of South Tucson's taxpayers. This effort caused a "frantic" response by South Tucson's defenders, who threatened to organize a boycott against the businesses of those who had signed the disincorporation petitions.[13] The South Tucson leadership had criticized the City of Tucson's threat to shut off the water as a crass and cynical effort at political manipulation. Once challenged themselves, however, South Tucson's leaders hauled out their own heavy political artillery, threatening opponents with vituperative pressure politics. Instead of one obtrusive government in the metropolitan area, there were now two.

South Tucson officially became a ghost town when the board of supervisors accepted the request by petitioners to disincorporate the city, but court fights followed the disincorporation, and the town's legal status remained in limbo. Harry O. Juliani, South Tucson's volunteer attorney, vowed to take the issue to the Arizona Supreme Court if necessary, and in fact did so after Superior Court Judge Albert R. Thurman of Nogales ruled in favor of the board of supervisors' disincorporation of South Tucson. On November 28, 1938, the Supreme Court upheld Judge Thurman's decision.[14]

Despite the court's clearance, Tucson postponed its annexation of the area, partly due to uncertainty over the process of annexation. A Phoenix annexation had been challenged in court and was before the Arizona Supreme Court for final dispensation. Tucson officials announced that until the Supreme Court clarified annexation laws, which could take a year or longer, the city would hold off on annexing South Tucson.

The City of Tucson also agreed in court to a temporary injunction not to annex South Tucson. The injunction resulted from a suit by L. M. Calhoun, a "secondhand furniture dealer" from South Tucson. Calhoun had also sued the Pima County Board of Supervisors, asking the court to force the supervisors to hold an election to determine if residents in fact wanted to disincorporate.[15] Calhoun's county suit resulted in an election on March 27, 1939, in which reincorporation of South Tucson passed by seven votes, 70–63. Once again the Hispanic majority seemed to have absented itself from the political squabble. The *Arizona Daily Star* reported "great jollification among the townspeople as the word spread. . . . After a few sashays up and down South Sixth Avenue, main artery of the town, the celebrators descended on downtown Tucson, blaring their automobile horns and shouting jubilee."[16]

Dissidents, accounting for those 63 "no" votes, petitioned the board of supervisors to overturn the election. Meanwhile, the City of Tucson had passed an annexation ordinance bringing approximately two-thirds of South Tucson into the City of Tucson. Of course, legal action followed Tucson's effort to annex the area, and judges continued to determine the fate of South Tucson.

First, Judge Phelps of Phoenix ruled that Tucson's annexation had preceded the reincorporation vote, so the election was moot and the annexation stood. Tucson, nonetheless, agreed to "exercise no jurisdiction" until the courts decided the entire question of in-, un-, and reincorporation.[17] In July 1940, the Arizona Supreme Court overturned Judge Phelps's decision and approved South Tucson's reincorporation.[18]

Even though the Supreme Court had confirmed South Tucson's existence, political peace continued to elude residents. Avoidance of higher City of Tucson taxes simply required South Tucson residents to support services themselves, without enough population, industry, or commerce to support "a modern city government."[19] City services remained strained and, to some, inadequate, although inadequacy was in the eye of the beholder. As Emmert explained in her 1951 annexation study, some "individualist" residents preferred a limited government presence. Former Councilman Jesus Q. Elias described this libertarian attitude when he retired from the city council in 1975: "I've been against bars [South Tucson had fifty bars and liquor stores within its one-square-mile area in 1975], but I was always overruled. Unfortunately the other fellows thought we needed the tax revenue. It hurt the town because we get the scum of the drinkers. They chase out of the city [of Tucson] and they come down here because we don't have enough policemen."[20] Individualists may have also appreciated the lower property taxes in South Tucson.[21]

The individualist attitude surfaced in 1949 on the outskirts of South Tucson when the young town attempted its first annexation. South Tucson's effort to expand met with such vociferous resistance—"strong protest in which some of the town's new inhabitants said they were 'shanghaied' "—that the city council rescinded the annexation two weeks later.[22] Ultimately, dissidents failed to muster a majority to disincorporate the town, but the pattern of politically motivated resistance to urban expansion continued on the fringes of South Tucson. The 1949 annexees avoided being shanghaied by South Tucson, but they were eventually shanghaied by the City of Tucson in the 1956 annexation that encircled South Tucson. Nevertheless, the continued existence of South Tucson marked the first successful political resistance to the expansion of the City of Tucson. The Amphitheater and Flowing Wells districts attempted the same incorporation strategy in the late 1950s, but failed. Oro Valley, to the northwest of Tucson, attempted the strategy in the 1960s, and succeeded.

South Tucson accomplished one small annexation in 1953 and planned a larger expansion in 1956 into industrial areas to the east. A lack of industrial tax base had limited South Tucson's prospects since its incorporation in 1936, but these industrial areas were tempting targets for the City of Tucson as well. Tucson Mayor Don Hummel acted accordingly, springing the city's freshly devised annexation strategy on an unsuspecting public, and an encircled South Tucson. South Tucson residents complained bitterly, but the town government found itself unable to undertake the long and costly legal battle necessary to overturn the annexation.

The legal disputes continued into the 1960s as county officials investigated South Tucson's governmental officials and town finances. Elizabeth Martiny, South Tucson clerk from 1946 to 1961, attributed the investigations to ambitious county attorneys seeking to generate publicity for themselves, and collusion between the county and the city, which still wanted to annex the town.[23]

South Tucson has preserved its one-square-mile independence to this day, but does this constitute a victory? Political independence in South Tucson translated into "a strong sense of community" with an early commitment to ethnic and racial integration.[24] Political independence also translated into an impotent town government, surrounded by poverty, but without the material means to address the needs of its residents. The political victory may have been a Pyrrhic one, accomplished at the expense of many of the newly incorporated city's residents.

By the time South Tucson confronted the City of Tucson for the second time, in the 1950s, the ethnic character of the community had surfaced in its political representation. Several Hispanics served on the town council and as mayors in South Tucson from the 1940s. Frank Benitez was elected mayor in 1940, and Pat Gonzales in 1949.[25]

Non-Hispanics maintained prominent roles in the community, primarily in the commercial sphere. The founding members of the South Tucson Chamber of Commerce in 1954 were Ted Walker, Dr. Jack Klein, Don Gaskill, Ray Weaver, Soleng Tom (Chinese-American), Meyer L. Rutz, Don Depagh, Fred Duff, Monte Mansfield Jr., Miss Allair Bennett, Fred Dotson, and Ray Dunn.[26] In 1956, businessmen in the South Tucson Chamber of Commerce and Lions Club voted to support annexation of South Tucson by the City of Tucson, but nothing came of the annexation move. The political leadership of the community in 1956, predominantly Hispanic, continually protected their community's political independence.[27]

The barrio neighborhoods in South Tucson and the city of Tucson range from quaintly ethnic to distressingly blighted. The "wrong side of the tracks" image of South Tucson springs from its perceived ethnic character, made palatable for tourists only through a nostalgic haze. A 1969 Junior League guidebook described Tucson from the focal point of Sentinel Peak, " 'A' Mountain," which casts an afternoon shadow over "an area inhabited by Tucson's earliest settlers, the Pima Indians."[28] The guidebook directed visitors to explore Tucson's history, culture, and recreational facilities "Beyond the Shadows." Although the guidebook contained no overt racism, in the Junior League's schema, stereotypical barrios lay within the shadows. Even before the urban redevelopment efforts in the 1950s led to the labeling of the areas south of downtown as blighted, an ethnic transformation had taken place. The term "blight" itself implied a process at work as cities evolved from a state of urban health to sickness. Roy Drachman, one of Tucson's most prominent developers, described the process in terms of middle-class and Anglo flight from the barrios: "My brothers and I lived on the wrong side of the tracks during the early part of our lives in the old adobe family house. . . . The neighborhood on south Main Street was at one time one of the better residential districts, with many of the more affluent families in that part of town. However, by the time I was growing up all but three of the Anglo-American families had moved to other neighborhoods." [29]

Drachman's reminiscence sums up a common image of South Tucson and the barrios—one of relative poverty, more Hispanic than Anglo, and suffering in general from middle-class flight. The blight image applied to areas irrespective of their location in terms of the Southern Pacific railroad tracks. [30] Perhaps there was a time when barrios were "next door," rather than "over there." Sheridan mapped the ethnic neighborhoods and described them in positive terms. Drachman described his old neighborhood as "the wrong side of the tracks"—but it had not always been so. It had become a bad neighborhood. Drachman's assessment turned on cultural assumptions that he shared with most urban planners. The blight image stuck to working-class and ethnic areas, more densely settled than the sprawling suburbs. "Blight" made barrios targets for urban renewal, but there is intriguing irony in the fact that the barrio residents—far down on the ladder of generally recognizable political status in the 1950s—were the first to successfully resist "development."

Drachman's memoirs illustrate the common misconceptions that plagued urban planners throughout the redevelopment projects. In Drachman's lexicon, affluent equaled Anglo, and neighborhoods became less desirable when they became predominantly working-class and Hispanic. These assumptions appeared clearly in Drachman's explanation for the "failure" of the El Rio golf course and subdivision.

It was on the wrong side of the tracks. The residential lots around the golf course were not bought by those who could afford to build the kind of homes which might have triggered the successful development of a nice subdivision. The developers finally gave up on the idea of selling large lots, and sold off the land facing the golf course, in small lots, to Mexican-

American families who lived in that general area. There was no sewer line to serve the area at that time, and every homeowner had an outhouse in the back of the house, facing the golf course.[31]

Implicit in Drachman's view is his definition of a "nice" subdivision: Anglo, middle class or wealthier, no outhouses. Drachman's use of passive voice handily ascribed the lack of a sewer line to some higher cosmic order. Would the "nice" homes on larger lots have been equipped with outhouses or septic tanks, or would the city government or developer have found the resources to install sewer lines? "Mexican-American families who lived in that general area" eventually purchased the lots and homes. Sheridan described the El Rio barrio after World War II as a "prosperous working-class and middle-class neighborhood," but it was still, in Drachman's eyes, less than "nice."[32]

Discussions of "blight" assumed demographic movements: either the "right" sort of people moved out, or the "wrong" sort of people moved in. A 1968 redevelopment study explicitly stated this assumption: "Concurrently with the deterioration of the physical environment, there develop in the deteriorating areas also economic and social problems. As the value and rental of housing in the deteriorating areas decrease, economically and socially disadvantaged families and persons are attracted to them and thus physical, economic and social problems overlap and are interrelated."[33]

An earlier analogy of blighted areas as a malignant virus appeared in Mayor Don Hummel's 1957 application for federal funds to prepare an urban redevelopment project. Hummel described one of the major goals as being the "prevention of the spread of blight into good areas of the community." Like Drachman and others, the mayor defined blight as those areas south of downtown harboring "dirt, disease and delinquency."[34]

These characterizations of blight failed to acknowledge the degree of continuity within neighborhoods and made the assumption that deterioration is inevitable once middle-class, or Anglo, residents leave a neighborhood. The possibility of working-class, Hispanic neighborhoods maintaining a sense of continuity and solidarity did not occur to Drachman, the mayor, or the professional urban planners. Simply stated, they did not consider the possibility that residents in barrios liked living in barrios.

Sheridan provided a more positive image of barrio life in *Los Tucsonenses*:

Most Tucsonenses lived sober, industrious lives, building their homes and raising their children in relatively stable and peaceful surroundings. To them, the term *barrio* was positive rather than negative, embodying the virtues of social solidarity and ethnic pride. Within the barrios, Mexican culture flourished, and bonds of kinship, neighborliness, and *compadrazgo* enabled families to survive economic depressions and the growing dualization of Tucson society.[35]

In the mid-1950s, Roy Drachman attempted to buy property in the barrios near downtown as part of his own private redevelopment project.[36] Drachman, like others involved in urban renewal, thought of himself as a knight in shining armor seeking to revitalize his old neighborhood on South Main Street by creating shops, businesses, and convention facilities. The old neighborhood would disappear, but good riddance, he thought. As far as Drachman was concerned, it had become a slum. But residents had different ideas about the future of the barrio, and they successfully resisted Drachman's proposals.

Tucson's city government took up the mantel of urban redevelopment in 1957, when Mayor Don Hummel obtained federal funds to study urban renewal. Tucson's proposed 400-acre redevelopment project was similar to hundreds of projects throughout the country. Federal money flowed into cities—admittedly a trickle compared to the later deluge of Great Society funds—and redevelopment projects sprouted like so many well-fertilized mushrooms.[37] In the process, cities bulldozed working-class and poor neighborhoods willy-nilly, yet provided little commensurate accommodation for the residents of those neighborhoods.[38] Mayor Hummel addressed the issue of displaced persons in a 1958 speech to Tucson's Rotary Club defending the renewal project, saying the plan would affect 1,795 families, for whom "new homes will be found . . . and for others, reasonable rentals."[39] The assistant city manager, S. Lenwood Schorr, who was hired specifically to supervise the renewal project in 1961, also recognized the potential problem of displaced persons—"We fully realize our responsibilities to the people living there"—and he, too, pledged that the city would help residents find affordable housing.[40]

Unfortunately, Hummel and Schorr failed to match these comforting assurances with concrete proposals. As Schorr later acknowledged, "that was not handled with anything like the sensitivity it deserved."[41] Hummel had outlined the city's low-cost housing program in his 1957 request for federal funds: one project, La Reforma, with 160 families, with no plan to expand the program except in "low-cost housing projects to be built by private builders."

Hummel had planned to rely on the private sector to provide low-cost housing for more than a thousand families, and the Tucson Home Builders Association did express a willingness to study "the feasibility" of building low-cost units. Hummel also promised to "set up liaison with various civic and charitable organizations" to alleviate housing shortages,[42] citing as an example the Alianza Hispano Americano, a Hispanic mutual aid organization that had been making low-interest building loans to individuals since 1919.[43]

However, Hummel's reliance on the private sector to provide low-cost housing failed to meet the needs of residents who would be displaced by redevelopment. It also failed to assuage the philosophical concerns of conservatives. Local conservatives quickly labeled the public aspects of redevelopment as socialistic. A former Republican city councilman, Richard V. Ageton Jr., described the plan as outright socialism in a speech to the Young Republicans in 1961. Ageton said the renewal plan was a "menace to property owners. . . . Nothing can stand in the way of the bulldozers once an urban renewal plan is under way. Small businessmen, store owners who have spent a lifetime building up a small business are ruthlessly uprooted."[44] The opposition to renewal also drew on national conservative connections, as evidenced by the appearance of Bruce Alger, a Republican representative from Texas, who criticized urban renewal specifically, and President John Kennedy generally, at the 1961 Lincoln Day Dinner in Tucson.[45]

Hummel had addressed the socialist bugaboo three years earlier: "The urban renewal project planned for Tucson has no socialistic implications. . . . It is the purpose of the project to reclaim slum areas and return them to profitable and legitimate use under free enterprise. . . . Condemnation of land for slum clearance is no more socialistic than taking land for the construction of highways, a procedure which brings no objection."[46]

Although Hummel tipped his hat repeatedly to private enterprise as he struggled to garner support for the plan, urban planners working for the city too often revealed their enthusiasm for social engineering. Planners felt themselves working for the public good, operating on the assumption that residents in barrios were "trapped" there—unwilling prisoners in an ever declining social and economic morass. Redevelopment would break the cycle of poverty and prevent the cancerous spread of blight into "good" neighborhoods. In 1961, as the push for renewal continued, Schorr borrowed a phrase from Ageton's invective and labeled blight a "contagious menace . . . like a dagger pointing at the heart of downtown." [47] Unfortunately for the urban planners, conservatives like Ageton feared the menace of socialism more than they feared the menace of "blight."

Hummel and the planners also had to cope with the price tag of urban renewal projects. Federal money generally came in the form of matching funds, which meant that Tucsonans would be forced to come up with some portion of the costs. [48] In 1936, Tucsonans raised only $600 and thus failed to "match" federal money to build a dam in Sabino Canyon. [49] In 1958, however, Tucsonans passed a $14,660,000 bond issue to upgrade the city's infrastructure, an effort spearheaded by a citizens' committee led by Frank Drachman (Roy's older brother). [50] Perhaps the success of the bond issue convinced Mayor Hummel and the renewal planners that taxpayers would agree to fund the urban renewal plan.

Unfortunately for Hummel and the planners, opposition intensified. William R. Mathews, editor of the *Arizona Daily Star*, led the resistance of conservatives, although other spokesmen like Ageton confronted the plan with more gaudy language. The political climate in the community and the nation made conservative opposition inevitable. Goldwater Republicanism was on the rise, and Arizona enjoyed (or suffered from) a reputation as conservative territory. As Schorr recalled: "At that time the thing that was breaking it more than anything was, 'Oh, we don't want to have federal control. If we take federal money we'll have federal control.' To one who had recently come from Manhattan, that sounded rather ludicrous. But there was that spirit. It was epitomized in the remarks and platform of Barry Goldwater, whose star was at its highest in those years, and who had great influence locally and all over the state." [51]

Mayor Hummel repeatedly addressed this opposition throughout the planning process, but still resistance spread. In 1961 the Historic Sites Committee of the Arizona Pioneer Historical Society (later the Arizona

Historical Society) announced that the renewal plan "does not include the preservation of certain historic sites and of an area representative of the Old Pueblo era!" The Historical Society therefore opposed the same plan that the mayor described as culturally sensitive.[52]

Opposition also arose from the local chapter of the NAACP. In 1961, Schorr debated the issue of renewal with Mrs. T. D. Sprague after a regular meeting of the NAACP. In the debate, Sprague suggested that "a revision of the minimum housing code could force the landowners to improve the condition of the property or else." Schorr said that such an approach would not work, except in the sense that property would be condemned, resulting in "eviction of persons for whom no provisions were made."[53] Revisions of the plan after 1957 paid more attention to displaced persons but never included anything resembling one-for-one replacement of housing.[54]

In January 1962, a bipartisan effort by the outgoing and incoming city administrations modified the renewal plan. Don Hummel had lost his re-election bid to Republican Lew Davis, but the two cooperated in devising a modified renewal strategy. The 392-acre project was pared down to 76 acres, so as to "concentrate on the hard core of blight encroaching into the Central Business District." Planners had listened to area residents who argued for the preservation of their neighborhoods. Not coincidentally, Hispanic residents recently had become more politically active in the wake of John Kennedy's election in 1960.[55] The planners described the areas deleted from the project as containing "a high incidence" of home-ownership, and several historical sites. The cost of the plan was reduced to $6.4 million, with the city's share reduced to $523,000.

The modifications failed to satisfy the philosophically conservative and/or tax-conscious opponents, however. The Citizen Urban Renewal Enterprise (C.U.R.E.) committee favored the plan, seeking "to offset rising public opposition to any urban renewal plan using tax money here." Opposing the plan was the Citizen's Committee for Facts on Urban Renewal, which sought to distinguish between "federal urban renewal and modernization and development by private enterprise." Both sides of the issue mounted public relations campaigns, offering statistics to prove what a boon the project would be for Tucson—or what a boondoggle.[56]

In the midst of all the shouting, a University of Arizona sociologist conducted a poll in the targeted area to find out what residents thought

about the plan. Dr. Julius Rivera found that 71 percent of property owners in the targeted 76-acre area favored renewal, and 77 percent of the
residents favored the plan. Rivera reported, "The population in the area
is rather young, hopes for a better future, and as a group favors urban
renewal."[57]

Even after the homeowners to the south had been excluded from the
renewal project, opposition to the plan remained. A public meeting held
by the city council on April 24, 1962, to discuss the plan attracted approximately eight hundred concerned residents, including Luis Martinez,
who owned the AAA Sign Company at 166 South Meyer, within the project area.[58] As reported by the *Arizona Daily Star*, Martinez said that "statements by proponents that the minimum housing code cannot be enforced
are 'so much hooey.' The fault may lie in the city inspector or fire chief
or health officer or City Council, he said. Inspection and enforcing the
code can cure the cancerous growth in the area."[59]

Support for the plan within the new Republican administration began
to crumble. First, the mayor and council proposed a citywide referendum
on the renewal plan, but this tactic failed when the city attorney informed
the council that calling a referendum election would require their en-
dorsement of the renewal plan: a referendum could only approve or dis-
approve their decision, not the plan itself. At the same council meeting in
which the attorney offered this opinion, Luis Martinez appeared to repeat
his demand that "the council order city officials to start enforcing city
building, trash and sanitation codes within the sprawling district." Rather
than endorsing the renewal plan, the mayor and council followed Martinez's suggestion to drop it and instead ordered city officials to upgrade
enforcement of city regulations in the "blighted" area. Two weeks later,
the council passed a resolution encouraging the "private sector" to undertake renewal projects in the blighted areas, and urban renewal efforts
in Tucson ceased.[60]

But not for long. Conservative fortunes crashed in 1964 as Arizona's
favorite son, Barry Goldwater, lost in a landslide. Great Society programs
flourished, and the torrent of federal money into cities began.

The 1965 effort to jump-start redevelopment chronicled the earlier
failures: "up to 3,000 acres are blighted and in need of substantial treatment whether through redevelopment or rehabilitation. . . . The area
south of the Central Business District is by far the worst." According to

the Pueblo Center Redevelopment Project planners, the reduction in 1961 of the originally proposed 400 acres to 76 acres was due to "a lack of public support, and considerable editorial opposition from both newspapers," and the project was "closed out" in 1962.[61]

At the outset of the renewed push for redevelopment, planners sought to cultivate public support. The planning effort became professionally slick, and "blighted" appeared more and more in newspaper articles describing the redevelopment area. The plan remained scaled down, however. Planners acknowledged that Tucsonans would never finance the 400-acre project. As the project was reassessed, viable neighborhoods remained exempt from the plan, and the project area was reduced even further, from 76 acres to 52 acres.

The activism of the residents provided clear evidence to planners that barrios were not synonymous with slums. Residents approved of the redevelopment of truly blighted areas nearby. The old Gay Alley district, home of Tucson's prostitution in territorial days, remained part of the plan. Tucson's prostitution had long since migrated beyond the city limits into the county, where a succession of sheriffs tolerated it.[62] However, the old cribs (the narrow storefronts where the prostitutes worked) remained south of downtown, near the abandoned and dilapidated railroad sanitorium, and barrio neighborhoods supported the removal of these eyesores.

Removal of cultural icons was another matter. Mrs. Elva B. Torres chaired the Committee to Save La Placita in October 1967. The committee circulated petitions advocating the preservation and renovation of the site of the original Plaza de la Mesilla, where only the month before, 14,000 people had gathered for a Sixteenth of September celebration of Mexican independence.[63] Torres said, "We hope to make the area a bridge between Anglo and Mexican-American cultures. Our heritage as Tucsonans is being lost. It is not just for the Mexican people, but for all Tucsonans that we want to preserve a little bit of the Old Pueblo."[64]

This time redevelopment proceeded beyond the planning stage. Resistance did help shape the project, but not to the complete satisfaction of many residents. Tucson's downtown today shows the results of planning and compromise: the Tucson Convention Center, La Placita, a hotel, restaurants, and Barrio Historico. The Committee to Save La Placita had advocated renovating the plaza with shops, an arcade of *puestos* (small booths), a theater for Spanish-language productions, and an interfaith

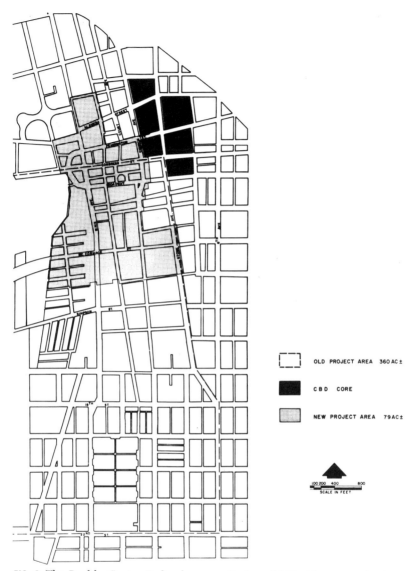

OLD PROJECT AREA 360 AC ±

C B D CORE

NEW PROJECT AREA 79 AC ±

100 200 400   800
SCALE IN FEET

FIG. 9 The Pueblo Center Redevelopment Project, 1965. The original urban renewal plan in Tucson targeted 360 acres near the central business district (CBD). Community resistance ended the plan. City leaders offered a more moderate renewal plan in 1965, the Pueblo Center Redevelopment Project, with the targeted area reduced to 79 acres (the lightly shaded area). Community resistance continued, eventually causing the further reduction of the renewal area to 52 acres. (Source: University of Arizona Library Special Collections)

chapel.[65] The La Placita that exists today—with its boutiques instead of puestos—obviously conforms only partially to the committee's vision. In the same manner, Barrio Historico differs greatly from the barrio that existed before renewal. As Bonnie Henry recalled, "Pretty pastels and law offices began to dot the remaining neighborhoods. What was left of the barrio became trendy. These days 'historic' translates to 'high priced.' "[66]

The Great Society and earlier federal programs provided financing for many urban redevelopment projects that deprived poor and working-class residents of their homes. In Tucson, working-class neighborhoods organized and resisted these redevelopment efforts, also using Great Society assistance. The efforts to empower poor people by providing organizational assistance paid off for some of Tucson's barrio residents who managed to preserve their neighborhoods.[67] Opposition did not pay off for Luis Martinez, nor for any of the shopkeepers in the northernmost blocks of South Meyer. Renewal leveled their low-rent commercial district. But more than property was lost.

Bertha Valenzuela described the impact of renewal on an old family friend who had been a lifelong resident of the barrio: "When she had to leave, she became very depressed. I don't know if she willed herself to die or whether she overdosed on her medicine, I don't know, but anyway she died. She preferred to die than to move somewhere else where she didn't know anybody."[68] As Don Bufkin recounted in later years, urban renewal in Tucson "was social and human tragedy even though it was physical renewal for some fifty acres down there."[69]

The Old Pueblo name signifies Tucson's cultural diversity, and the Chamber of Commerce continues to market Tucson's Hispanic past, but only in the most romanticized sense. The smell of frijoles and tortillas cooking in barrio streets may add to the charm of the Old Pueblo, but the visuals sometimes distract.

Public policy—such as urban renewal strategies—rarely focuses on private grievances. The Tucson Convention Center serves a broad population, audiences of everything from symphony music to monster truck rallies. Many of those patrons never knew the old barrio, or if they did, feel few reservations about the changes in the area. They would probably agree with Roy Drachman that the barrio was a slum. To many Tucsonans, "barrio" means chickens in the alley, cars on blocks, and spoken Spanish, and at times it seems that residents' biculturalism extends no further than a taste for margaritas and Mexican food.

Whether due to willful ignorance, romanticized nostalgia, or a combination of both, the social and human tragedy of urban renewal in Tucson slips further and further from view.

4 ENVIRONMENTAL RESISTANCE

■ ■ ■ ■ ■ ■ ■ ■ ■ ■ ■ ■ ■ ■

"Bottomless Towers"

Resistance to urbanization in Tucson based on an increasing environmental awareness became explicit in the 1950s. Boosters and planners initially ignored the environmental critique, despite the clear expression of concern over degrading natural surroundings. By the 1970s, the environmental critique had become the focal point for otherwise disparate forms of resistance as residents sought to preserve Tucson's natural setting and lifestyle.

The desert and mountain "visuals" have been important to Tucson's growth since at least the 1920s. To both tourists and prospective residents, boosters promoted a physically and morally healthful lifestyle made possible by Tucson's "uncitified closeness to nature."[1] The alluring photographs in Chamber of Commerce promotional literature often featured ranch-style homes in the foothills to illustrate the closeness to nature that Tucsonans enjoyed. But Tucson's other residents—who lived in barrios, tract-home suburbs, and rabbit-hutch apartments—could also claim a tie to, or at least an awareness of, nature in their midst because of the startling proximity of the mountains. Although definitions of nature rarely intruded into civic consciousness during the early 1950s, the valuation of the environment continued to increase. Eventually, environmental awareness helped to shape the argument in the community about growth.

The vociferous slow-growth movement that appeared in Tucson in the 1970s critiqued urbanization on the basis of its inevitable degradation of the natural environment. Slow-growth Tucsonans described Los Angeles and Phoenix as sprawling models not to be followed. The city's plan to construct a crosstown freeway repeatedly failed to gain public support, due at least partly to the negative example of Los Angeles. Bumper stickers appeared saying, "Leaving Tucson? Take a Friend." Historians, including Samuel Hays, argue that the first Earth Day in 1970 culminated a series of incidents that together resulted in the environmental movement.[2] Bufkin and Sonnichsen describe the resistance to urbanization in Tucson as an evolving movement that mirrored the growing national awareness of the environment.

However, even though the 1970s can be described as a watershed for environmental awareness in Tucson, the origins of that awareness appeared much earlier. Although the environmental link remained implicit, much of the political resistance to growth in the 1950s was based on environmental factors as urban development threatened quasi-rural lifestyles. The loss of natural surroundings rarely surfaced explicitly as a motivation for resistance, at least until 1956. Even then, the addition of environmentally based resistance to the previously described political and ethnic opposition to growth left the naysayers in the minority. Still, another voice had been added to the opposition, forcing pro-growth advocates to maneuver around another set of objections.

Perhaps the failure of the resistance to stop urban sprawl in Tucson was inevitable given the demographics of Sunbelt boomtowns: there were always too many recent residents who enjoyed Tucson just the way they had found it. By the time these new residents began to feel alarmed at the rate of change in the community—the rate at which development degraded natural surroundings—they, too, had been demographically pushed into the minority by the thousands of new residents, recently arrived, who enjoyed Tucson just the way *they* had found it.

The environmental resistance sought to preserve what its supporters saw as Tucson's unique lifestyle. Although references to nature fueled the debate, activism in defense of the natural environment itself came later.[3]

Instead, defense of a threatened lifestyle motivated the first environmental resistance. As Joseph Wood Krutch remarked in 1956, "I came to Tucson because I wanted a more attractive way of life, a more natural environment."[4]

Even boosters faced the reality that Tucson's marketability would be damaged if natural attractions like saguaro cacti or views of the mountains were destroyed by too much development. Despite their ridicule of environmentalists as alarmists, cautionary pronouncements and programs began issuing forth from the Chamber of Commerce.[5] Often the argument over growth devolved into shouting matches between pro-growth and slow-growth partisans, but in fact neither side could claim homogenous purity.

From the earliest tourist promotions, natural surroundings largely defined Tucson's lifestyle. The Sonoran Desert offered lush vegetation, but limited opportunities for casual strolls. As the cowboy song reported, in the desert there are "thorns on cactus and horns on toads" and "to sit down you need to have soles on your pants."[6] However, the Arizona-Sonora Desert Museum provided safe sojourns into the incredible variety of vegetation and animal life in the desert.

The idea for the museum originated in 1950 out of the environmental concerns of three Tucsonans who loved the desert. Organizers, with the support of the Pima County Parks Advisory Committee, created "an outdoor interpretive center where people from all the states could see and learn about the land itself; about the birds, reptiles, insects, mammals of the vast American desert; the plants, life!"[7] Visitors expecting barren sand dunes were no doubt surprised, not only by the lush vegetation but also by the startling landscapes that characterize basin and range topography. The Tucson, Catalina, and Rincon Mountains dominate the city on three sides, and the Santa Ritas provide a distant panorama to the south.

The Chamber of Commerce rolled out hyperboles galore when marketing Tucson's desert beauty and Old West traditions. Still, a heightened, if somewhat tailored, awareness of the environment was emerging, as illustrated in the following sketch, which appeared in 1962: "Tucson is located in a desert valley, surrounded by ranges of mountains. Unlike the Sahara, our desert contains much natural growth, such as green mesquite, palo verde and cottonwood trees. There are also many varieties of cacti, which, from April until late May, are in colorful bloom."[8]

Despite the Chamber of Commerce's assurances, the Sonoran desert remains primarily brown even in the midst of riotous spring. Mesquite trees are mostly black and spindly; palo verde trees offer green bark rather than green foliage; and cottonwood trees grow only near streams or in canyons with subsurface water, rarely appearing on the desert floor. Cacti do bloom colorfully, but delicately, and viewing the blooms of the trademark saguaro requires binoculars. Boosters' descriptions of the desert accentuated the exotic qualities of plant and animal life, such as those displayed in *Arizona Highways* and in photography books. Samuel Hays attributed the heightened sensitivity to the desert's beauty to the proliferation of nature photography books in the 1970s.[9]

Of course, there are other ways to define natural surroundings. The barrios near downtown, with their chickens, adobe walls, and wood-burning stoves, might be defined as more natural than the steel-and-glass, petroleum-fueled, sewer-served, electrified, ranch-style homes sprouting in the desert foothills. But boosters would have expressed no such ambivalence, confidently defining nature in its most material—and marketable—sense as "the desert." The climate, visual oddities like saguaro cacti, and western panoramas of "wide open spaces" all appeared in the promotional literature aimed at tourists and prospective residents. The Chamber of Commerce sold Tucson's lifestyle as shirt-sleeve golf in December and backyard barbecues in January.

The desert itself, though, fascinated some who, as Wallace Stegner observed, could let go of their prejudice for green. For these desert lovers, the Chamber of Commerce published guides to desert vegetation around Tucson, and realtors touted the "carefree," desert-landscaped suburban "lawns" of rock and cacti that required no mowing.[10]

The Tucson lifestyle also relied on Old West traditions, and suburban homes became "ranchettes" if accompanied by more than a sliver of land: "In the foothills, within 20 easy minutes from downtown, there are many suburban ranch home sites, commonly 4 acres or more in size. There is ample room for swimming pools, putting greens, shuffleboard and badminton courts, playground equipment and stables. Ranch living has become almost standard with Tucson executives who still are within easy driving distance of all the city's commercial and industrial areas."[11] Thirty-four dude ranches ringed the city in 1950, and eight riding stables provided access to horses for residents hankering for a ride.[12]

The Chamber of Commerce portrayed ranch life as an integral part of Tucson's environment. In 1964, NBC aired Barbara Walters' interview of Joseph Wood Krutch at a working cattle ranch, and the Chamber of Commerce trumpeted the broadcast as presenting a "true picture of the Old Pueblo."[13] The ranch motif even worked its way into industrial recruiting brochures. The Hughes Aircraft Company described the ranching lifestyle as akin to their own high-tech pursuits: "Arizona was settled by men who dared to be different, who rejected being part of a stereotyped pattern, and carved out a new life in their own frontier. . . . If you are interested in not only a new way of personal life but a different concept of professional life, we would like to talk about specific opportunities for you at Hughes-Tucson."[14] Hughes apparently had in mind the transmogrification of cowboys into aerospace engineers.

Of course, the values being advertised bore little relation to a careful definition of ranch life or the pioneer experience—which, of course, was not exclusively male. Ranchers continue to defend their way of life as nearer to nature than the broader, urbanized society. When economic arguments against their continuing federal subsidies hit too close to home, ranching interests trot out the lifestyle argument that ranching should be preserved as part of our culture, even if it makes little economic sense.[15] By ranch living, the Chamber of Commerce had in mind less-dense development, bridle trails, and panoramic views of city lights. Absent from the Hughes brochure and other promotional literature was any reference to spring branding and the castration of steers, spur-scarred horses, or cowboys missing fingers and teeth. "Old Tucson"—originally constructed as a movie set for the filming of "Arizona" in 1939—provided a properly sanitized version of the Old West appropriate for tourist excursions.[16]

Climate, however, was probably the most consistently marketed aspect of nature in Tucson, which boosters dubbed "the Sunshine City." Residents and visitors alike took sunshine for granted, and more than two consecutive days of rain brought howls of unfairness. Tucsonans "naturally" had the highest incidence of skin cancer in the continental United States.[17] Despite cancer statistics, the Chamber of Commerce made grandiose claims for the healthfulness of Tucson's climate:

Tucson has much to offer in the way of good health. Located in the Great American Desert, its climate is superb—comparable only to that of Egypt.

There is glorious health-building sunshine all year around, with a minimum amount of rain and no fog, snow or ice to retard good health . . . no dark, gloomy days to depress spirits. . . . Because of its warm atmosphere and mild winters, people in Tucson are fresh air and sun-worshippers and spend much time out-of-doors. This type of living always tends toward better health.[18]

The pamphlet went on, however, to list Tucson's eighteen hospitals and rest homes, forty-eight doctors, five osteopaths, two "chiropractic," three "chiropodists," and one "naturopath."[19]

Of course, the Chamber of Commerce touted Tucson's sunshine at every opportunity. A 1933 brochure, bound impressively in pressed copper metal etched with a scene of a saguaro cactus, announced the establishment of the Saguaro National Monument near Tucson with sunshine as a prominent selling point: "This is the Tucson Chamber of Commerce signing off—operating under a frequency of 300 days of golden sunshine by authority of our Lord."[20]

In November 1950, the Sunshine Climate Club even managed to take advantage of an East Coast blizzard. Arthur Godfrey, host of a popular radio show, sought to distract his stormbound listeners by reading about warmer weather as reported in the New York Times: "Miami, 68; El Paso, 76; Tucson, 85." Godfrey then wondered aloud if Tucson's temperature on November 28 had been "a freak." The Sunshine Climate Club responded with a telegram that Godfrey read on the air the following day: "Sincere condolences to our Eastern friends. Shirtsleeve temperature eighty-six yesterday here in Tucson no freak. Maximum temperature was above seventy-five for twenty days so far this month. You are invited to visit Tucson the sunshine city this winter. Thaw out your prostate." The Sunshine Climate Club practically crowed over this public-relations bonanza: a free advertisement broadcast to ten million listeners![21]

Arizona Highways profiled Tucson in 1956, 1958, and 1965, consistently emphasizing the outdoor western lifestyle. Residents enjoyed backyard pool parties and barbecues in the midst of natural desert vegetation. Tourists wore gaudy cowboy costumes as smiling wranglers gingerly shepherded them along spiny desert trails. And just to make sure prospective tourists understood what a genuine experience awaited them in Tucson, the Chamber of Commerce spelled it out: "For nine months of the year the city goes all out to cater to its winter visitors. Facilities for enjoyment of active sports are offered everywhere. The favorite pastime is riding out into the desert on old Indian trails or up into the foothills for a picnic by moonlight, western style. . . . vistas are spacious and the western atmosphere is genuine."[22] The Old Tucson Development Company tried to capitalize on those spacious vistas by issuing a film-recruiting brochure in 1972 describing "thousands of acres of unspoiled wilderness" starting—miraculously—just fifteen miles from downtown Tucson.[23]

The children of residents also enjoyed the benefits of western living. "Private Schools of Tucson Arizona, 1952" described open-air classrooms in "ranch schools" where students played football on bare desert ground and received lessons in hard work and self-reliance by doubling as wranglers.[24]

The maintenance of Old West traditions as part of Tucson's lifestyle required an unspoiled natural environment, but even then, questions of boundaries arose. In "Selling the Desert," historian Kerwin Klein discusses the process by which mythical definitions of the western landscape became ingrained in the culture and are still accepted despite increasing boundaries of space and time. The Old West became something to experience in parks and monuments and on scenic highways. According to the boosters' promotional literature, however, the palpable reality of the Old West peacefully coincided with modern Tucson. Boosters sold prospective residents the notion of inconsequential material boundaries: nature and/or the Marlborough Man just on the other side of the chain-link fence: "Off for a ride in the desert! Nothing can offer sharper contrast to big city living than the care-free individualistic life of the western range, especially when the trees aren't trees, but saguaros!"[25]

Boosters marketed nature and lifestyle with happy abandon after World War II. Although there was political resistance to growth, the environmental resistance developed later. Historians characterize the increasing opposition to growth as based on the rise of this environmentally based resistance, founded on the growing realization that the natural environment within and surrounding the city was degrading.

Awareness of potential trouble in Tucson's environment appeared in scientific studies conducted during the 1950s, some of which the Chamber of Commerce had commissioned in the hope of obtaining reassuring data for their promotional literature. In 1953, the Chamber of Commerce issued a pamphlet providing "The Truth About Water in Tucson." Despite the fact that Tucson relied solely on groundwater (at that time the largest American city to do so), the Chamber of Commerce claimed that declining water tables posed no threat. Eventually boosters, and Tucsonans in general, came to rely on the Central Arizona Project, a grandiose, multibillion-dollar federal project that began delivering Colorado River water to Tucson in 1992 (with some interesting, unforeseen results, discussed in chapter 5).

Another future problem, pollen counts, began appearing in 1956, but also with the assurance that no problem existed.[26] The Chamber of Commerce's first reference to pollen counts in 1956 comes out of nowhere. Why would the Chamber of Commerce even mention pollen counts unless it was trying to short-circuit concerns that were already present and circulating, or at least foreseen just beyond the horizon? As late as 1968, the Chamber of Commerce still maintained that pollen levels were inconsequential: "From late November to mid-February the pollen count in the Tucson area is practically nil and even during the spring and fall when there is a certain amount of pollen, the count is extremely low compared with that of Eastern states."[27] Despite these assurances, by 1968, Tucsonans sneezed with distressing regularity. The proliferation of olive trees and other nonnative plants, imported by immigrants seeking to make the brown desert more closely resemble the green landscape they had left behind, had created an allergy problem in Tucson. Eventually, in 1984, the board of supervisors banned the sale of olive and mulberry trees in Pima County.[28]

In the mid-1960s, a University of Arizona researcher studied air pollution in Tucson and also arrived at a laudatory, although cautionary, evaluation. The study found that air pollution similar to Los Angeles's smog reduced visibility only twice in Tucson from 1959 to 1964. The sources of the smog were emissions from automobiles and from the copper smelter in San Manuel, on the other side of the Catalina Mountains. The cautionary note at the end of the report recommended further monitoring of air quality but offered no plan for curbing or eliminating the problem.[29]

"Sprawl" threatened the natural environment most directly as the city spread inexorably over the desert basin. Although the regional plan of 1945 recognized the "rapid and often haphazard subdivision of land,"[30] the same pattern of development continued throughout the 1950s and 1960s. The push for urban renewal in 1968 cited "leapfrog" development as indicative of Tucson's urbanization: "Flat topography, aggressive development of major arterials, and the availability of utilities, coupled with low density of construction have caused development to leapfrog vacant lands. Substantial scattered vacant lands thus exist throughout the community and even near the Central Business District."[31] According to Emmert, as many as half the platted lots remained undeveloped within the city limits in 1951.[32] Developers avoided these lots, given the availability of cheap land beyond the urban fringe. "In-fill" became a campaign slogan of the slow-growth candidates in the 1970s.[33]

The aesthetic qualities of the community came under scrutiny in the early 1960s. The Chamber of Commerce formed the Tucson Beautiful Committee in 1961 to promote "parks, picnic areas, and trailways . . . and keep our atmosphere clean."[34] The committee lobbied for "effective smog control" and mounted cleanup campaigns, one of which collected "over 400 tons of tumbleweed and other debris."[35]

In 1965, the city council appointed the community goals committee to come up with suggestions to preserve Tucson's "pleasant, healthful and harmonious environment."[36] The committee's report offered a cheerleading call to action, focusing on the need to accentuate traditional architecture and native landscaping (although the palm trees pictured in their report were decidedly nonnative). The report also advocated commonsense solutions to visual pollution, such as the placement of power lines underground. At least implicitly, urban growth had taken on menacing qualities. The committee's description of the Tucson basin as having "gradually succumbed to urban land use" cast urbanization as a conquering rather than civilizing influence.[37]

Efforts to analyze the aesthetics of urban environments proliferated in the 1960s. One report, "The Tucson Visual Environment," drew on a methodology for studying urban landscapes developed by Kevin Lynch in *The Image of the City*. By the late 1960s, when the report appeared as part of continuing urban renewal programs, analysts could recognize a general uneasiness, or "perceptual stress," among residents who felt their lifestyle was being threatened. The report described Tucson as "a city of low imagability, difficult to describe as to form, and dominated by the beauty of its surrounding natural environment. . . . Many of the citizens indicated a nostalgic and strong attachment to the Tucson of the past—its way of life, its architecture, and history, its 'small town character.' Unfortunately many of these citizens seemed bitter and resentful of changes."[38] One resident summed up citizen bitterness by placing Tucson's charms firmly in the past tense: "Tucson was charming, a small city in a spot of incredible natural beauty. Now . . ."[39]

"The Tucson Visual Environment" sought to explain the environmental degradation that troubled so many residents. Based on Lynch's methodology for determining "imagability," the report described Tucson as suffering from low-density development "resulting in monotony and disorientation," a decentralized downtown area, an undifferentiated grid system, perceptual stress (an awareness of increasing traffic, smog, and slums), and problems of "visual quality and legibility." Legibility referred to concepts such as "bottomless towers," an idea generally applied to urban skyscrapers, whose tops define the urban silhouette, but whose entire height is rarely seen. In Tucson, residents recalled seeing the entire height of their natural skyscrapers, the mountains. As the city expanded across the floor of the desert valley, the foothills and lower reaches of the mountains became obscured, and the mountains became "bottomless towers."

It is difficult, however, to quantify the impact of this visual change on residents.[40] Was it enough to cause another manifestation of political resistance to growth in the 1960s? Obviously many immigrants arrived in Tucson not out of a love for the desert, but a desire for snow-free winters. Many Tucsonans pushed the desert away by planting Bermuda grass and fir trees in their lawns. Desert landscaping was always acceptable in Tucson, and in some neighborhoods, the rule. But in other neighborhoods, lawn mowers droned every weekend. And Tucsonans sneezed.

Although quantification of the growing awareness of environmental degradation in the 1950s proves elusive, there was an observer in Tucson who took note of the changes in the environment and criticized them eloquently.

Naturalist Joseph Wood Krutch wrote about the desert from his retirement home on the outskirts of Tucson. His earlier career in academia and as a prominent social critic gave his observations of desert life added significance. When Krutch wrote about the desert, he was critiquing modern industrial society and the "modern temper." Krutch moved to Tucson from New York City in 1952. He had been visiting Tucson since the late 1930s, and in 1950 he spent a sabbatical year there before returning to Columbia University in 1951. The following year Krutch retired permanently to Tucson.[41]

Krutch's residence in Tucson coincided with the city's growth from a small desert town to a sprawling metropolis. Several other cities in the West also experienced rapid urbanization in the years following World War II, but few cities contained such a sterling voice to comment on the change in urban landscape that was taking place. Nature and lifestyle drew Krutch to Tucson, but the change in the natural environment caused by rapid urbanization threatened the way of life that Krutch, and many others, found so attractive in the early 1950s.

As a naturalist and social critic, Krutch decried the loss of natural environment in Tucson's urban fringe, and suburbanization's intrusion into the pristine beauty of the Sonoran Desert. But to what degree can any suburban area be considered "natural"? As with most preservationist critiques, Krutch offered a personal view of what constituted an acceptable intrusion upon the natural environment: one house per five acres.

Krutch's complaints joined the already-established resistance in the community, which was both politically and ethnically motivated. These other manifestations of resistance lacked Krutch's philosophical foundation or rhetorical eloquence but were similar to his critique in that they were individualistic, apolitical (or unstructured), and mostly ineffective.[42]

Krutch first toured the southwestern deserts in 1938. As an amateur naturalist, Krutch observed with fascination the exotic flora and fauna of the desert. More immediate, however, was the attraction of the southwestern climate: "health was the decisive factor without which mere inertia would probably have persuaded me to continue in the way I had been going. . . . to have a really good excuse for living in Arizona is just what I [had] been unconsciously waiting for."[43] Krutch brought a sensitivity and curiosity to his surroundings beyond that of the typical retiree, but nonetheless he was part of the early "snowbird" migration to the Sunbelt.

In the debate over the growth of Tucson, Krutch spoke from an economically independent perspective common to the middle-class retiree. He could argue against "progress" from a position of personal security, requiring no extractive or despoiling industry to secure his living.[44] As a new resident in 1952, Krutch built a modest home on five acres of undisturbed desert beyond the city limits, joining the large number of fringe residents looking askance at the expanding behemoth called Tucson. By 1956, Krutch voiced opposition to Tucson's growth.

Krutch recognized the futility of arguing for no growth but still offered a critique of Tucson's expansion: "If we can't keep Tucson small, can't we at least keep it different? . . . Tucson has a community personality which we should take care not to destroy. People smile more here and are happier than in the larger cities. We should endeavor to keep the things about Tucson which are unique."[45]

The natural desert surrounding his home epitomized what was unique about Tucson for Krutch. The horse owners on the fringe of Tucson might have agreed, as long as a few bridle trails were included. To other residents of Tucson, the flat, easily graded valley floor invited development, with cacti, birds, and lizards just inconsequential casualties of human presence. Development proceeded unencumbered through the 1950s, but not without opposition, as the preceding chapters have shown. It was not until 1956, however, that an explicit environmental critique was offered. After a series of large annexations were completed in 1955 and 1956, which even city officials admitted to be "a bit indigestible,"[46] Krutch spoke out. In a speech to Tucson's Rotary Club in October 1956, Krutch made his argument for preserving Tucson's uniqueness: "Whenever I see one of those posters which reads 'Help Tucson Grow,' I say to myself, 'God forbid.' I suggest that the Rotary Club adopt a new motto: 'Keep Tucson Small.' "[47] Krutch later acknowledged that his environmental concerns remained peripheral to the community at large in the 1950s.[48] The *Arizona Daily Star* reported his speech as possibly a tongue-in-cheek exercise: "Dr. Krutch left some Rotarians wondering whether to take him seriously, or whether he was speaking more or less in a humorous vein."[49]

On the same day that Krutch spoke to the Rotary Club, the planning and zoning commission approved a controversial rezoning request in the suburban area beyond Krutch's five-acre homestead. Of the three plans proposed, the commission approved the plan for the most intensive development, increasing business zoning by sixty-five acres within a one-mile-diameter area, despite the protests of residents of the area "who sought to retain the suburban ranch type of zoning [then] in existence." Concern over the diminishing natural environment may have motivated the rezoning protest at some level, but on the surface at least, increasing taxes and a conflict of interest by one of the commissioners propelled the "heated 3-hour discussion."[50]

Krutch described his controlled-growth ideas in "Man's Mark on the Desert" in 1962. The spread of the city across the desert floor had left Tucson "no longer recognizable as the town I came to live in some dozen years ago." He faulted the blind allegiance to "development" and "progress." Krutch recognized the futility of government regulation as he described the realities of zoning ordinances: "When an area is zoned as for residence only, that means merely that you can't put a commercial building there—until someone wants to. Then the zoning will be changed."[51] Krutch understood the minority standing of environmental awareness and found solace only in "partial solutions":

> Does all this mean that the desert, with all it has meant to many of us and might mean to generations still to come, is doomed to disappear in the not too distant future—unless indeed a fundamental change of heart should take place in the majority of the citizens who direct our destinies? Perhaps. Perhaps, on the other hand, there is a partial solution—namely the reservation of some sections of it as public land explicitly reserved in Parks, Monuments, and Wilderness Areas. It is far more rewarding to be able to live in the desert than merely to visit it. But that is at least better than nothing.[52]

The Saguaro National Monument and the Arizona-Sonora Desert Museum provide examples of Krutch's "partial solution." Krutch supported the museum early and often; Sonnichsen credits him for naming the museum's van, "The Desert Ark," used in outreach programs throughout the community.[53]

The Desert Museum and Saguaro National Monument remain prized assets of the community, valued by boosters as well as ardent desert preservationists. The definition of the desert's value, with or without a pecuniary element, separates boosters and preservationists, but a value attached to the desert remains. Preservation results have been sufficient for some, but considered inadequate by others.

Development continued into the 1980s as the sparsely settled urban fringe approached the topographical barriers of the mountains that border the Tucson valley. Development intensified as townhomes replaced ranchettes. Even Krutch's "partial solution" became threatened in the 1980s as the debate over Tucson's expansion reached the Saguaro National Monument: How closely can the fragile ecosystem of the monument be ringed by tract homes and golf courses before the monument is destroyed both aesthetically and materially? Development has continued despite a fractious history of protests and warnings. Krutch represented one part of the resistance: "Is it not obvious that the process of mechanization has passed its optimum point when it has ceased to make life more leisurely, less tense, and more comfortable and become instead a burden to maintain?"[54]

When Krutch opposed growth, he was thought to oppose progress. Superficially, this anti-progress critique put him on the fringe of resistance, but because of his acknowledged intellect, he was considered more eccentric than lunatic. But in Tucson, boosters had a stake in preserving the environment and showed an awareness of environmental degradation early in the 1950s, even if they did not admit to such an awareness in their promotional brochures.

The case of foothills development perhaps displays most clearly the dynamics of environmental resistance to growth, and the limitations of local political efforts to preserve natural surroundings.

John Murphey, the developer most responsible for Tucson's spread into the Catalina foothills, often limited development and preserved natural surroundings in such a way as to create the "foothills lifestyle" that became prized as Tucson's most desirable. Murphey never opposed Tucson's growth—as a developer he fostered it, and profited greatly from it—but he did offer a sort of resistance in that he distrusted zoning regulations and politicians' long-term stewardship of the community. Murphey controlled growth through his own private business dealings, preserving much of what was considered traditional in Tucson. With the assistance of architect Josias Joesler, Murphey devised strict covenants and deed restrictions to make sure homes and neighborhoods in the foothills "fit the terrain."[55] As Dave Ellwood, former county/city planner in the 1950s, recalled, "Murphey was a visionary guy and he had a built-in sensitivity to the land. He would walk or ride the whole area before he laid it out, and he took care to site houses on the land in the best way. Without him,

God knows what would have happened to the foothills." By creating the foothills lifestyle, Murphey increased his personal wealth while preserving natural surroundings. He became a model for other developers in the area who also used deed restrictions and covenants to control "such matters as the color of roofing material and placement of garbage containers."[56]

The impact of Murphey's development in the foothills became more obvious after his death in 1977. The low-density housing patterns preserved by Murphey's own initiative fell under the purview of county zoning regulations. Critics of the more dense development in the foothills called the county's incremental zoning a hodgepodge following no master plan, which resulted in "a sort of aesthetic holocaust." Townhomes and condominiums sprang up, much to the chagrin of ranch-home residents who maintained that their "tread-softly" (although sprawling) presence in the desert offered an acceptable intrusion on the natural landscape. The one-house-per-acre residents referred to the new construction as "rabbit warrens for people." Resorts and golf courses " 'Californicated the foothills' by imposing elegance where wilderness once reigned." Denser development led to increased resistance in the late 1980s as the population in the fifty-square-mile area reached about 40,000. The hue and cry increased when residents learned that zoning for the area would allow a total population of 80,000. Even developer Roy Drachman voiced his dismay: "What's happened has not been pleasing to me. I am distressed to see some of the things developers have done in the foothills—things that don't make sense. They've created scars that will take a long time to heal. Some of the developers who did this are friends of mine, but that's the way I feel."[57]

Murphey had purchased 1,700 acres in the foothills in the 1930s and then had proceeded to create "the city's most prestigious residential area."[58] The Shields family had owned the Flying V Ranch in the foothills since the early 1900s. They also sought to preserve the rural lifestyle of the foothills by maintaining their 830 acres as a working ranch and, of course, dude ranch. In 1979, however, the Shields sold 272 acres to the Estes Company, one of Tucson's busiest homebuilders. "We didn't have much choice," Reed Shields told the *Arizona Daily Star*. "The last year we had all the land, our taxes were over $30,000. My dad said, 'That's awfully expensive horse pasture.' "[59]

Krutch, Murphey, and Shields all expressed a sensitivity for the natural environment, although how each defined that environment, and defined an acceptable intrusion upon it, differed. Krutch spoke from a position of economic independence that allowed for a purer preservationist critique. Murphey became a millionaire as a developer, primarily in the Catalina foothills, and in the process created a prestigious residential area that was criticized as elitist (a critique shared with environmentalism generally). As journalist Douglas Kreutz phrased the question, "Should the foothills remain a special, protected place of wide-open spaces and top quality construction—and thereby be the exclusive domain of the affluent?" [60]

The Shields family has managed to maintain their ranch in the foothills, sandwiched between a resort hotel and golf course on one side and a residential development on the other. All three, Krutch, Murphey and Shields, considered themselves defenders of the "natural surroundings."

5 TUCSON EPILOGUE

■ ■ ■ ■ ■ ■ ■ ■ ■ ■ ■ ■ ■ ■

Monkey Wrenches and Mountain Lions

From the 1970s, throughout the 1980s, and into the 1990s, contentious resistance has confronted virtually every proposed development in Tucson. Residents within the city limits and beyond the urban fringe, motivated by political, ethnic, and/or environmental concerns, have opposed growth in the 1990s with greater visibility and volume than the opposition of the 1950s. Newspapers regularly chronicle the fights over development—the squabbles make good copy—but rarely with a recognition of the deep roots of the controversy. The visibility of contemporary resistance obviates the need for a precise recapitulation here. Rather, this epilogue briefly summarizes recent opposition to Tucson's urbanization within the context established in the previous chapters.

Faith in the beneficent qualities of progress and growth has continued to motivate boosters, planners, and politicians. The city government further entrenched the effort to lure businesses and residents to Tucson with a formalized structure staffed by city workers and funded by tax revenues. In the mid-1960s, Democratic Mayor James N. Corbett created the Development Authority for Tucson's Economy (DATE) to facilitate the recruitment of businesses to Tucson. DATE's first major success occurred in January 1965 when Burr-Brown Industrial Research Company announced its plans to establish a facility in Tucson.[1] By 1974, DATE officials claimed to have attracted fifty-two companies to the city. In 1978, the Tucson Economic Development Corporation replaced DATE, and companies continued to migrate to Tucson. IBM established a plant southeast of the city in 1978, and National Semiconductor arrived in 1979.[2]

Business recruitment continued gung-ho, but the city's efforts proved vulnerable to national economic downturns. When IBM announced the end of manufacturing operations in Tucson in 1986 (an engineering and research staff of approximately 1,000 remained at the Tucson facility as of the summer of 1994), city leaders began questioning the strategy of relying on a few large employers for the city's economic health.[3] "Diversification" became the call in city hall. However, this sobering reassessment of recruitment strategy remained firmly entrenched within the old assumptions about "progress." City leaders continued to describe economic stasis or recession as anathema. Reductions at the Hughes plant, the closing of National Semiconductor, and the loss of the Gates Lear Jet facility at the airport all cast a pall over boosters and politicians in the 1980s.

Of course the city survived, but within the assumptions and worldview of the boosters, a state of health was not restored until a new wave of business migrations into Tucson in the 1990s. The major coup, trumpeted loud and long by city leaders, was the transfer of Hughes's southern California operations to Tucson, announced in 1993. In the boosters' *weltanschauung*, the struggle between cities is Darwinistic, and Los Angeles's loss is Tucson's gain.

The city government also further formalized its planning and zoning structures in the 1970s. The community goals committee of the mid-1960s gave way to the comprehensive planning process, "convened" by the city council in 1973.[4] The planning process resulted in a draft plan in March 1975 that divided the city into fourteen separate planning districts. Each district had its own planning organization, designed to foster citizen participation through mandated open meetings.[5]

Despite these new functional bureaucracies, in the 1970s the impact of planning and zoning on Tucson's urban sprawl remained minimal. The rule of thumb seemed to be "zoning for the asking."[6] Developers continued to spread low-density housing tracts over the desert floor, at least until "low-cost peripheral land" began to disappear in the late 1970s. High interest rates in the late 1970s also pinched development by reducing the viability of sprawling, low-density, suburban housing, except for the most affluent.[7] More recently, Tucson's suburbanizing sprawl has resumed, mostly toward the far southeast and northwest. The improving employment picture at Hughes and other companies has created another boom for home builders and realtors.

Zoning decisions continue to baffle residents and professional planners. In 1992, the board of supervisors adopted the "Comprehensive Plan for Eastern Pima County." The plan appeared after three years of study and was to be implemented in one month. Before it went into effect, however, the supervisors approved a controversial proposal for a resort development in the mouth of Pima Canyon, which had been identified in the plan as an "environmentally sensitive" area.[8] Krutch's prediction about zoning decisions—that they last until someone with money wants them changed—seems to hold true.

Political resistance to Tucson's expansion has continued full bore, and opposition appears in the traditional ad hoc protest of fringe residents resisting annexation and zoning changes. In the mid-1960s, Mayor Corbett encountered resistance to the city's annexation policy that was similar to the opposition Mayor Hummel faced in the 1950s. Corbett acknowledged that the protesters would have to be dragged into the city "kicking and screaming." Soon thereafter, a new batch of stickers appeared on Tucson bumpers: "Kicking and Screaming, Yes. Annexation, No!"[9]

The 1970s saw the election of controlled-growth supervisors and councilmen, under the leadership of Ron Asta, who served on the board of supervisors from 1972 to 1976. The "Astacrat" movement espoused environmental concerns similar to those expressed by Krutch fifteen years earlier. Asta proposed restrictions on urban sprawl, and he advocated in-fill and commercial/industrial development more in harmony with the desert environment.

However, in 1977, three controlled-growth councilmen lost a recall election after vigorously pushing a water-rate hike, and after appearing unsympathetic to "growth" even though a stagnant job market gripped the city.[10] Asta served only one term on the board of supervisors. His personal flamboyance wore thin with voters at the same time that pro-growth partisans targeted him for defeat. But the controlled-growth agenda was kept alive in succeeding boards by Supervisor David Yetman (who later became director of the Tucson Audubon Society). Environmental awareness has possessed a voice in Tucson electoral politics consistently since the 1970s.

The best recent example of resistance on Tucson's urban fringe is the opposition to the proposed Rocking K development southeast of Tucson. Developer Don Diamond, in conjunction with Estes Properties, proposed in 1989 to build two resorts and a "planned community" of about 30,000 new residents on 6,380 acres of the old Rocking K ranch east of the Saguaro National Monument.[11] Area residents—who as neighbors of the Saguaro Monument enjoy a low-density, quasi-rural lifestyle—vehemently protested the new development, but the debate quickly became more complex than simply a "growth versus no-growth" argument. B. Paleck, superintendent of the monument, actively involved himself in planning for the new development, seeking to preserve the environment of the monument as much as possible given what appeared to be inevitable growth.[12] The resistance scenario was thus complicated as the ranger worked with developers, and as area residents, who considered themselves to be the best of neighbors to the monument, failed to question whether their presence already constituted an unacceptable intrusion on the Sonoran Desert. Meanwhile, the trademark saguaro cacti continue to die from unknown causes.

In a more structured manifestation, neighborhood associations have increased their visibility and political effectiveness throughout the 1980s, regularly challenging development plans and revisions of city regulations within their neighborhoods. Neighborhood associations constitute powerful players in city politics, and electoral success regularly greets candidates endorsed by the associations.[13] The neighborhoods use strategies to defend themselves beyond a simple reliance on electoral politics. The Sam Hughes and West University neighborhoods use historic-building designations to control development within their communities. Thus, the expanding University of Arizona, sandwiched between these neighborhoods to the east and west, has found the path of least resistance to the north and south.

Neighborhoods, and the community in general, continue to oppose freeway construction in Tucson. Citizen participation in the development of transportation plans has failed to prevent NIMBY-like (or "Not in my back yard") protests. As Sonnichsen describes, "Nobody wanted a freeway to go past his place. Nobody wanted a bantam interchange on his corner."[14] The "Butterfield route" plan for a crosstown freeway appeared in 1960. Opposition grew until the city council dropped the plan in 1974.[15] New plans for freeways along the Rillito and Pantano washes appeared and disappeared in the 1970s. The Pima Association of Governments approved one of five plans in 1981, proposing two "high-speed" parkways "through landscaped areas dotted with parks." Protest created stalemate. Opponents of freeways in Tucson still point to the Los Angeles model as the course not to follow.[16]

The external opposition to Tucson's expansion, following the South Tucson model, reappeared in the 1960s with the incorporation of Oro Valley to the northwest. Originally the community surrounded a golf course and country club, but now the town has begun its own expansion policy, seeking to acquire tax-generating areas coveted by Tucson itself. Marana, a long-established farming community farther northwest, is also pursuing an aggressive annexation policy aimed at acquiring tax-generating shopping areas on Tucson's northwest fringe.

Internal divisions now rankle Oro Valley and Marana as residents oppose their communities' expansion policies. Marana farmers see their lifestyle threatened by burgeoning development. Oro Valley residents, who have long cast a suspicious eye on Tucson's city hall, now spend their time organizing recall elections within their own community.

In the meantime, the City of Tucson, still expansionist at heart, seeks to paint itself as the "sensitive" annexing agent, better able to accommodate residents' desires and needs. In court challenges brought by the City of Tucson in 1994 to halt Marana's annexations in the northwest, Tucson claimed itself to be the appropriate annexer. Marana pictured itself as the "little guy" struggling for civic survival against the metropolitan "bully" of Tucson. So far, the courts have validated Marana's annexations. The story continues.

South Tucson and the barrios have continued to struggle for their existence. South Tucson remains surrounded and frozen in its one-square-mile niche. A tragedy in 1978 nearly bankrupted the community when a South Tucson police officer accidentally shot and paralyzed a City of Tucson police officer during a joint operation. The resulting legal suits and $3.59 million settlement almost outstripped the town's resources.[17]

Insufficient tax revenues continue to plague South Tucson. Despite a gleaming new city hall (financed with federal grants), South Tucson struggles to provide basic services. In early 1994, the town manager proposed cutting costs by eliminating the community's police and fire departments and instead contracting out for such services. At the eleventh hour, sufficient funding materialized to meet the police and fire department payroll.

Tucson's barrio neighborhoods continued to face renewal efforts aimed at "blighted" areas throughout the 1970s. The Tucson Community Center project, resulting from the city's first implemented renewal plan, opened in 1971. The La Placita development of shops and restaurants near the TCC opened in 1974 but struggled financially throughout the 1970s. Meanwhile, the gentrification of the Barrio Historico continued, with rents rising as commercial occupants replaced long-time residents.[18]

The conundrum of urban renewal and residential viability appears most clearly in the effort to preserve the Armory Park neighborhood near downtown. In 1974, the city's zoning board declared Armory Park a historic district, which qualified the area for tax reductions and government loans.[19] Many residents took advantage of the proffered financial assistance to improve their property, but they soon found that the investment made on their property surpassed its market value. Home improvement became a financial quagmire.[20]

Renewal plans in the late 1970s continued to target barrios near downtown. The Snob Hollow and Rio Nuevo projects were opposed by area residents who asserted that the neighborhoods were not blighted. These plans, plus downtown renewal plans in 1975, 1978, and 1980, failed due to resident resistance and broader community opposition based on the perceived unacceptable tax burden.[21]

Successful renewal did occur on North Main Avenue, where the city established the Tucson Museum of Art. The ten-year project culminated in 1975. A new city hall and county and federal buildings also sprouted downtown in the 1970s, generally on the sites of their predecessors.[22]

Nature and lifestyle are still major selling points in Tucson. But how does a metropolitan population of almost one million peacefully inhabit such a fragile ecosystem as the Sonoran Desert? Residential areas on the city's fringe still revel in their surroundings: the cooing of quail and mourning doves, and the howling of coyotes. The resistance at Rocking K and elsewhere on the urban fringe largely arose from residents' efforts to preserve their lifestyle based on one house per three acres, two acres, or even one acre. Many developers now realize that environmental sensitivity, at least rhetorically, must accompany any plan to bulldoze the desert.

Upscale resorts have proliferated, adding sophistication to the traditions of dude ranches. Guests may still ride horses at sunset, but they are equally attracted to golf, tennis, and health spas. Pink and yellow Jeeps with canvas tops trundle tourists daily into the desert for outings. Mild winters and sunshine dominate tourist promotions, just as they did fifty years ago.

Despite the glowing sales pitches, degrading environmental circumstances have become impossible to ignore. Pollution concerns range from the spectacular to the mundane. In 1979, the American Atomics Company closed after a nearby school found its swimming pool tainted with tritium.[23] In 1981, southside wells began producing water contaminated with the carcinogen trichloroethylene, an industrial solvent used at U.S. Air Force and Hughes plants in the 1950s. Hughes and USAF workers had dumped the solvent in the desert, and thirty years later it had percolated into the groundwater supply.[24]

Air pollution presents the most ubiquitous case of environmental degradation. The EPA ordered the Pima County Air Quality Control District to institute clean-air programs in 1975.[25] In Arizona, only the Phoenix and Tucson metropolitan areas are required to conduct emissions tests on automobiles. Tucson motorists use oxygenated fuel during winter months.

Splashy activism in defense of the desert arose in the enthusiasm following Earth Day in 1970. In 1972, "eco-raiders" vandalized newly built homes and construction equipment in fringe developments. Their graffiti proclaimed, "Stop Urban Sprawl." The culprits turned out to be four University of Arizona students, arrested after several months of headline-grabbing antics.[26] The purported willingness to use violence in defense of nature gained its widest notoriety in Earth First!, the environmentalist group cofounded by Tucsonan Dave Foreman. The current cause celebre of Earth First! and other groups is the preservation of Mount Graham, which according to activists is threatened by the University of Arizona's multi-telescope project on the southern Arizona mountaintop. In sit-ins, camp-ins, rallies, and legal suits, activists argue for the value of biological diversity versus the hubris of arcane science.

Tucson resident Edward Abbey provided the narrative line for the environmental resistance in the 1970s. The eco-raiders seemed to embrace the ethos promoted in Abbey's novel *The Monkey Wrench Gang*—or was it vice versa?[27] At his most pessimistic, Abbey predicted the end of urban society in the desert Southwest by the turn of the century. On the surface, a bad call, as we near Abbey's literary deadline. Or then again, maybe closer to the mark than most Tucsonans would care to acknowledge. The purported godsend of CAP water has proven to be problematic, to say the least. In some older homes and neighborhoods, CAP water leached rust out of pipes, turning tap water a dirty orange, and in the most extreme cases, bursting pipes. The reader can imagine the howls of protest.

In a less human-centric vein, the latest casualties to development in Tucson seem to be the big horn sheep on Pusch Ridge in the Catalina Mountains. Development often impacts in less obvious, cataclysmic ways than doom-and-gloom literature predicts. Some plants and animals do quite well in the face of urbanization, for example, russian thistle, or tumbleweed, thrives on every vacant lot, and coyotes dine quite nicely on house cats and toy poodles. But other species suffer. The big horn sheep on Pusch Ridge have dwindled in numbers (about twenty individuals survived as of May 1994), below the level of viability. The decline in population results from human encroachment on their habitat: both development up the slope, and intrusions by hikers and horseback riders into the shy creatures' private haunts. Human development and activity has not only shrunk their habitat but has also changed the nature of their habitat. Lightning-caused fires are now suppressed to protect people's homes and property, resulting in brushier terrain that shifts the advantage within the fragile ecosystem to the predator of big horn sheep: mountain lions.[28]

When the sheep are gone, will the lions move down the slopes and join the coyotes to feast on house pets? The prospect would no doubt make Edward Abbey smile.

PART 2

ALBUQUERQUE

At first glance, the process of urbanization in Tucson and Albuquerque seems eerily similar: topographically inviting terrain to the east, increasingly influential spending by the defense industry, and flocking snowbird migrations. Differences arise upon closer study, but the likenesses remain.

By the 1920s, Albuquerque's new neighborhoods in the Heights to the east of the Rio Grande River were being serviced by an electric trolley.[1] By the 1930s, neighborhoods had appeared on the mesa above the Heights, which stretched about ten miles to the Sandia Mountains. The University of New Mexico had established its main campus on the Heights, and even farther east, Kirtland Air Force Base, along with Sandia Laboratories, occupied mesa land that originally had been outside the urban fringe but was now well within it.[2]

The boom following World War II pushed development farther onto the mesa to the northeast. Increased spending by the

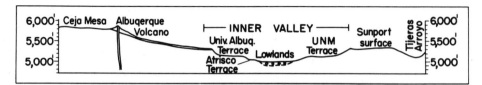

FIG. 10 Profile of the Rio Grande Valley. As in Tucson, geography determined Albuquerque's early development. The original settlement in the lowlands spread first to the University of New Mexico (UNM) terrace to the east, and then onto the East Mesa, labeled here as "Sunport Surface." Later development spread to the west. The volcanic escarpment of the Petroglyph National Monument is below the "Albuquerque Volcano," with the subdivisions on the "Univ. Albuq. Terrace" abutting the monument. (Source: "Albuquerque: Its Mountains, Valley, Water, and Volcanoes," p. 14)

defense industry brought thousands of new residents, creating a population explosion and all the commensurate problems: housing shortages, traffic congestion, and inadequate social services. Similarities with Tucson abound, including observers' analyses of growth in Albuquerque, which especially in the boom period following World War II suffered from the same myopia that marked analyses of Tucson's growth.

Just as in Tucson, political contentiousness accompanied Albuquerque's population explosion. Historians such as Robert Turner Wood and Bradford Luckingham focused on the political wrangling that resulted, for example, in a city charter change in 1972 that replaced the commission form of government with a mayor and council structure. The push for reform in city government originated with the Citizens Committee in the 1950s, composed of "technocrat" types from the eastern suburbs who were employed by what Wood and Luckingham described stereotypically as "efficiency-conscious" defense organizations. These engineers were said to abhor the old-fashioned city government's inefficiency and so pushed to replace it with a more standardized sort of bureaucracy.

However, a focus on political structures results in a superficial depiction of Albuquerque's development. As in Tucson, resistance to Albuquerque's growth appeared across a broad political spectrum at the earliest stages of the boom—in suburban areas to the east, ethnic neighborhoods to the west and south, and later in environmental concerns voiced by residents throughout the community.

Although generally comparable, the opposition to urbanization in Albuquerque manifested itself somewhat differently than in Tucson. Each city's unique cultural mix, within the bounds of a similar regional identity, caused the resistance to take shape according to political, geographic, and ethnic factors particular to each city.

An early, unique feature of Albuquerque's growth arose in 1880 with the arrival of the Santa Fe Railroad. Anglo dominance in Tucson and Albuquerque began with the arrival of the railroad, but in Albuquerque the railroad bypassed the original settlement near the river. More than a mile separated the town and the railroad because the inhabitants, mostly Hispanic, were unwilling to grant the Santa Fe a right-of-way through town.[3] The real-estate boom around the new railroad tracks (which eventually connected the "Old Town" with "New Albuquerque")[4] thus contributed to an ethnic enclavement that occurred in Albuquerque earlier and with more geographic certainty than in Tucson. While the Anglo-dominated commercial center of Albuquerque straddled the railroad tracks along Central Avenue (also known as Railroad Avenue), Old Town remained pastoral and Hispanic. One indication of Old Town's declining status appeared in 1926, when the Bernalillo County Court House moved to New Albuquerque.[5]

Until the 1950s, the new Albuquerque grew faster and earlier than Tucson, partly because of environmental factors. Agriculture along the Rio Grande surpassed that along the Santa Cruz, and a cooler, less deserty climate gave Albuquerque an early advantage over blistering hot Tucson, at least until technological advancements softened the impact of Tucson summers. Built on a semiarid plain at 5,300 feet, Albuquerque is almost 3,000 feet higher than Tucson (2,400 feet), and temperatures average about 10 degrees cooler.[6]

Boosters in Albuquerque pushed the city's development with a cohesiveness lacking in Tucson, perhaps due to the greater degree of enclavement and the lack of an in-state rival such as Tucson faced in Phoenix. Albuquerque's self-image as the commercial center of the Southwest appeared repeatedly in promotional announcements and programs. Although similar to those in Tucson, promotional efforts in Albuquerque generally started earlier and shouted louder, expressing a community pride that at times approached arrogance.

6 THE PRO-GROWTH PARTNERSHIP

■ ■ ■ ■ ■ ■ ■ ■ ■ ■ ■ ■ ■ ■

"Step Lively"

As in Tucson, developers in Albuquerque sought to profit from the city's natural attributes. Promotions advertised Albuquerque's sunny climate, its location on the Rio Grande River, and its Indian heritage. However, even though Tucson and Albuquerque shared these characteristics of regional development, the specific pattern of urbanization differed as the process of development diverged in the two cities. For example, Albuquerque's boosters enjoyed a closer working relationship with the city government. As a result, Albuquerque enjoyed greater expansion than Tucson achieved in the first half of the century.

Boosters had been vigorously pushing Albuquerque's development since territorial days. New Albuquerque businessmen and developers founded the Board of Trade in 1882 and the Commercial Club in the 1890s to promote commerce in the city.[1] The Commercial Club also served as a social organization and hosted dances at the club's hall.[2]

One man who exemplified the early type of individualistic promoter and developer was Colonel D.K.B. Sellers. In 1905, Sellers developed the Perea addition and the Grant tracts in the valley. He then went on to plat University Heights east of the city, an area advertised as "the coming aristocratic residence section of Albuquerque."[3] In the Perea addition alone, Sellers marketed seven hundred lots, and the Grant tract on North 5th Street sold out in thirty days. In addition to his real-estate dealings, Sellers promoted Albuquerque's Territorial Fair and other "city enterprises."[4]

Turn-of-the-century Albuquerque boosters expressed a remarkable degree of confidence. As University of New Mexico buildings rose to the east of the town in 1890, a *Daily Citizen* editorial proudly proclaimed that "Albuquerque is already recognized by the country at large as the railroad and commercial center of the Southwest, and the advance we have already made in the way of institutions of learning show[s] that the town is to be recognized hereafter as also the educational center of the country."[5] The Commercial Club also issued a pamphlet describing the city as "the educational center" of the region.[6]

The Commercial Club also marketed Albuquerque as a mecca for tuberculosis patients. A series of pamphlets in the early 1900s proclaimed the city to be "Eden" and "the land of sunshine." The "Killgloom Gazette" was issued briefly in 1914 as a newsletter for patients and staff of the six local sanatoriums. In 1914, the Commercial Club issued a pamphlet titled "Why Albuquerque, New Mexico, Will Make You Well"; the reasons were clean air and "ozone."[7]

In 1916, boosters reorganized the Commercial Club as the Albuquerque Chamber of Commerce, and the expansive promotions continued full bore. The new Chamber of Commerce advertised the city through a series of pamphlets describing "climatic conditions . . . soil of the valley, land prices, cost of irrigation, varieties of crops produced, stock raising . . . [and] the public lands of the state for sale and lease."[8]

City promoters instituted the "Step Lively" campaign in 1920, issuing a pamphlet that catalogued Albuquerque's enticements and concluded with the bilingual invitation, "Sabe, Señor? Let's Go!"[9] Among Albuquerque's charms were "60 miles of graded streets." In 1925, the Chamber of Commerce announced the formation of the Albuquerque Civic Council, which coordinated the promotion of Albuquerque's health-resort image. The council was a nonprofit organization composed of "our leading citizens," and the group enjoyed the benefit of financial support from the city government.[10] Tax levies also supported an advertising campaign that described the city as "The Heart of the Well Country."[11]

This early example of tax-supported boosterism (which in Stephen

Elkin's urban regime schema is a stereotypical privatist regime) is a departure from Tucson's experience. Although many political leaders in Tucson came out of booster organizations such as the Sunshine Climate Club and Chamber of Commerce, the booster organizations themselves remained financially independent—and usually strapped.

Promotion efforts in Albuquerque continued into the 1930s under the enthusiastic leadership of ex-officio Mayor Clyde Tingley, who except for his 1935–38 term as governor of New Mexico served on the city commission into the 1950s. Tingley, along with other boosters, supported the First America fair and eventually the state fair, established in 1938, which became Albuquerque's biggest annual event.[12]

Predictably, the Depression years slowed growth, and strains in the booster organizations appeared. In 1939, *Albuquerque Magazine* noted that among the "obstacles" encountered in trying to establish the magazine were potential advertisers who were "wary of pure advertising schemes [as] their generosity in sponsoring community projects had been imposed upon."[13]

Perhaps as a result of flagging confidence, promotions in the 1930s slipped in their universal claims for Albuquerque's metropolitan splendor. A market study prepared by the city's two daily newspapers in 1939 described "greater Albuquerque" as an area "four miles in all directions from the Post Office."[14] But it was not clear whether the city's dimensions were meant to startle readers with images of gargantuan size, or tempt them with visions of metropolitan trappings amidst small-town coziness.

By the 1940s, promotions regularly included references to Albuquerque's small-town qualities, a mixed message that was also apparent in Tucson's promotions. In Albuquerque, however, appreciation for "smallness" appeared much later and contrasted more clearly with earlier boasts. Urban sophistication remained the theme of many promotions in Albuquerque, but the solid front of big-city hyperbole crumbled, as evidenced by a 1941 brochure proclaiming Albuquerque "the most metropolitan little city anywhere."[15]

In 1942, the Albuquerque Chamber of Commerce distributed ten thousand "Come Live in Albuquerque" brochures, although the subsequent wartime expansion obviated the need for such promotions. The allure of the city as described in the brochure was both metropolitan and Main Street. Boosters cited well-known war correspondent Ernie Pyle as a prominent example of a new resident who had sampled life in all the great cities of the world and had decided in 1941 to make Albuquerque his permanent home. Pyle explained his decision to settle in Albuquerque in *New Mexico Magazine*, focusing more on small-town qualities than metropolitan sophistication: "We [Pyle and his wife] like it because you can cash a check almost anywhere in Albuquerque without being grilled as though you were a criminal. And because after your second trip to a filling station the gas-pumper calls you by name." [16]

By 1949, the Chamber of Commerce was back in stride in its promotions of the city, expressing the same sort of optimism that motivated progress-minded developers in Tucson: "Only as a community prospers . . . do its citizens prosper." [17] As Wood describes, boosters took "immense pride" in the city as it pursued metropolitan status in the period following World War II. At times, "it seemed that they regarded it as the most outstanding municipality in the number-one country in creation." The migration of Easterners "certified Albuquerque's attractiveness," and added to the city's size—an obvious mark of health and vitality.[18]

The local newspapers supported the city's claims as a health mecca. The *Albuquerque Journal* heralded the story of Janet Atsha, an asthma sufferer who arrived in Albuquerque in 1949 at the age of six, apparently dying. After a few months of hospital care in Albuquerque, Janet had recovered sufficiently to "jump rope and climb." Her mother, also an asthma sufferer, declared, "Albuquerque will be our home from now on. This must be what heaven is like." [19]

The *Albuquerque Journal* also championed "headlong growth" and urged comparisons with other cities in the region, such as El Paso and Santa Fe, extending the tradition of favorably comparing Albuquerque with other regional cities.[20] For example, the health promotions of the early 1900s boasted of Albuquerque's advantages over Denver, Colorado Springs, Pueblo, El Paso, Phoenix, and Tucson.[21]

Even as Albuquerque's population neared 100,000 in the 1950s, promotions continued proclaiming Albuquerque's virtues in a standard effort to attract tourists and develop commerce.[22] In 1951 the Chamber of Commerce sponsored a contest for the best slogan for the city. The winning entry was "Albuquerque—Land of Mañana—Wonderland of Today." [23] The Chamber of Commerce also issued "Pause in Albuquerque: In the

Heart of the Picturesque Indian Country" and "See New Mexico From Albuquerque," which described the city as "thriving, metropolitan" and the "gateway to these scenic wonders (Indian pueblos, mountains, and fishing)."[24] In 1963, the Chamber began issuing "The Turquoise Trail," a brochure describing a scenic loop drive centered on Albuquerque.[25]

Hordes of new residents continued to arrive, and "population figures brought forth exultation." In 1954, Albuquerque's two newspapers published a series of brochures referring to themselves as "New Mexico's leading daily newspapers" and promoting Albuquerque as "America's most dynamic city."[26] A 1958 editorial in the *Albuquerque Journal* chortled over the "miracle city": "We who have been here for some time have difficulty in keeping on top of our capabilities and our potential. The outsiders see the picture and come swarming into our midst. We live in a miracle city with many of us not realizing the magnitude of the miracle."[27] The count of residents in 1960 brought forth editorial back-slapping: "In 200,000 Class," at last.[28]

Albuquerque also took the lead in promoting regional comparisons presenting the Southwest as the preferred destination of sun worshipers. In 1964, both tourists and prospective residents were targets of the "sun challenge" thrown down to Florida and Hawaii by the Southwest Sun Country Association, a booster organization composed of the Chambers of Commerce of Albuquerque, El Paso, Tucson, and Phoenix. (The association had no physical structure but was purely a public relations effort, with the Albuquerque Chamber of Commerce coordinating press releases and advertising campaigns for the four cities.)[29]

Albuquerque enjoyed (or perhaps suffered from) a close working relationship between boosters and the city government. Albuquerque's city commission represented business interests in a manner typical for growing communities (and privatist regimes), but the connection between city government and business went further than in Tucson. Examples of the cohesive pro-growth partnership abound. Tax levies supported the Albuquerque Civic Council's promotions of Albuquerque as a health resort. Clyde Oden, owner of a Buick dealership, served on the city commission concurrently with his tenure as president of the Chamber of Commerce.[30] Although Oden lost his commission seat in the 1946 election, the business-government connection persisted. After Oden's departure from the city commission, the Chamber of Commerce established a "liaison committee" to "study, on behalf of the members of the Chamber of Commerce on behalf of the people of the city of Albuquerque, certain problems confronting the city." The Chamber of Commerce asked the city commissioners to cooperate with their study committee, and the commission duly promised to do so.[31] No such direct connection between boosters and city government ever existed in Tucson.

The boom years following World War II changed the face of Albuquerque, but the pro-growth partnership survived intact. Suburban development spread onto the mesa east of the city, and developers like Dale Bellamah became millionaires. The population within the city limits increased from about 50,000 in 1945 to 96,815 in 1950, and to 201,189 in 1960. Many of the new residents were veterans who had been stationed in the West during World War II and returned to Albuquerque for its moderate climate, informal atmosphere, and defense jobs.[32]

The size of Albuquerque in 1946 was 11.61 square miles after achieving a few small annexations during World War II.[33] In 1946 a "Better Government" ticket of city commission candidates swept into office on a platform of "business growth and municipal expansion." Clyde Tingley opposed rapid growth because of the financial pressures it placed on the city. Despite running against the booster tide, Tingley maintained his seat on the commission. However, he lost the chairmanship—and control— just as the Chamber of Commerce announced a plan to expand Albuquerque's boundaries based on its study committee's deliberations.[34] The resulting annexations in the late 1940s and 1950s expanded Albuquerque's physical size to about 86 square miles, engendering vociferous resistance in the process. (Resistance to annexations will be discussed in chapter 7.)[35]

The partnership between business and government in Albuquerque remained in place throughout the city's development. The freeway construction plans of the 1950s serve as an indication of this fundamental alliance. Unlike Tucson, Albuquerque began construction of "crisscrossing freeways" in 1956 to solve the traffic problems brought on by the population explosion. The freeways were completed in the 1960s.[36] The attitude toward freeway construction marks a difference between the two cities; Tucsonans repeatedly rejected the idea of a crosstown freeway, seeing it as a step toward the model of Los Angeles—and a step in the wrong direction. Conversely, Albuquerque's boosters were always able to convince the city commission, if not their neighbors, to support big-city "improvements."

Unanimity of purpose marked Albuquerque's booster efforts. Individual boosters like Sam Hoffman went broke as the housing boom went temporarily bust in the 1960s, but the city government and booster alliance pushed the city's development relentlessly. The "growth machine" acquired new faces but continued to hum along contentedly even as resistance began to materialize. The turbocharged power of the machine suggests one reason why opposition to growth was steamrolled so quickly in Bernalillo County. Even the civic reformers seeking to modernize city government fit comfortably behind the wheel of Albuquerque's growth machine.

In 1953, a comprehensive zoning ordinance was passed without major protest.[37] In 1954, a reform group elected members to the city commission, pushing for efficiency and the orderly expansion of city services. The resulting increase in the city budget required the imposition of a city sales tax (one cent in 1956) and the reassessment of land values. Rapid growth had necessitated the increase in the city's budget so as to provide city services to more residents over a wider area.[38]

Development in the 1960s reached the foothills of the Sandia Mountains. Other milestones appeared: the first shopping mall in 1961; redevelopment of Old Town Plaza in the 1960s as a tourist attraction; and the first annual International Balloon Fiesta in 1972.[39] New "company-made communities" sprang up on Albuquerque's fringes in the 1960s and early 1970s: "the people kept pouring in, many of them retirees from the east seeking a pleasanter, less congested life than they had known before."[40] A trend toward more pastoral lifestyles on the fringe of the metropolis fueled a mini population boom in the traditional villages of Tijeras, Bernalillo, Corrales, and Placitas, and in the "company-made" towns of Paradise Hills and Rio Rancho to the north and northwest.[41] On the fringe of the city, "the pace of life seemed slower [and] traditional cultures or natural beauty was closer at hand."[42]

Development in Albuquerque also differed somewhat from Tucson's in its relatively uniform grid system for streets. New developments on the fringes tended to conform to established patterns of shape and block size, making newly developed areas as readily accessible as established parts of town.[43] The uniform pattern of development increased the liminality, clearly demarcated, between the urban setting and the natural surroundings: green lawns and trees contrasting with the predominantly brown mesa (to be discussed more fully in chapter 9). Conversely, the acceptability and popularity of desert landscaping within Tucson decreases the liminality between the city and surrounding environment.

The partnership between government and business groups survived the various reform movements that reshaped the city commission and ultimately restructured the city government. In 1960, the Chamber of Commerce agreed to support wealthy businesses, which donated $1,000 each to fund the independent Albuquerque Industrial Development Foundation.[44] In 1966, "dynamic and progressive" candidates for the city commission, including Pete Domenici, took control of the city commission and continued the business-government alliance. Domenici, as chairman of the commission, assigned three city employees to work with the Chamber of Commerce, the Albuquerque Industrial Development Service, and the Albuquerque Industrial Foundation to coordinate the boosters' efforts to attract new industry to the city.[45] Once again city government, in the form of tax-paid employees, worked hand-in-hand with boosters in Albuquerque. Although Tucson's city government cooperated with boosters, this degree of mutual assistance had rarely appeared.

Civic reformers like Domenici expressed a faith in the efficacy of rational growth through the management of development. In 1967, Domenici announced a shift to "planned annexations" in an effort to calm tempers raised by years of controversial expansion efforts by the city. As Domenici explained, "annexation" had become "a dirty word."[46] By 1971, controlled growth was an issue in the city commission election with "none of the front-running candidates favor[ing] headlong expansion."[47] The most significant structural reform of the city government was proposed in 1971 when City Commissioner Pete Domenici argued for the change to the mayor/council form of city government. Domenici hoped the new form of government would establish strong, full-time leadership to deal effectively with emerging problems, including growth issues.[48]

Did city-government reforms indicate that Albuquerque offered a better example of planned growth than Tucson? On the surface at least, planners in Albuquerque received the cooperation of businessmen and politicians. In 1953, Arizona banker Walter R. Bimson gave the commencement address at the University of New Mexico, describing for the graduates a "new business code": "An important point in all this change is that by use of traditional democratic processes we have almost done away with the old concept that the owner of property and wealth has a right to use his property any way he pleases."[49] A test of Bimson's thesis had occurred in 1950 when the Albuquerque City Planning Commission's function changed from advising the city on growth issues to regulating development. The initial impact of this change was negligible due to the commissioners' ties to the real-estate and construction industries. In 1952, however, the planning commission proposed an ordinance requiring builders to pay for paving roads and installing utilities in new subdivisions. The city commission unanimously rejected the ordinance, but the following year the commission passed the controversial measure to stop the financial drain that rapid expansion had placed on the city. In this instance, financial necessity had proved to be more influential than appeals for orderly growth.[50]

Although cooperation generally marked the business-growth partnership in Albuquerque, dissension occasionally surfaced among the politically conservative. When the city government took over trash collection from private companies and acquired the animal shelter from the Humane Society, political conservatives questioned the government's intentions.[51]

Another example of splits within the boosters' consensus appears in the divisions in Albuquerque's commercial associations. The depiction of 1950s harmony and consensus points to the conjoining of the geographically diverse business groups in the midst of the postwar boom. But although the groups did join together, they were never completely at peace. In 1953 the Heights Businessmen's Association (six hundred businesses east of the University of New Mexico campus) joined the Albuquerque Chamber of Commerce as an affiliated organization. The North Albuquerque Association also joined the Chamber of Commerce on similar terms.

The rivalry between downtown and Heights businesses "came to a head" a few years later as traffic congestion increased downtown and expansion of the city continued toward the east. Heights business owners felt that maintaining downtown as a viable commercial center was not in their best interest. A formal break occurred on February 7, 1958, when the boards of directors of the H.B.A. and N.A.A. voted unanimously to split from the Chamber of Commerce. In 1962 the two groups voted to rejoin the Chamber of Commerce, even though many business owners sensed the need for separate organizations.[52]

Differences between the Heights and downtown surfaced again in 1960–1962 in the argument that developed over where to build the new city-county hall: downtown or in the Heights. Predictably, Heights businessmen favored a site in their own neighborhood, while downtown businessmen argued for a downtown location. Others also argued for a downtown site so as to strengthen the city's urban core. The city commission skirted the issue by appointing the Albuquerque Growth Committee in December 1961 to study the issue. Ultimately the committee recommended the downtown site.[53]

Perhaps the split within business groups was inevitable given the personal judgments of profit potential related to the geographic diversity of commerce in Albuquerque. In addition to the geographic factors, a basic split between business owners occurred in relation to growth issues. Some businesses, such as real estate development and home construction, require legions of new residents to assure their own prosperity. Others, such as those in the service sector with an established clientele, find their own prosperity assured given the existing population.

Despite potentially diverging interests, the generalization holds in Albuquerque, more so than in Tucson, of a remarkably uniform push for growth. Splits among boosters appeared, but the pro-growth partnership steamrolled the early resistance to annexation, as the next chapter will show. The push for growth in Albuquerque in the 1950s was gung-ho, optimistic, self-righteous, and unstoppable. Only when the boosters attempted their most grandiose annexation in 1964—an effort to annex the entire county—did resistance succeed in stifling the spread of the city.

7 POLITICAL RESISTANCE

■ ■ ■ ■ ■ ■ ■ ■ ■ ■ ■ ■ ■ ■ ■ ■

"Land, Lots of Land"

Political opposition to Albuquerque's expansion appeared throughout the post–World War II boom. Anglo and Hispanic residents resisted continuous, aggressive annexations by the City of Albuquerque. Some sought to preserve their culture and lifestyle, whereas political conservatives opposed the expansion of city government. The pro-growth partnership of boosters and city government had overwhelmed the early resistance but in so doing engendered ever more harsh criticism and opposition. Annexations became so rancorous that in 1964 the New Mexico state legislature imposed a two-year moratorium on annexations by the City of Albuquerque. By 1967, city leaders were advocating planned growth in an effort to rehabilitate the city government's image.

The spread of Albuquerque into the inviting open spaces east of town mirrored Tucson's expansion across the desert floor. Albuquerque's natural barrier to the east, the Sandia Mountains, allowed for substantial sprawl before development reached the escarpment. As George Fitzpatrick and Harvey Caplin describe: "Until the post–World War II boom started, East Central Avenue beyond the Fair Grounds looked like this . . .

land, lots of land."[1] When Ernie Pyle moved to a more pastoral Albuquerque in 1942, he said that he liked Albuquerque because "we have a country mailbox instead of a slot in the door. . . . [and] because our front yard stretches as far as you can see, and because Mt. Taylor, 65 miles away, is like a framed picture in our window. We like it because when we look to the westward, we look clear over and above the city of Albuquerque and on beyond, it seems, half way to the Pacific Ocean."[2] But as development spread, pastoral scenes disappeared, replaced by suburban monotony, with only the mountains on the horizon to remind residents of the once-open spaces.

In 1946 the recently elected, reform-minded city commissioners presented a huge annexation plan to the district court for validation. The annexation, as proposed, would double the city's population and bring the area within the city limits to approximately one hundred square miles. Only Clyde Tingley, the old New Deal Democrat still ensconced at city hall, voiced opposition to the annexation plan, arguing that providing basic city services to the area would cost at least $12 million. Meanwhile, within the fringe area, a "storm of protest" was brewing.[3]

At the center of the controversy over the proposed annexation was the Chamber of Commerce's role in creating the city's ambitious annexation policy. The *Albuquerque Journal* metaphorically described the targeted area as a helpless calf when it reported that "at the behest of the Chamber of Commerce, the city commission Monday flexed a gigantic legal riata with which it [hoped] to rope in all of its densely-populated suburbs."[4] The "densely-populated suburbs" included the established, although not incorporated, communities of Old Town, Barcelona, Arenal, Armijo, Five Points, Los Duranes, Los Candelarias, Los Griegos, and Santa Barbara.

The city commission had initiated the annexation by instructing the city attorney to petition the district court to recognize the annexation on the basis of New Mexico's 1939 annexation law known as the Roswell Law.[5] The law allowed cities to annex certain areas by simple resolution, provided the areas bordered the city on two or more sides and were "platted into tracts containing five acres or less, and . . . substantially built up, [with] two or more businesses or commercial establishments located thereon, and the inhabitants thereof are enabled to secure the benefits of the city (police, fire), or could be furnished with (light, water) . . ."[6] The annexation would be accomplished when the district court filed the city's

resolution. This method of annexation circumvented the gathering of signatures on petitions required by the traditional method of annexation.
Although annexation by petition remained the most common means of
bringing areas into the city limits, the Roswell Law gave city commissioners an alternative when resistance among suburban residents ran high.

Resistance was still possible under the Roswell Law, but limited. The
Roswell Law stipulated that any annexee "feeling himself aggrieved by
the action of the council, shall have the right to appeal to the District
Court by filing his petition praying a review of the council's action within
30 days." The court would them decide if the annexation could proceed,
considering primarily the ability of the city to provide services in a timely
fashion.[7]

Evidence of resistance is found in the Chamber of Commerce's statements in support of the 1946 annexation plan. The Chamber of Commerce's new president, C. C. Broome, painted a threatening image of
"encirclement" in Albuquerque if fringe areas, with a population of
35,000, continued to grow outside the boundaries of the city. Broome
also recognized that resistance to annexation ran high in the fringe areas,
and he noted that "it would be impossible to get half the 35,000 to approve [i.e., sign annexation petitions] under the present circumstances."[8]

As protest against the annexation plan mounted, especially in Old
Town, city commissioners disavowed their association with the plan, attributing it solely to a Chamber of Commerce initiative. In a February
1947 *Albuquerque Journal* article, Al Buck, chairman of the city commission,
was quoted saying, "We of the Commission have not been carrying the
flag. The plan is sponsored by the Chamber of Commerce."[9] But the previous April, the city commission had appointed an "extension committee" of twenty-five residents "from inside and outside of the city
limits . . . to investigate areas east and north for possible annexation," and
chairing the extension committee was W. C. Oestreich, president of the
Albuquerque Board of Realtors.[10] Oestreich had rationalized the sweep-
ing annexation plan by quoting the committee's planning consultant Ken
Carmichael: "it would be well to consider that there would be no use in
taking in only a few city blocks and therefore, I have based my city limits
line on the very great possibilities of our city's future growth."[11]

The annexation plan obviously grew out of Albuquerque's cohesive
government-business partnership. Both the Chamber of Commerce and

Board of Realtors influenced the formulation of the plan, with the city commission rubber-stamping their decisions.

The argument over the city's annexation plan found its way into the New Mexico legislature, where opponents of annexation had a valuable ally in Representative Joseph Montoya, a Democrat from Albuquerque and chairman of the House Taxation and Revenue Committee. By February 1947, four bills were working their way through the legislature: two (one each in the house and senate) that would facilitate annexation, and two that would restrain it. The bill supported by Montoya and other opponents of Albuquerque's annexation plan "would require cities to obtain the written consent of the majority of residents and property owners." [12]

The hearings in the legislature provided a forum for both sides of the controversy. Broome and the Chamber of Commerce representatives described the issue in terms of progress versus silly recidivism. Opponents of the plan described Albuquerque's city commission as virtual lap dogs of the Chamber of Commerce. Gilbert Espinosa, a resident of Duranes, criticized Broome's characterization of the resistance to the annexation as crank or eccentric, and he said the plan was "grandiose" and motivated by the desire of the city commission to raise revenues. According to Espinosa, "90 per cent of the people don't want to come in." [13]

In the end, the legislature passed a "compromise" annexation bill, despite some last-minute theatrics by Montoya. Two days before the end of the legislative session, Montoya disappeared along with the single official copy of the compromise bill. Montoya had been "a bitter foe of every annexation plan advanced by the Albuquerque city government" and viewed this "compromise" as simply a watered-down augmentation of the city's annexation powers. Montoya's family said he had traveled to California on doctor's orders following an asthma attack, but the next day Montoya appeared in El Paso, professing dismay over the brouhaha his unannounced departure had created. The "embattled law" passed on the last day of the legislative session in the spring of 1947. [14]

Under the 1947 annexation law, disputed annexations would be handled by an arbitration board composed of seven members. Three would be appointed by the city government, three elected by residents living in the area designated for annexation, and the seventh member, presumed to cast the deciding vote, would be elected by the six members, or if no consensus could be reached, appointed by the district court. The board's decision was to be based solely on "whether the benefits of the government of the municipality are or can be available within a reasonable time."[15] What was reasonable to the city government, however, was often unreasonable to various groups of residents. The single criterion by which the arbitration boards were to base their decision—which did not include the weight of opinion for or against annexation—indicates the sentiment of the state government favoring annexation plans.

Thus, after 1947, Albuquerque's city commission had three methods of annexation available to them: petitions, the Roswell Law, and arbitration boards. Although the arbitration boards were intended to forestall controversy, the boards' operation fell short of allowing for democratic processes to function freely and ended up serving primarily as forums for fringe-resident rancor without commensurate political power. Resistance was given a voice, but no authority.

Robert Turner Wood's thesis of Albuquerque's harmonious growth in the 1950s required a depiction of early expansion as orderly and painless. Consequently, annexation resistance appeared in his study more in terms of individual conflict on the city commission as Tingley continued to resist the spread of the city and ever-mounting financial burdens. Grassroots resistance continually surfaced, however, both against the physical expansion of the city and the intrusion of a city government thought to be in the hip pocket of the Chamber of Commerce. Even though the 1946 annexation effort had stalled due to the wrangling in the state legislature, the opponents' independence was short-lived; the following year, city commissioners figuratively reached across city boundaries when they voted to double the water rates for residential customers living in the county.[16]

In 1948, city residents from a broad political spectrum protested the city's takeover of trash collection from private contractors. In the process of acquisition, the city commission had voted to raise collection rates from forty cents per month to one dollar per month. After a clamorous protest, the commission lowered the monthly rate to seventy cents.[17] The political squabble within the city no doubt reinforced the reluctance of resistance-inclined fringe residents to join the city.

As the controversy over the 1946 annexation plan played out, the city commission continued to annex smaller parcels of land using the traditional petition method, which required the owners of at least half the property to request annexation. In the fifteen months from June 1946 to September 1947, the city commission enacted nineteen annexations. Twice during that period, on May 6 and July 16, 1947, the commission annexed three separate parcels at a single meeting.[18] Many of the annexations involved property under development on the East Mesa. Thus, for instance, the March 11, 1947, annexation included "94 unsold lots."[19]

The first protest of a petition-based annexation occurred in 1948. On May 25, the city commission accepted an annexation petition from residents west of the Rio Grande River, forwarding the petition to the city manager for verification of the percentage of property owners requesting the annexation. On June 1, as the verification process continued, another group of residents within the area presented a "protest" petition to the city commission, arguing that the petition method of annexation was unconstitutional: "We the undersigned [94 signatures] . . . have a fundamental right, as American citizens, to have a voice in deciding the type of municipal government under which they are to live, and for us to be annexed merely by your consenting to said Petition would be a denial of such right."[20]

In arguing for fundamental rights, opponents offered a logic for resistance akin to the "natural" rights of John Adams and Thomas Jefferson; in Albuquerque's case in the 1940s, no annexation without representation. Opponents of the annexation maintained that only those specifically requesting annexation should be annexed. The petition method of annexation ran afoul of this desire. Opponents described the city commission as exemplifying a tyranny of the majority, an opinion confirmed one week later when the commission annexed proponents and opponents alike.[21]

All in all, the city managed to annex about thirty-seven square miles in the late 1940s. After these "victories," the city commission announced further plans to annex areas to the west and north: the 1946 plan revisited.

The city fought a two-front annexation war. In June 1948, the commission designated the North Valley area as a target and set about establishing an arbitration board. On July 20, 1948, the commission availed itself of the Roswell Law and passed a resolution to annex Old Town to the west. While the arbitration process continued to the north, the city struggled to contain the legal challenges that developed in Old Town. Eventually, legal challenges also developed in the northside annexation.

On August 14, 1948, the arbitration board for the North Valley area approved the annexation of three square miles of "highly developed northside suburban area," bringing approximately six thousand residents into the city limits. The board had modified the original proposal, formulated by a Chamber of Commerce committee, by eliminating "the northernmost mile of the north valley tract, which was mostly farm land." The board's decision approving the annexation was based on the view that "municipal services could be extended within a reasonable time." Apparently, "reasonable" meant two years, since City Manager Charles E. Wells said it would take the city about two years to install sewers and water mains, provided citizens approved a new bond issue.[22]

The legal challenge to the northside annexation resulted when property owners in the area (John Cox, J. Leatherwood, and "others similarly situated"), represented by attorney Martin A. Treet, questioned the constitutionality of the 1947 annexation law. The property owners maintained that arbitration boards represented an unlawful "delegation of legislative authority."[23] On June 28, 1949, the New Mexico Supreme Court upheld the 1947 annexation law, thus preserving the northside annexation.[24]

The Old Town annexation also found itself disputed in the courts. On July 20, 1948, the city commission used the Roswell Law to "ram through" the annexation of Old Town "after a long bitter wrangle." From the outset, residents (mostly Hispanic) protested vigorously, terming the move "a scruff-of-the-neck" maneuver and "the least democratic method of annexation."[25]

Opponents of the Old Town annexation, represented by former governor A. T. Hannett and attorney Milton Seligman, challenged the city's actions at the August 3, 1948, meeting, before the district court had recorded the city's annexation resolution. As a result of the ongoing protest, city commissioners voted to table the annexation for further study.[26] Eventually the city circulated petitions in the Old Town area and gathered signatures of the owners of half the property.

The city's pursuit of Old Town raised concerns within the old community over the preservation of their existing social ties. Old Town had remained relatively pastoral and predominantly Hispanic since territorial days. On August 24, 1948, City Manager Charles Wells related to the commission a letter he had received from Gilberto Espinosa requesting information on city statutes. At issue was the status of Old Town's Sunday evening dances at the Old Albuquerque Society Hall. Espinosa had asked the city manager if the dances would be canceled if the community was annexed into the city, due to Albuquerque's ordinance against public dancing on Sundays. Wells characterized the dances for the commission: "These dances have been held at Society Hall in Old Town as far back as I can remember. They have always been conducted in an orderly manner and have been well patronized by the residents of Old Albuquerque." [27] The city commission eased local concerns by assuring residents that the dances could continue after the area was annexed.

In the meantime, the legal opposition to the Old Town annexation shifted to challenge the city's petition signatures. At the January 4, 1949, meeting, Hannett questioned whether the city had in fact obtained the signatures of the owners of half the property in the area. Hannett claimed three signatures had been forged and that others represented non–property owners. As an example, Hannett pointed to the signature of a Catholic priest, which the city had used to claim the approval for church-owned property. Hannett maintained that only the archbishop could make such an assessment. [28]

In the end, Hannett and the commission reached a compromise. The city and opponents of the annexation agreed to a variation of the arbitration board process. The commission established a three-person arbitration board to settle the issue within two weeks, with Hannett representing opponents' views on the board. [29] Two weeks later, on January 17, 1949, the Old Town arbitration board asked the city commission for one more week since "a multiplicity of problems have arisen which we are quite sure were not anticipated by the City Commission or by the protestants of the annexation." The commission's response was to pass a resolution denying the request for more time. As a result, Hannett resigned from the arbitration board, and the next day the commission passed another resolution annexing Old Town. [30]

If the commission members thought they were rid of Hannett, they were mistaken. Hannett filed a motion in district court for a restraining order halting the annexation, and on January 30, 1949, Judge R. F. Deacon Arledge placed Old Town back outside the city limits, ruling that the city in fact had accounted for less than half the property in the annexation area.[31]

The city proved to be just as stubborn as Hannett. After the setback in court, the commission began another effort to annex Old Town through the standard arbitration process under the 1947 law.

On April 12, 1949, Old Town residents picked their three members of the arbitration board in a local election. As the *Albuquerque Journal* reported, election turnout was light (26.9 percent, or 572 votes cast out of 2,122 registered voters), but among those voting, the overwhelming opinion was anti-annexation. The three opposition candidates received twice as many votes as the three pro-annexation candidates. Despite the low turnout, opponents of the annexation celebrated their victory with "torchlights and speeches" in the Old Town Plaza.[32]

The opponents of the annexation seemed to achieve a second victory when the seventh member of the arbitration board was named by the court: Gilberto Espinosa, the Duranes resident who had opposed the annexation in 1946, and who had recently written the letter to City Manager Wells regarding the Sunday evening dances. The optimism of opponents was misplaced, however. On June 30, 1949, the arbitration board voted four to three to approve the annexation, with Espinosa casting the deciding vote.

Espinosa's rationale and underlying lack of enthusiasm for the annexation appeared in his explanatory statement: "It is inevitable that a small section like Old Town . . . should be part of the city. It is impossible for an area to exist in an unorganized form next to an organized municipality. . . . [But] I agree with certain things cited by the opposition, specifically neglect of certain areas and favoritism. And I am certainly not entirely satisfied with the type of city government. However . . . the question is whether the city benefits are or will be available [to Old Town] in a reasonable time."[33] Espinosa had grimaced and said "yes."

The disappointment of opponents flashed during the pivotal meeting. J. W. Hedges, one of the three anti-annexation board members, called city commissioners "iron-fisted Stalins and dictators." The *Albuquerque Journal* reported an exchange between Hedges and pro-annexation board member Irwin Moise. Moise urged Hedges to "come into the city and get rid of them [the Stalins and dictators]." Hedges responded, "Throw 'em out and we'll come in."[34]

Results of the annexation were both obvious and unforeseen. First on the city's agenda was the sale of revenue bonds totaling $1,410,000 for sewer and water construction throughout the city, now including Old Town ($150,000) and the North Valley ($600,000).[35] Perhaps unexpected was the fate of the Sunday evening dances. On January 10, 1950, six months after the annexation, twelve Old Town residents presented the city commission with a "petition of grievance." The residents specifically requested police protection and street cleanup due to "malicious and unlawful deeds" following the Sunday evening dances, after which "the street is cluttered up with whiskey bottles [and] vomiting on the sidewalk . . . is a common occurrence. We also request that the street be cleaned, cared for, the same as any other part of the city."[36]

Had the dances always been such rowdy events? Perhaps they had, notwithstanding the city manager's recollection a few months previously. Whether or not rowdiness had infected the area with annexation, or had always been present, it was now the job of Albuquerque city police and city street cleaners to maintain the area.

Albuquerque's largest annexation occurred three months later, November 22, 1949, but without the controversy surrounding Old Town and the North Valley. The annexation extended the area of the city by about eleven square miles, while adding zero new residents. The city used the petition method to annex the 7,325 acres of undeveloped mesa land to the east. Dale Bellamah, one of Albuquerque's busiest home builders, advocated the annexation as an example of "planned development." Bellamah used his positions on the city planning commission and the Albuquerque Home Builders Association to push for the expansion.[37]

The Bel-Aire annexation a few months later included people—and therefore protest. Residents of the Bel-Aire development, mostly middle-class and Anglo, petitioned the Bernalillo County Commission in December 1949 to incorporate as a village so as to forestall the city's annexation efforts. On January 17, 1950, the city announced its plan to annex the area by petition ("acreage in petition: 1701," "acreage not in petition: 1539"). This effort met with vigorous protest, including a letter to the commission from L. J. Lippett, owner of 80 acres in the annexation area: "this so-called voluntary petition for annexation has been presented without my knowledge, signature, or consent, although the said petition included the above described land owned by me." Lippett also reminded the city commission that the area to be annexed included part of the proposed "village of Bel-Aire." On January 17, the city commission tabled the annexation due to the legal questions surrounding the annexation of a nascent village.[38]

On January 24, 1950, the city commission annexed 3,300 acres surrounding the Bel-Aire development, despite the protest by Milton Seligman, the attorney representing property owners in the area. (Seligman, along with A. T. Hannett, previously had represented Old Town residents.) Seligman had reminded the commissioners that one and a half square miles of the addition was part of the proposed village of Bel-Aire. In response to Seligman's protest, the city attorney rendered an opinion to the commissioners as follows: "1. That the areas are not identical. 2. That the proceedings for incorporation filed with the County Commission are untenable."[39] Why the proposed village was legally untenable was not explained, but the commissioners took their attorney's word and annexed the 3,300 acres.[40] The annexation brought fewer than twenty new residents into the city, but the annexed land surrounded the Bel-Aire development and made it a target for annexation under the Roswell Law. Annexation quickly followed, and the proposed village of Bel-Aire was never established.[41]

The election of two "Better Government" city commissioners in 1950 resulted in continued expansion of the city and more "heated wrangling" between Tingley and the new commissioners.[42] The most glaring issue facing the commission was the strain of rapid growth on the city's water system. The 1947 master plan for upgrading the water system had been rendered obsolete by the city's rapid growth. In 1952, after water shortages forced rationing in 1946, 1948, 1951, and 1952, the city's water board announced an "ambitious program of new construction."

Tingley and the Old Guard opposed the program as too expensive, waging an "I told you so" campaign during commission meetings and in the press. In frustration, Don Johnstone, chairman of the water board, resigned. Johnstone's letter of resignation specifically blamed Tingley for the problems in the city's water system: "[shortages were] not the fault of the master plan, or of the men who are operating the system, but of the short-sighted, penny-pinching, obstructionist tactics in regard to financing in which you [Tingley] are indulging. It seems you are unable or unwilling to grow with the City."[43]

Late in 1953, after the city was again forced to ration water, the commission and the voters approved a compromise bond issue for $2.4 million to improve the water system.[44] In 1954, "Citizens Committee" candidates swept into office after running on a platform of orderly and efficient city government. The new commissioners passed a one-cent city sales tax in 1955, using the increased revenue to expand services commensurate with the added demand.[45]

Resistance to higher city taxes surfaced in the late 1950s in areas of the city previously assumed to be acquiescent. Residents of the Heights area formed the Property Owners Protective Association (POPA) in 1959 to fight an increase in their taxes to pay for flood-control projects in valley neighborhoods. Development in the Heights had increased the runoff into the valley, but Heights residents remained unconvinced of the flood danger in the lowlands.[46]

The election for city commissioners in 1959 pitted the POPA against the Citizens Committee. The Citizens Committee maintained its control of the commission, but one POPA candidate won a seat. The contentious, tax-conscious mood of voters also appeared in other results: defeat of a proposed city-county merger (13,506 opposed, 5,777 in favor), and defeat of a bond issue to build a new city-county building.[47]

Voters who may have quietly acquiesced to annexation were now voicing resistance to higher taxes and an intrusive city government. Wood describes this dissension as new: "Increasingly they [Heights residents] were willing to clash with established authority."[48] Wood was correct to describe the protest in the Heights as new, but he makes the mistake of conflating the area with its residents. The city commission had annexed most of the Heights and mesa land to the east as undeveloped land, yet whenever annexations had scooped up people as well as land, resistance had appeared.

The Albuquerque Citizens Committee voiced its awareness of opposition within the community but seemed to ascribe the opposition to the growing size of the city: "This city is growing to such a size that we know that from now on there will be organized opposition of one kind or another."[49] Their awareness indicates acknowledgment of organized, potentially successful resistance. Typically, boosters, planners, and pro-growth politicians in Tucson as well as Albuquerque noticed resistance only when it posed a viable threat. Although the lack of political viability in the late 1940s had made the resistance invisible to later historians, annexation resistance had sometimes included a voting majority of the residents. But because resistance could easily be overcome by legal fiat, it appeared inconsequential.

Another tax controversy split the community in the mid-1960s, this time over a proposed gasoline tax to pay for road improvements, primarily in the Heights neighborhoods. Opposition to the tax surfaced among valley residents and petroleum industry workers, who forced a referendum election. The tax lost 11,734 to 10,943, with the narrow margin provided by valley precincts. Perhaps ominously for city commissioners contemplating reelection, "significantly greater numbers" voted in the referendum than in the previous commission election.[50]

The expansion of Albuquerque continued to the northwest in the 1960s with the success of the Rio Rancho development. Beyond this satellite community, a pastoral vestige survived in the North Valley. Another "booming residential area" appeared to the south of the city and west of the Rio Grande River, and this area became a target for annexation in the spring of 1960. The protests that surrounded the city's annexation of Old Town and Bel-Aire paled in comparison to the contentious opposition that greeted the commissioners' new annexation plan for the southwest valley.

More than a thousand residents of the southwest valley met on April 6, 1960, to hear the city's plan explained by Dick Bennett, a member of the city planning commission. Bennett bore the brunt of the residents' ire when he admitted that their taxes would go up with annexation, but he sought to reassure residents by explaining that their insurance rates would go down and their property values would go up. When pressed, however, Bennett acknowledged that city water and sewage service might take ten years to establish in the area. As the *Albuquerque Journal* reported: "A chorus of boos ended Bennett's part of the meeting."[51]

Several other speakers supported the annexation, suffering the same inhospitable responses as Bennett. One insurance agent assured residents that their rates would go down with annexation. Anonymous comments recorded by the newspaper included: "I'd rather pay double the insurance premiums than one-fourth of the tax increase and wait 15 years to get services the city is promising." "If we wanted to live in the city we'd move there. There are plenty of houses for sale in town." One recently annexed resident said, "Our taxes tripled when we were annexed. We haven't gotten very much out if it. All we have accumulated is more taxes."[52]

Justice of the Peace A. P. Darden presided over the clamorous meeting. At one point he asked for a show of hands for or against the annexation. Only three hearty souls raised their hands in favor of the move. Later Darden asked for a show of hands in favor of the Southwest Valley Booster Club, which had formed to lead the opposition to the annexation: "A veritable forest of hands went up."[53]

The protest certainly got the attention of the city commission. Commissioners passed a resolution at the April 19, 1960, meeting seeking to explain their desire to annex the area. First the resolution sought to pacify the angry residents: "It is not the intention of the City Commission of the City of Albuquerque to annex isolated or remote areas or lands the owners of which will not be benefited by such incorporation." Then the commissioners tried to explain the rationale behind annexation: "The growth of large cities, particularly in the eastern United States, to a point where they touch and surround small towns, has created real difficulties in the way of duplicating government, overlapping functions and confusion as to responsibility so that tax money had been wasted, efficiency has been lost, and the principal beneficiaries had been organized crime."[54]

The city commission then moved to establish an arbitration board to settle the annexation controversy. The resolution's mention of the threat of organized crime was typical of the boosters' habit of defining opponents of growth as beyond the pale, but assertions of Mafia opposition to annexation never reappeared. No doubt mobsters would prefer a less rigorous civil structure, but the opponents of annexation in the South Valley were quasi-rural residents, not casino operators.

In the meantime, the Southwest Boosters Club had hired attorney Milton Seligman, the old foe of city annexation plans, to begin the legal process of incorporating the ten-square-mile area as a town or village, to be known as South Albuquerque.[55] At the meeting in which Seligman was hired, Commissioner W. W. Atkinson tried to convince residents of the folly of their move. Atkinson said a "South Albuquerque" would have "disastrous results. It would set a pattern for a very undesirable future." The move also made little economic sense, according to Atkinson. The per capita budget for Albuquerque was $56. For South Albuquerque's projected population of 27,000, the per capita budget would be $66. The Southwest Boosters remained unconvinced.[56] (The experience of South Tucson twenty years earlier seems to corroborate Atkinson's warnings, but no mention or comparison with South Tucson appeared in the South Albuquerque debate.)

There was little doubt among city officials concerning the dominant opinion in the area. At an April 20, 1960, meeting with Seligman, City Attorney Frank Horan acknowledged the desire of most county residents to live outside the city. Horan said that if an incorporation vote were held in the area to forestall annexation, "I have little doubt it would carry easily."[57]

In fact, the protests did succeed in stopping the annexation. On April 26, 1960, the city commission rescinded their action of April 19 and canceled the annexation: "Whereas, it has come to the attention of the City Commission that a large number of residents of the proposed area have expressed their objection to said proposed annexation; and Whereas, it is not now, nor has it ever been, the desire of The City Commission to annex to the City areas contrary to the desire of the residents of said area."[58]

Residents of Old Town and Bel-Aire might have disputed the commission's last assertion, but the shift in policy away from forced annexations was genuine. More than a year later, the commission again passed a resolution assuring residents that "this Commission will not annex an area against the wishes of the people that live in the area."[59] In return, the Southwest Valley Boosters had agreed to a truce, promising to suspend their incorporation activities for a year.

However, the change in policy applied only to the southwest valley, and only to this commission. The "truce" conveniently left in place the mechanisms for facilitating annexations of tracts under development but still owned and controlled by individual investors or corporations. In this way, the city commission, thwarted in one thrust to the south, succeeded in a second effort.

In September 1960, developer Ed Snow requested that the city annex his Hoffman City subdivision southwest of the city. Snow was attempting to complete the development of 2,800 acres of the old Atrisco land grant, which had been purchased for development by Sam Hoffman in the late 1940s. The development had passed into Snow's hands after Hoffman's death. The trust officers for the land grant's heirs opposed the annexation into the city, arguing that they remained the owners of the vast majority of the land. (Land-grant property rights and politics are explained more fully in chapter 8.) The trust officers claimed that so far, the developers, Hoffman and Snow, had paid for only 640 acres of the land. Nonetheless, the city commission annexed "Snow Vista" on September 27, 1960.[60]

The annexation of Snow Vista proved that the government-business partnership was still fully functional despite the years of turmoil over the expansion of the city. Snow's request for annexation was only one part of a full-blown proposal requesting simultaneous zoning changes and infrastructure development. Snow's construction company was paid $184,000 for water, sewer, and paving work done within the development. And when the question of ownership arose between Snow and the trust officers of the Atrisco land grant's heirs, the city commission simply took Snow's word: "[we] must assume Snow petitioned as owner in good faith."[61]

Meanwhile, back at the first "southern front," opponents of annexation in the southwest valley resumed their organizational efforts when the truce expired. Incorporation partisans forced a vote in September 1961 in the villages of Atrisco, Arenal, Five Points, and Armijo on the proposal to form an independent municipality. Residents defeated the proposal 1,903 to 443, indicating an overwhelming opposition to any municipal ties, be they to Albuquerque or South Albuquerque.[62]

The state government stepped into Albuquerque's annexation drive in 1963 and 1964, mostly on the side of the city. In September 1963 the legislature prohibited the incorporation of any village within a five-mile "urbanized area" surrounding an already incorporated municipality unless that municipality approved the incorporation. Village residents did receive one benefit from the state when the attorney general rendered an opinion removing the tax motivation for annexation: "Where a village is annexed to a town, the property within the village at that time would not be subject to ad valorem taxes to retire the present general obligation bonded indebtedness of the town."[63]

The following year, the state legislature again stepped into the annexation dispute on the side of Albuquerque, establishing a new process for annexation: "an incorporated municipality could take in by simple resolution any unincorporated area which had been completely encircled by the municipality for five years."[64] This law, in conjunction with the recently devised "shoestring" method of annexation, gave rise to the largest of Albuquerque's annexation schemes: an effort in 1964 to annex the entire county.

The city's easiest way to annex was through the Roswell Law, the simple resolution process which permitted them to annex contiguous areas. If a tract was separated from the city limits, however, the city would make the tract "contiguous" by annexing a sliver of land, referred to as a "shoestring," often along county roads and easements.

The shoestring precedent had been established in 1946 when City Attorney Donald B. Moses gave city commissioners the means to annex the Mesa del Norte development. At the time, Mesa del Norte was half a mile beyond the city limits. Moses suggested that the city seek a 100-foot right-of-way from Bernalillo County along Las Lomas Road, and then "notwithstanding the fact that a very narrow corridor would connect the said land with the present city boundaries, this property would be contiguous."[65] In 1964 a convoluted shoestring annexation brought in the 127-acre Paradise Acres subdivision two miles south of the current city limits by also annexing the right-of-way along several roads and a narrow 1,000-foot-long strip through property belonging to the Atrisco land grant.[66]

The city's aggressiveness in pursuing annexations had increased in response to mounting financial pressures on city services. The city also faced an increased threat posed by independent sewer districts and water companies outside the city. Several utility companies had been established in response to state health department inspections that had shut down local wells and septic tanks in congested areas.[67] The construction of sewer lines might have been welcomed if not for the competition such independent companies posed for the city. After all, providing city services to "deprived" county residents was the primary inducement offered by city officials for annexation, but fringe areas in the southwest valley were obtaining city-like services without being annexed.

The city's policy then became the aggressive construction of sewer lines and water mains into the county, justified by city commissioners as viable "inroads" into the South Valley. Central to the policy was the fact that the extension of city services into the area would make independent water districts and sewer districts uneconomical "by denying them rights-of-way over direct paths." [68] The city commission had determined to drive the independent companies out of existence, and this fracture in the business-government partnership cast some businessmen as outsiders. Others, such as developer Ed Snow, remained firmly connected to the city government.

Within this context of contested expansion, the most incredible example of Albuquerque's growth mania came in June 1964 when the city commissioners announced plans to annex 11,800 acres of county land, including a narrow strip along the perimeter of Bernalillo County. The strip around the periphery of the county was 50 to 100 feet wide, totaling 649 acres. The purpose of this encirclement was to give the city the ability to annex the entire county in five years by simple resolution. The city justified their annexation as democracy in action: "more than half the land being brought in was done so by petition of the owners."

The "owners," however, turned out to be the city itself, the University of New Mexico, and W. W. Falls, Inc., a development company that planned to subdivide the Volcano Cliffs on the West Mesa. The city planning department had arranged the annexation maps so that the rest of the land in the proposal was "contiguous" to that of the three "owners." Also included in the annexation were strips of land, like the spokes of a wheel, projecting out from the city to the peripheral strip. All in all, it was a tortured manipulation of geography. The author of the plan, "Project 1970-Plus," was City Manager Edmund Engel.[69]

Ominous grumbles of complaint greeted the plan. A land owner in the area, Rex Mattingly of Corrales, announced his intention to seek an injunction to stop the annexation. Although not recorded in the minutes, others spoke against the plan at the June 23 commission meeting. George Hensley, chairman of the Rural Property Owners Association, agreed with the need to control the proliferation of independent water and sewer districts but criticized the city's methods, saying that "an attempt is being made to usurp the constitutional rights and privileges of some 62,000 residents around the city of Albuquerque . . . by merely twisting legislation."[70] Ultimately the plan would set a precedent "destroying the rights and liberties of any citizen anywhere in the United States." As the *Albuquerque Journal* reported, "Hensley's talk . . . was greeted by loud applause."[71]

Once again the courts determined the outcome of an annexation controversy in Albuquerque. In July 1964, District Judge D. A. MacPherson agreed with Mattingly and issued a permanent injunction stopping the city's plan. MacPherson based his decision on two concerns. First, the judge questioned two "nontaxpaying bodies" (the city and the University of New Mexico) uniting "to force taxpayers into the city against their will." MacPherson also based his decision on "an authority on municipal corporations" who labeled the city's plan "unreasonable." Judge MacPherson had then concluded that "if the territory is sparsely settled, situated remotely from the thickly settled portion of the municipality, would receive no advantage or benefits from annexation but would be burdened with additional tax, and the residents of the territory prefer to remain without the municipality, it should not be annexed." Most telling to MacPherson was the fact that the peripheral strip contained no houses, and the city expressed no intention of extending city services into the area.[72]

The city seemed to ignore this rebuke from the court and went right ahead with its aggressive policy in an attempt to annex 8,200 acres in the West Mesa and North Valley areas. To accomplish the annexation, "a connecting strip of ten miles of roadway" would be annexed to make all the areas "contiguous." Two commissioners, Ralph Trigg and Emmanuel Schifani, voted against the annexation plan. Trigg remarked that "It seems to me the public feeling is about fifty to one against this. In fact, I have had only one phone call from a person favoring the annexation."[73] Once again Judge MacPherson ruled against the annexation, declaring it "arbitrary and capricious" and therefore "unreasonable." As an example of capriciousness, the judge pointed to the ten-mile connecting strip, which included a "proposed" bridge over the Rio Grande River.[74]

At this point the city turned to the arbitration board method of annexation for the North Valley. Late in 1964, the city appointed three members to the board, and in January 1965 the residents of the designated "annex unit" elected their three members, all of whom opposed the annexation. The leader of the opposition delegation was Gerald Cornelius, former chairman of the Bernalillo County Commission.[75] The district court appointed the seventh member of the arbitration board: South Valley resident Ralph Wolf. In February 1965 the arbitration board voted four to three against the annexation, with Wolf casting the deciding vote. Cornelius defended the board's decision by pointing to an area annexed by the city eleven years earlier that was still without city water and sewer service. The city officials, he said, are "like a bull in the china shop. It's their way or else."[76]

One result of the furor over the city's annexation drive was passage by the state legislature of a two-year moratorium on annexations by the City of Albuquerque unless it had the approval of 100 percent of the property owners in the area to be annexed. Ten parcels totaling 951 acres were annexed during this time, often on a lot-by-lot basis.[77] By the time the moratorium expired, city commissioners had come to the conclusion that bringing people into the city against their will made little sense. Ralph Trigg, now the commission chairman, announced that "there would be no forced annexations."[78]

The more cautious approach to annexation became entrenched under the chairmanship of Pete Domenici in 1967. Domenici announced that the city would extend city services into county areas before they were annexed, and "by utilizing planned annexation we will do away with the friction and ill will which in many cases in the past has earmarked annexation."[79] As a result, controversies over annexations died down.

Also, the general awareness of the difficulties resulting from the headlong rush toward bigness was beginning to surface. The earliest such report appeared in 1962 when City Manager Edmund Engel chronicled problems brought on by growth in a series of newspaper articles.[80] By the early 1970s, "more residents seemed to worry about the growth than to brag about it."[81]

Opposition to Albuquerque's expansion appeared so frequently and from such seemingly disparate angles that perhaps a brief summary and effort at generalization would be helpful.

A very specific form of political resistance originated in the individual actions of politicians like Clyde Tingley and Joseph Montoya, who opposed Albuquerque's growth out of personal judgments of propriety and political viability. Tingley, for example, began opposing growth and development in Albuquerque once he lost control of the city commission. He apparently perceived his role on the commission to be the steadfast opposition to anything the civic "reformers" attempted.

Tingley based his opposition to expansion on the burdensome taxes such growth would require. Tax-based protest formed a major component of the general, community-wide resistance to Albuquerque's growth. County residents voiced a strong desire to avoid the higher city taxes. The city regularly promised increased services commensurate with the higher taxes, but as expansion of the city proceeded with gaps in such services, southwest valley residents became increasingly skeptical of the city's sales pitch.

Antitax sentiment also motivated political restiveness within Albuquerque. The Heights/valley disputes over flood control and road construction turned on the issue of one region paying for improvements for another region.

Ideological concerns motivated much of the resistance to Albuquerque's expansion. A general "liberty versus tyranny" argument appeared throughout the community, from Old Town to the North Valley, with "fundamental rights," "constitutional rights and privileges," all threatened by the "Stalins and dictators" who inhabited city hall. Specifically, northside residents questioned the legality of the 1947 annexation law, arguing that arbitration boards constituted an improper delegation of legislative authority. Old Town residents described the same law as "the least democratic" form of annexation.

Finally, opposition to growth sought to defend and preserve neighborhoods and lifestyle. Hispanic areas struggled to stay outside the city limits, and then, once part of the city, fought to maintain their neighborhoods and culture. Particularly in the barrios, activists in community associations sought to preserve traditional patterns of housing and kinship (to be discussed in chapter 8).

Rural lifestyles also motivated resistance. Without offering any precise definition of "rural," residents often spoke of their disdain for "the city." As one southwest valley resident had said, "If we wanted to live in the city we'd move there." Rural residents also organized themselves in the

North Valley, although they phrased their opposition to Albuquerque's expansion in stark "freedom versus tyranny" terms. Of significance is their own self-identification as rural property owners.

Although the city governments of both Tucson and Albuquerque met strong opposition to their annexation drives during the post–World War II boom, the reach of Albuquerque's political leadership far exceeded that of Tucson's. Nothing resembling the city commission's plan to annex all of Bernalillo County appeared in Tucson, although both cities pursued annexations in the name of planned and controlled growth. Perhaps Albuquerque's ambitious annexation policies resulted from the closer working relationship between the city commission and Chamber of Commerce. The 1946 annexation plan was formulated by the Chamber of Commerce and the commission's advisory committee, made up of business leaders including the president of the real estate board. Tucson's boosters exerted influence on city leadership, but rarely, if ever, to that degree. But while toeing the booster line more rigorously allowed Albuquerque to expand more forcefully, such harsh feelings arose toward the city's expansion policy that "annexation" became a civic profanity.

8 ETHNIC RESISTANCE

■ ■ ■ ■ ■ ■ ■ ■ ■ ■ ■ ■ ■ ■

"The Enchilada Floor"

Albuquerque's Hispanic population in the 1940s and 1950s participated in political activities such as annexation resistance to a greater degree than Tucson's Hispanic population. Nonetheless, the early ethnic resistance in Albuquerque, such as the fight to keep Old Town out of the city, was no more successful than middle-class, Anglo, suburban resistance. On the other hand, Albuquerque's Hispanic population was able to preserve viable neighborhoods by opposing urban renewal plans that targeted their neighborhoods for destruction.

The range of Hispanic leadership, from Joseph Montoya to Gilberto Espinosa, is one indication of a broader political participation by Hispanics in Albuquerque than in Tucson. Whether denoted by the European-referenced "Spanish American" or by the federally approved "Hispanic" label, Albuquerque's ethnic population maintained a political involvement from the earliest days of statehood.

By 1945, Albuquerque's approximately 18,000 Hispanic residents composed about 35 percent of the city's population of 50,000. Their involvement in city commerce was generally limited to small business, but they were more successful in politics, where their influence is evidenced

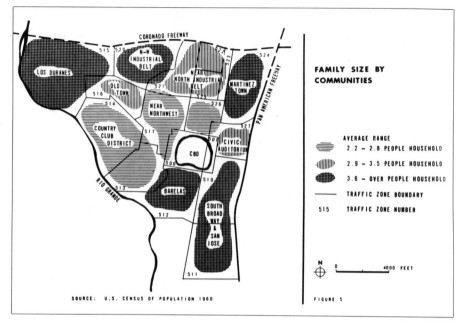

FIG. 11 Family Size by Communities. Urban renewal of the central business district (CBD) in Albuquerque inevitably impacted surrounding neighborhoods. This 1965 map clearly illustrates the proximity of residential areas to downtown. (Source: Albuquerque Planning Department Central Area Study, 1965, p. 28)

by the numbers of Hispanic politicians elected to local, state, and national offices. Also, Hispanic organizations such as the League of United Latin American Citizens (LULAC) and the Alianza Hispano Americano were active in the Albuquerque area. From 1950 to 1960 the percentage of Hispanics within Albuquerque declined to 27 percent of the 201,189 population, mainly due to the influx of new residents, including many Anglo, middle-class defense workers. In 1970, after a slowdown in Anglo migration, the percentage of Hispanic residents increased to 39.2 percent of the 315,774 population.[1]

Hispanics were active at all levels of political activity. Nine of New Mexico's thirty-two counties remained under the control of Hispanic political machines until the 1960s, when more radical Chicano groups began to exert influence.[2] A typical example of Hispanic representation in state government can be seen in 1939, when Hispanics held the positions of secretary of state, attorney general, state auditor, and corporation commissioner. There were also two Hispanic district-court judges (out of nine), four state senators (out of twenty-four), and eighteen state representatives (out of forty-nine). The most prominent Hispanic political figure in the 1940s was U.S. Senator Denis Chavez, a Democrat from Albuquerque elected in 1936.[3]

But even though Hispanics consistently held offices, they never dominated the state government. An indication of their relative position appears in the accommodation that resulted in the election of an Anglo governor and a Hispanic lieutenant governor. Joseph Montoya served as lieutenant governor for eight years until 1957, when he was chosen to fill a "Hispanic" seat in Congress left vacant by the death of Antonio Fernandez. Montoya served as a representative until 1964. He then ran successfully for the U.S. Senate.[4]

On a cultural level, Albuquerque's ethnic identity clearly held sway compared to Tucson. Tucson goes by the "Old Pueblo" sobriquet even though there was no Indian pueblo, in the sense of communitarian adobe dwellings, anywhere near Tucson. The Indian villages in the area of the original Spanish presidio and mission along the Santa Cruz River in Arizona bore little resemblance to the multistoried structures of the New Mexican pueblos.

Albuquerque, on the other hand, lies in the heart of "pueblo country," but its nickname, "Duke City," refers to the aristocratic, Spanish viceroy of New Spain in the 1700s: the Duke of Alburquerque. In 1706, the governor of the province of New Mexico, Don Francisco Fernandez Cuervo Valdez, established a new settlement on the Rio Grande River, naming it after the viceroy. More than a century later, the first "r" was omitted from the name. As Erna Fergusson describes, "That extra r was dropped . . . by the sort of people who would still like to lose a q or two."[5] (Fergusson was referring to the Anglos who began arriving with the railroad in the 1880s, residents who would have happily erased all trace of Albuquerque's cultural heritage.) The 1992–93 telephone book lists thirty-nine businesses prefacing their names with the words "Duke City," and the city's AAA baseball team goes by the moniker "Albuquerque Dukes."

The architectural style of the buildings in "new" Albuquerque through the 1880s and 1890s remained staunchly brick with nary a trace of indigenous or regional influence. "Pueblo" or "Santa Fe" style buildings came as a self-conscious afterthought at the turn of the century.[6]

Albuquerque's Indo-Hispanic pastoral heritage persisted through the post–World War II boom in the old villages beyond the city's fringe, where "the pace of life [was] slower, traditional cultures or natural beauty closer at hand, and yet access to the city only a matter of minutes by car."[7]

The Indian and Hispanic cultures in Albuquerque started with a substantial degree of cultural enclavement, unlike Tucson, where enclavement developed gradually over decades. V. B. Price, in City at the End of the World, took an optimistic view of this bicultural tradition as having created a unique urban character (endangered recently by growth). It is true that a degree of harmony and tolerance actually existed within the community, despite continuing contentiousness, but too much optimism is misplaced. Much of the annexation resistance arose from the unwillingness of old communities, often Hispanic and pastoral, to come into the city. Their calls for independence, and pleas to be left alone, fell largely on deaf ears among city planners and boosters. The threat to Albuquerque's bicultural identity is not recent but longstanding, and the only cause for optimism is that so many have been so willing to fight for so long.

One indication of a continuing ethnic resistance is Albuquerque's pattern of development. Developers initially built new homes in the northeast because the land there was cheap and held with clear titles free of land-grant ties.[8] Much of the land to the west of the river remained in the hands of the original Hispanic owners and their heirs, the primary example being the Atrisco land grant. These owners, possessed of a "tradition of attachment to the land," successfully resisted the incursion of "outsiders" for more than 250 years.[9]

The Atrisco grant covered 51,000 acres on the West Mesa. The heirs numbered about three thousand in the 1950s, about a thousand of whom still lived on the grant. A board of trustees—nine heirs, each elected to three-year terms—administered the grant's holdings. Contentiousness generally marked the board's deliberations as heirs aligned themselves with "majority" and "minority" factions.[10]

Pressure by city leaders and developers to sell large tracts of grant land mounted in the 1950s. In October 1957, the city offered to purchase

10,240 acres of grant land on the West Mesa for a new airport. The city first proposed to buy the land for $15 an acre. After the laughter died down, the city offered $35 an acre, but this bid, too, was rejected as ludicrously low. Grazing land at the time was going for $200 an acre.[11]

In 1959, developer Sam Hoffman offered the trustees $312 an acre for 3,840 acres: $1.2 million. Hoffman had made a fortune developing the East Mesa, but land prices there had grown prohibitive. Now Hoffman's gaze rested firmly on the West Mesa, where he planned to build "Hoffman City," with 12,000 to 13,000 homes.[12]

The Atrisco board of trustees approved the sale and scheduled a meeting of the heirs, who would make the final determination. Three heirs who opposed the sale filed suit to stop the meeting, arguing that the trustees had settled for less than fair market value, which the opponents placed at $800 an acre (the price of East Mesa land at the time). The opponents also questioned who would get the money, or more specifically, how the fortune would be divided among the heirs. The district court, acting in a fiduciary role for the grant's heirs, denied the suit and allowed the meeting to proceed as scheduled.[13]

Approximately two thousand heirs and onlookers met on May 2, 1959, to hear the terms of Hoffman's proposal read in both Spanish and English. Hoffman was both "lauded and attacked." In general, proponents of the sale argued that the price was more than they could get from any other source and that the development would raise the value of the rest of the grant's holdings. Opponents at the meeting ignored the monetary issue and referred to the grant as culturally valuable, and they called for the preservation of the grant for their children "just as their ancestors had done for them." In the end, the heirs voted 4-1 in favor of the sale (432 for, 115 against). Only heirs who were residents of the grant were allowed to vote. The 158 ballots cast by heirs who were not residents were "disqualified."[14]

In the end, Hoffman's grand undertaking failed as regulatory obstacles mounted in 1959, and as Albuquerque's housing boom soured.[15] After Hoffman's suicide, developer Ed Snow successfully completed the development, over the renewed objections of the land grant's heirs (see chapter 7).[16]

Ethnic identities fractured Albuquerque's "harmony" in issues other than annexation and suburban development. In 1959, a dispute involving the

Sandia Conservancy District split the city geographically and ethnically. Flooding near the river led the city to attempt a flood-control project that would require higher taxes throughout the city. In response, Heights residents formed the Property Owners Protective Association to protest the increased taxes that would fund the project, from which they would receive no benefit. Even though the development of the Heights had, in fact, denuded the watershed, and consequently increased the runoff to the lowlands, Heights residents felt no obligation to pay for flood control.[17] This dispute split Albuquerque not only geographically but also ethnically because Heights residents were generally Anglo and middle class, and the lowland residents were primarily Hispanic.[18]

In another Heights versus valley dispute, the lowland precincts provided the winning margin for opponents of the half-cent gasoline tax in 1965. The increased gas tax was required to build roads, mostly in the Heights. Lowland precincts swung the vote to the opponents.[19]

As described in the previous chapter, resistance to annexation surfaced in ethnic villages and neighborhoods along the Rio Grande River, including Old Town, as the city expanded in the late 1940s. The old communities of North Barelas and San Jose also were brought into the city in 1949. The vote taken in Old Town showed a two-to-one majority opposed to annexation, but the light turnout at the election probably indicated that many residents were willing to accept the city's plans. Acquiescence was tempered, however, by concern for preservation of the community's lifestyle, as indicated by the inquiry over the fate of the Sunday evening dances. The city's assurances no doubt caused some residents to shrug off the resistance to the annexation.

The relations between the city and neighboring communities had been generally cooperative in the 1940s. In 1947, residents of a Hispanic neighborhood just outside the city limits complained to the city commission that city wells were tapping their water supply. In a memo to the commission, the city manager acknowledged that the city's nearby well field had lowered the water table below the level reached by the residents' "shallow wells." As a solution, the manager recommended that the city build a water main into the neighborhood, even though it was five blocks north of the city limits. The city commission agreed, and the county residents were provided city water.[20] After this relatively benign beginning, relations between the city government and "poorer neighborhoods" deteriorated, and by the 1960s they were "uneasy."[21]

In an effort to preserve the identity and culture of the communities coming under the control of the city, neighborhood associations were formed. The East San Jose Community Improvement Association was organized in the 1950s, and seven more associations were established in the 1960s under the auspices of the Peace Corp Training Center at the University of New Mexico.[22] In 1965, the *Albuquerque Journal* remarked on the associations' "novel" distance from politics. The South Barelas Improvement Association's constitution stipulated that the association "shall be not for profit or for political gain." The North Barelas Community Development Association was even more explicit in its disavowal of politics: "No district precinct chairman, chairwoman or justice of the peace shall be on the board of directors of the association, and no person shall use the association in any manner to further his political ambitions."[23]

Blaise Padillas, assistant director of a home-improvement project in South Barelas, described residents' attitudes toward politics as distinctly suspicious: "The poor people here in Barelas don't trust the politician. They think of community development as their problem, and they don't want anyone to take advantage of their desire to do something. To these people a politician is your friend during his campaign. If he's elected, he's no longer interested."[24]

As community associations proliferated in the 1960s, a federation of groups formed. Rudy Baca headed the federation from his position as president of the Santa Barbara–Martineztown Advancement Association. Baca described the goals of the federation as coordinating development projects, helping associations acquire federal funding, and making sure "the community development associations continue to follow democratic principles [and] keep out sectarian and political groups."[25]

A note of radicalization can be heard in Baca's "democratic" exclusiveness. The democracy within the associations manifested itself in a profound sense of solidarity within the communities. Perhaps the best example of this neighborhood cohesiveness occurred in East San Jose. As juvenile delinquency increased throughout Albuquerque in the early 1970s, residents of East San Jose pointed with great pride to the lack of such increases within their neighborhood. Residents attributed their relative peace to the community's youth center. The East San Jose Community Improvement Association had raised funds to match city funds from the recreation department to build a youth center that included gymnasiums, craft shops, and meeting rooms. David H. Vargas, president of the East San Jose Association, defined the neighborhood's approach to improvement as "self-help." All projects in the area relied on matching funds. The "handouts" from Model Cities and other federal antipoverty programs were steadfastly refused.[26] While conducting a tour of their new woodworking shop, Vargas described one of the community's fund-raising efforts: "This is what I call the enchilada floor. I call it the enchilada floor because we sold so many enchiladas to buy the cement for this floor that we almost had them coming out our ears."[27]

Suspicion of city politicians had developed as city planners and politicians pushed redevelopment plans and programs in the 1950s and 1960s. The same types of coalitions of urban planners, developers, and politicians that had attacked the problem of "blight" in Tucson began targeting Albuquerque neighborhoods, especially the barrios, for urban renewal. Such areas were discussed as if they were "to be cured of a disease and the unwholesome structures in the area to be amputated."[28]

The first effort at redevelopment in Albuquerque occurred in 1957 when local merchants funded a city planning department study seeking to cure the congestion and lack of access in the downtown area.[29] The resulting "Central Business District Study: Land Uses, 1957" advocated the division of downtown between office and shopping areas. Local residents, primarily Hispanic, who occupied neighborhoods surrounding the downtown area were given no place in the plan. The downtown area was to be organized as a service center for the city, accommodating a "high concentration of pedestrian traffic" in shopping areas to the north and office areas to the south. The plan ended with a salutary call for further study and resulted in no new construction.[30]

The first area actually to come under renewal was the South Broadway neighborhood, south of downtown, some five blocks wide and twenty blocks deep. The area contained approximately 1,700 houses and a population of 6,000. The estimated median income of residents was $200 to $300 per month.[31] The city deemed the project a "pilot program," using no federal funds for clearance or redevelopment but rather "encouraging

residents and property owners in the . . . area to clean up and remodel."
The city's plan called for low-interest loans to be issued by local lenders
to stop the spread of "blight," after which the city would use federal
funds to "backtrack and clean up the mess where clearance programs
might be called for."[32]

The director of the city's effort in South Broadway was Vernon Doaks,
coordinator of the city's new Urban Renewal Agency. Doaks emphasized
the self-help nature of the program and placed the stress on "preventative
rather than curative action, with an eye toward catching deterioration in
specific areas before a really serious situation develops."[33] To handle the
"serious" situations, the city planned to use federal funds and so established the Albuquerque Community Improvement Committee in 1960 to
formulate a plan and a grant proposal. According to Doaks, the city intended to "go slow" in their redevelopment effort so as to avoid the pit-
falls encountered by other cities that had cleared large areas with the ex-
pectation that the private sector would move in and redevelop, only to be
left years later with large tracts of vacant land in their downtown areas.[34]

Under the personal tutelage of Doaks and his two assistants, who were
on a first-name basis with most residents and property owners, South
Broadway commenced to paint and remodel. Property owners tore down
six thoroughly dilapidated houses that were condemned by city inspec-
tors. One bank approved fifty-seven loans in the area from January to June
1962. The city spent $50,000 to acquire six acres and develop a new park,
and Piggly Wiggly opened a $250,000 supermarket that took up an entire
block. During a 1960 "clean-up" drive, eight hundred tons of trash were
collected. City leaders cited the decline in area fire calls as one result of
the improvements, and the newspaper reported that South Broadway's
"face [had begun] to shine."[35]

One measure of the success of the South Broadway project was the
personal contact between Doaks and his staff and the residents. As a result
of efforts by planners and property owners, homes were preserved and
slated for remodeling rather than destruction. Only roofless shells fell to
redevelopment. At the time, the *Albuquerque Journal* deemed the program a
great success, and bemoaned Doaks's resignation in June 1962.[36]

Perhaps the reason Doaks resigned was the election of new city commissioners in April 1962. The Albuquerque Citizens Committee had run
a slate of candidates who opposed the use of federal funds for urban plan-

ning. Opposition to urban renewal had arisen among businessmen, "particularly those in the housing and real estate industries," and among political conservatives in general.[37] The Citizens Committee candidates defy simple categorization as liberal or conservative (they defined themselves as "better government reformers"), and the particular issue of urban renewal created multiple fractures along political, economic, and ethnic lines. In general, however, as in Tucson, federally funded renewal programs generated conservative resistance.

With their election in April, the majority on the city commission established the "building inspection team"—not to replace urban renewal but rather to pursue it on a self-help basis while the city continued independently to formulate redevelopment plans. The building inspection team consisted of Fire Chief Simon Seligman, Health Director Larry Gordon, and Supervisor of Building and Inspection A. P. Garland. The team's mandate was to strictly enforce codes to encourage residents and property owners in the downtown area to rebuild. Archie Westfall, chairman of the city commission, predicted that "in most, if not all, cases corrective measures short of condemnation probably will be possible."[38]

The meager results of the inspection program resulted from "the inability of householders to obtain loans."[39] In the meantime, planning continued on several fronts, both within and without the city government. Albuquerque's planning department began to study downtown redevelopment in 1963, completing the "Central Area Study" in 1965. On a different tack, the city commission in January 1964 established the Albuquerque Metropolitan Development Committee to study the issue of sprawl in relation to "core" development. As Chairman Westfall explained, "For the past year and a half or so a number of people in Albuquerque have become keenly and greatly concerned over our little condition of 'sprawlitis.' " Westfall went on to explain that the commission approved of Albuquerque's spread outward, but not at the expense of the city's core. The eight businessmen on the Metropolitan Development Committee were to develop a plan for the revitalization of downtown.[40] The committee's ideas became public in 1965 and were published in 1966 as the "Albuquerque Core Redevelopment Plan." The businessmen called for open space in the downtown area, overpasses to provide easy access, and "high density residences" near downtown.[41]

Despite the plan's formulation by businessmen, it failed to materialize in any concrete way, due, ironically, to the resistance of downtown businessmen. The *Albuquerque Journal* publicized this split within the business community in February 1964. Without explanation or preamble, the newspaper quoted at great length C. K. (Bud) Redd, "veteran real estate man," who explained the certain failure of all voluntary redevelopment plans downtown. At fault, according to Redd, was the "warped philosophy" of downtown businessmen who abhorred going into debt for the sake of a high-rise downtown. "I don't know this for sure but I'll bet you that 90 percent of the property in what we call the downtown area is debt free, and that's an unhealthy condition. You can't build a big fine building without going into debt. . . . They [downtown businessmen] operate on a cash basis, and they want to continue that way. This will result in a lot of one and two story buildings going up where high-rise buildings should go up." [42]

Redd's castigation of his fellow businessmen targeted their "independence," which allowed individual property owners to "clobber a whole program." Redd reluctantly concluded that federal intervention and support for urban redevelopment was necessary. "Those boys [federal renewal agencies] have been at it for years and they know what they are doing. They have the authority to condemn property and this is what we need." [43]

It was in this environment that the planning department's "Central Area Study" appeared in 1965. This study echoed Redd's conclusion by attributing the failure of earlier programs to the resistance of individualistic businessmen. The study also described "sociological" causes; i.e., the Hispanic, mostly poor, residents in the neighborhoods immediately surrounding the central business district generally opposed redevelopment plans. [44]

The Central Area Study described the surrounding neighborhoods as generally blighted. As evidence for slum conditions, the study quoted the 1960 Census of Housing, which described about one-third of the central area's housing as "dilapidated or deteriorated" (34.2 percent of 3,801 housing units). The lumping tendency of planners at this time appeared in this survey of the central area. A minor inconsistency, perhaps pointing to the danger of generalizations, appeared in the study's analysis of housing conditions. First, the study described dilapidated housing as resulting from poor original construction, specifically excoriating adobe construction. When pointing to the structures in worst condition, however, frame construction was the worst culprit.[45]

More egregious was the study's dismissal of the needs of area residents. Housing in the redeveloped central area was to be "attractive (and) high density." None of the eight objectives in the plan acknowledged the existence of current residents.[46] As the renewal plan progressed to a specific $2.5 million proposal, the human impact became clearer. In September 1965, the city's sanitarian, John Cordova, described the urban renewal project as including 980 families residing in 335 pieces of property "beyond repair," 240 pieces of property requiring an average $1,687.40 in rehabilitation, and 153 houses in good condition. Cordova said that most residents approved of the redevelopment plan, but he acknowledged that "quite a few older people [are] living there. There's long-time occupancy, and they don't want to move too far away."[47] A later survey of the area would show that many residents did not want to move at all.

The city commission pushed for the passage of urban renewal bonds to match federal funds for the $2.5 million project in the April 1966 election, and they were stunned when voters singled out the urban renewal bonds for defeat. City Manager Edmund Engel "expressed extreme dismay."[48] Although voters approved $20 million in civic improvement bonds for added fire, sewer, and water service (plus storm drain and street construction, which included an overpass into the downtown area), they defeated bonds of $2 million for a new Hall of Justice, $750,000 for a new museum building, and $475,000 for the city's share of the proposed $2,595,000 urban renewal project. The voters seemed to be saying that they wanted easier access to downtown (approving the overpass), but few changes once they got there.[49] "Urban renewal" had become the evil twin of annexation.

Despite the electoral setback, city commissioners continued to push for urban renewal. As planning progressed, the federal government named Albuquerque a participant in the Model Cities program, which in some ways overlapped with renewal. Conservative reaction was vehement. Some warned against the "perils of federal control," and one man declared, "We've got to start fighting the Communists at home."[50]

Nonetheless, the city commission forged ahead. Next on their agenda was the plan to develop Old Town Plaza as a tourist attraction. City planners identified three problems in the Old Town area: First, the area was "hard to reach by automobile. Second is that parking near the Plaza is in short supply and few motorists like to park on dirt. And third, that there are dirt streets, unsightly utility lines, dilapidated buildings and houses, non-historic businesses, and ugly signs in the fringe area." Planners had become aware of the federal-funding bugaboo and therefore explicitly downplayed the federal role in the plan. Only funds for the purpose of placing utility lines underground would be solicited from the federal government.[51]

Even while supporting the plan, the *Albuquerque Journal* acknowledged the city's clumsy handling of the proposal. "True, the planners made some mistakes in both the plan itself and in the manner in which it was presented to the public. Perhaps the biggest mistake was the mere mentioning of urban renewal."[52] A letter to the editor exemplified the "buzz-saw" of emotion that surrounded the plan. Warren Hawkins wrote: "Keep it as it is. I have been reading about urban renewal for Old Town Plaza. Preposterous! Can't we keep a few little quaint shops and at least one little old mud house in this neon-lighted world? Keep Old Town Plaza as it is!"[53]

Albuquerque's urban renewal efforts came to fruition in 1968 replete with ongoing political squabbling. Factions developed as various departments debated the specifics of the plan. How many fingers were in the urban renewal pie? At various times, five local and federal agencies claimed jurisdiction over urban renewal in Albuquerque: the Albuquerque Planning Department, Metropolitan Transportation Department, Urban Renewal Agency, Model Cities Administration, and Office for Economic Opportunity.

At the center of the controversy were the federal regulations pertaining to urban renewal. On one side of the issue were officials who "kow-towed" to "the feds." On the other side were those who "played it fast and loose" with federal regulations. Officials on each side accused each other of skipping meetings, lying, and sabotaging planning efforts,[54] leading Martha Buddecke to pose the rhetorical question "Who Plans the Planning?"[55]

Despite the political squabbling, Albuquerque received $25 million for the Tijeras Urban Renewal Project in June 1968. The project resulted from the loan and grant application (requesting $31 million) submitted by the

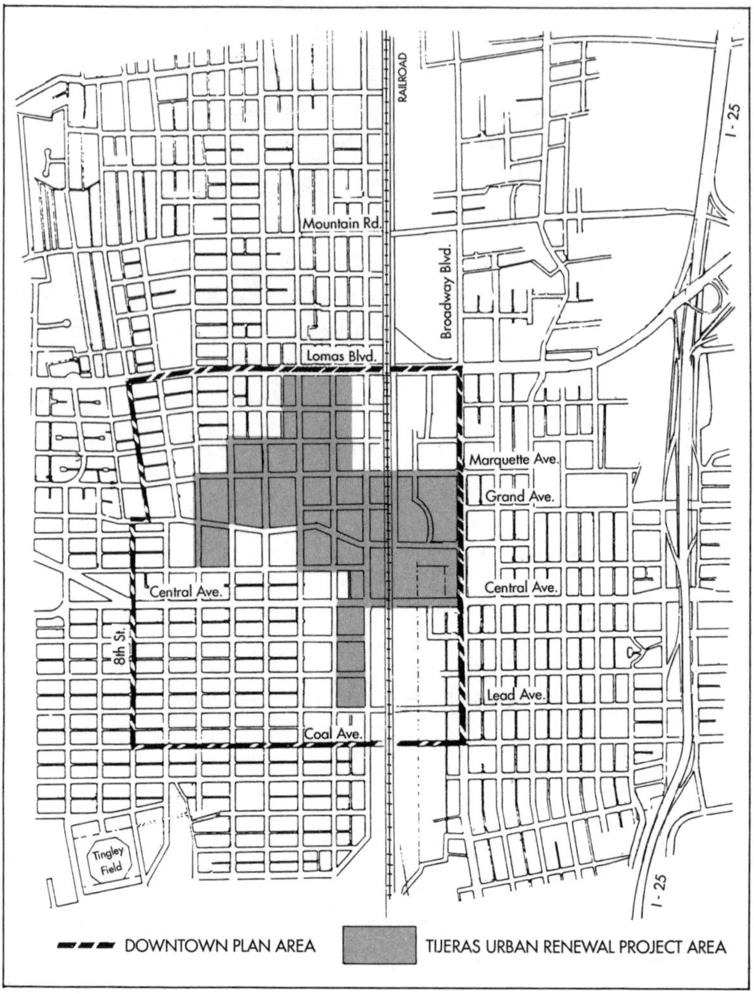

RAILROAD
I-25
Mountain Rd.
Broadway Blvd.
Lomas Blvd.
Marquette Ave.
Grand Ave.
Central Ave.
Central Ave.
8th St.
Lead Ave.
Coal Ave.
Tingley Field
I-25
DOWNTOWN PLAN AREA
TIJERAS URBAN RENEWAL PROJECT AREA

FIG. 12 Downtown Albuquerque in Relation to Public Renewal Areas. Multiple renewal projects, often overlapping, were proposed for downtown Albuquerque in 1970. The resulting bureaucratic conflicts between federal, state, and local officials caused one editorial writer to ask "Who Plans the Planning?" As in Tucson, barrio resistance in Albuquerque successfully fought to preserve established neighborhoods, such as the Tijeras project area. (Map based on the Albuquerque Planning Department Downtown Plan, 1970)

city's Urban Renewal Agency. The plan covered 182.6 acres near downtown and required that "all single family residential structures that [can] not be feasibly converted to uses allowed in the plan . . . be acquired and cleared."[56] The types of residences foreseen after redevelopment were "high intensity" warrens, not the original single-family homes.

Residents of the area formed the Citizen Improvement Committee to resist the renewal program. The residential resistance created more name-calling among the city and federal officials. The city commission and chairman of the Urban Renewal Agency accused local Volunteers in Service to America (VISTA) representatives of fomenting resistance in the renewal neighborhoods. John Goldsmith, VISTA supervisor in Albuquerque, explained that his workers were simply explaining the renewal process to residents (including the federal regulation requiring participation by residents in the planning process), and that residents' organizational efforts and demands for a seat on the board of directors of the Urban Renewal Agency were of the residents' own doing.[57]

As resistance mounted, flaws in the Tijeras plan appeared. Specifically, the *Albuquerque Journal* noted that a neighborhood slated for destruction actually had a split personality: "The northwest corner is a slum—mostly unpaved streets, dilapidated housing, overcrowding. The southeast corner is a quiet, well-kept neighborhood with houses built around the turn of the century." And even within the "slum" area, erroneous judgments were made. The "slum" house of Mrs. Lupe Cortez was described as "ramshackle outside," but "neat and warm inside." Contributing to the "slum" designation was Cortez's status as a renter (albeit at the same address for thirty years) and her use of a wood-burning stove to provide warmth.[58]

Perhaps a clearer example to the planners was the case of seventy-seven-year-old Otto Van Cleave, a homeowner who had lived in the same house since 1903. Of the renewal plan, Van Cleave said, "I think it's crap! I want to stay here. I'll do everything in my power to keep from moving."[59]

Meanwhile, residents of the Tijeras area continued to push for representation on the board of directors of the Urban Renewal Agency. Finally, in April 1969, the city commission voted to appoint Jack Candelaria. Candelaria was a resident of the San Jose neighborhood and had recently participated in Model Cities planning. Tijeras residents had nominated James

Hontas, president of the Citizen Improvement Committee, for the position, but the city commission picked Candelaria as a "representative for the whole renewal area."[60]

The resistance of the Tijeras residents paid off in the end. Their neighborhood had been slated for destruction to make room for a school complex, but federal planners amended the project and removed the education center. Most of the neighborhood was left in place.

Typically, federal funding shrank for areas where improvement in residential areas was needed.[61] In 1969, the city formally requested $8 million for neighborhood rehabilitation, including street repair, remodeling of housing, and the purchase of condemned property. The city received only $8,900 in Model Cities funds for these projects, but robbed Peter to pay Paul in order to do some of the work.[62] Renewal became an ad hoc affair. Smaller projects continued into the 1970s. For example, in 1971, local agencies moved approximately fifty families in the Barelas area away from the stench of a city sewage treatment plant.[63]

Perhaps the smaller size of projects allowed planners and politicians to manage renewal without trampling so thoroughly on the wishes of residents and taxpayers. Mirroring the city's turbulent annexation fights of the 1950s and 1960s, urban renewal generated loud protest until new political leadership in the late 1960s brought a softening of the city's approach to both renewal and annexation.

Finally, in 1970, the downtown plan was approved, and in 1975, the city's comprehensive plan went into effect,[64] but resistance to urban renewal, both political and ethnic in origin, had shaped the final outcome of redevelopment in Albuquerque. The appearance of downtown Albuquerque today bears the marks of both the planners' zeal and the residents' resistance.

9 ENVIRONMENTAL RESISTANCE

■ ■ ■ ■ ■ ■ ■ ■ ■ ■ ■ ■ ■ ■

"Sprawlitis"

The rise of environmental awareness in Albuquerque mirrored the national trends of the late 1960s and 1970s. In Albuquerque, environmental awareness resulted in calls for slow growth and preservation of open spaces on the fringe of the city in the 1970s. Although consciousness of natural surroundings appeared in the earliest booster promotions, an explicitly preservationist critique in defense of nature failed to materialize in Albuquerque until the early 1970s, late in the postwar boom.

Albuquerque residents seemed to have had a more diffuse view of natural surroundings than Tucsonans, with nature thought of as "out there" rather than within the city's midst. Nonetheless, even though it was not part of the early lexicon of protest, much of the early resistance in Albuquerque was based on "nature." The rural lifestyle defended by the RPOA inherently contained "nature" (albeit a "middle landscape" as defined by Leo Marx in *The Machine in the Garden*), but when rural residents voiced their concerns about growth, the focus of their critique was governmental transgressions rather than environmental preservation.

While Albuquerque's natural surroundings appeared in the earliest booster promotions, many people valued nature only as a marketable commodity, a business asset to be sold and utilized just as the fertility of the Rio Grande River had been used from the beginning of settlement. Albuquerque's promoters thought of nature in the useable forms of climate, topography, and culture. A preservationist view of nature, such as Joseph Wood Krutch offered in Tucson, did not appear in Albuquerque until the early 1970s.

Ernie Pyle might have arrived at Krutch's nay-saying extreme had not a Japanese machine gun on Okinawa ended his life in 1945. An early description by Pyle of his home on the outskirts of Albuquerque shows a sensitivity to nature such as Krutch felt:

> . . . the weirdest kinds of desert weeds are always springing up in our bare south lot . . . meadow larks hidden in the sage across the road from our house sing us awake in the summer dawn. . . . Every night around 9 two rabbits come to nibble on our lawn. And about once a week when we rise early, there are quail in our front yard . . . they don't fly away with a frightened whirring of wings, they just walk slowly across the road and inside the concealing sage.[1]

Erna Fergusson was another literary figure who might have offered a preservationist argument as a native daughter of the city, but Fergusson tended to valorize some aspects of nature and not others. In her book *Albuquerque*, sunsets and mountain views were glorious, but the surrounding sagebrush plains were "arid wastes."[2]

Albuquerque's boosters often spoke of the city's uniqueness, but they rarely offered a precise definition. The 1939 inaugural edition of *Albuquerque Magazine* described the city as unique, even if residents did not recognize it as such: ". . . living in the very center of the most interesting part of New Mexico, our residents all too frequently think of remote points as the proper localities to visit, and fail to appreciate the captivating possibilities of our own unique and lovable region."[3] In the 1941 promotional brochure "Pictorial Albuquerque," the Chamber of Commerce displayed the city primarily through photographs of city buildings, with some additional shots of the surrounding mountains and Indian pueblos.[4] In 1965 the city commission discussed the need to establish new taxing districts for infrastructure improvement "to the end that this community will continue to grow as one united in the essentials yet free to express the individuality of its people thereby retaining the flavor which has caused us all to cherish this as our own and permanent home."⁵ In these claims to uniqueness, the city's plurality of cultures plays an equal, if not greater, role than nature, but within this awareness of cultural pluralism, an assumption about natural surroundings remains.

In most of the promotions and self-evaluations of Albuquerque, even those focusing on cultural aspects of the community, nature appears as an inescapable element of the community's character. Perhaps this awareness of nature is unavoidable in southwestern cities due to the basin and range topography that makes vivid horizons the norm rather than the exception. In Albuquerque, the sun rises every morning over the mountainous eastern horizon: the Sandia Mountains, Tijeras Canyon, and Manzano Mountains.

Another obvious natural characteristic of the city is its climate. The earliest promotions touted Albuquerque's sunshine as a curative for tuberculosis, much as Tucson promotions sought to lure convalescents to local sanatoriums around the turn of the century. These health-targeted promotions continued throughout Albuquerque's development, although not to the degree of establishing a "Sunshine Climate Club." In the 1960s, Albuquerque took the lead in promoting the region's climate through the "Southwest Sun Cast." The city commission's proclamation announcing the "sun cast" started with typical booster hyperbole: "WHEREAS, the city of Albuquerque has successfully claimed and held the title of Sunshine Capital of the United States. . . ." The proclamation went on to challenge Florida and the rest of the country to match the Southwest's sunshine at the first annual Sun Cast, "in which representatives from the cities of Albuquerque, El Paso, Tucson and Phoenix will meet in special ceremony at the Albuquerque Sunport to present and compare respective sunshine records, and to challenge the rest of the nation in general and the Southeastern United States in particular to match this impressive array of sunshine statistics."⁶ The city's sunshine statistics were being kept by the *Albuquerque Tribune*, whose "sunshine record" for December 25, 1963, announced "740 consecutive days" of sunshine (meaning 740 consecutive days when the sun had peeked through the clouds at least once).⁷

One element of Albuquerque's natural surroundings that differed from Tucson's was the Rio Grande River, still running in a steady meander. In Tucson, the Santa Cruz River runs only after heavy rains. Albuquerque, however, maintains a pastoral identity based on the nearness of the river. Farming persists, and deciduous oaks, sycamores, and walnuts stretch in a ribbon up and down the river's course. Whereas Tucson shrugs off most seasons with monotonous heat, autumn can be witnessed in Albuquerque even from the sagebrush mesas because there are plenty of leaves to turn and fall in the river valley below.

Thus Albuquerque's "uniqueness" rests on perceptions of topography, climate, and culture. Mountains define the horizon in both Albuquerque and Tucson, probably to Tucson's advantage. The Catalinas' dramatic front range with its clearly visible features such as Pusch Ridge, Finger Rock, the Window, and Thimble Peak is arguably more scenic than the mostly featureless mound of the Sandias.

The valleys plainly differ. Tucson rests amidst the Sonoran Desert. Albuquerque lies on a high semiarid plain cut by the flow of the Rio Grande. The mesas above the bluffs that front the river are covered with sagebrush, which perhaps because it is perceived as "ordinary," engendered fewer defenders than Tucson's peculiar saguaro cactus, protected within a national monument bordering the city on two sides.

The cities' climates differ as well. Albuquerque receives less rainfall than Tucson, but the nearness of the river and a more congenial summer climate makes vegetation flourish more green than Tucson's prevalent brown.[8] Albuquerque's higher altitude and cooler temperatures probably were an advantage in attracting permanent residents in the days before air conditioning softened the desert's growl. But the coolness could be a two-edged sword, with "mild" becoming "cold." During the winter of 1929, Jimmy Walker, the mayor of New York City, paid a visit to Albuquerque, and photographs of the occasion show it was a blustery day. The city boosters, in cowboy regalia, came out to greet the celebrity and presented Walker with an Indian blanket. The mayor apparently appreciated the gift because he promptly wrapped himself in the thick wool blanket against the cold.[9]

Tucson also brashly claimed to be the "Sunshine Capital," but Albuquerque argued that its sunny days were comfortably mild rather than inhospitably hot. Perhaps it was ironic then that Albuquerque, not Tucson, faced water shortages in the late 1940s and early 1950s. Rapid growth outstripped the water delivery system and forced the city to adopt "emergency rationing measures" in 1946, 1948, 1951, 1952, and 1953.

(Although water was available in the river and shallow aquifer, the infrastructure required expansion.) [10]

Albuquerque's Indian and Spanish heritage also defines the city's uniqueness in many ways, but somewhat haphazardly, as exemplified by the rise of "regional" architecture. The stolid old brick architecture that characterized new Albuquerque began to give way to a revival of Spanish colonial and pueblo-style buildings. The first to go up, in 1901, were the Santa Fe Railroad Station and the adjoining Alvarado Hotel, whose native styles the Fred Harvey company hoped would appeal to tourists. [11]

The pueblo style appeared on the University of New Mexico campus in 1909 with the construction of the new administration building. The style became entrenched on the campus when the board of regents hired architect John Gaw Meem, who became a major promoter of Albuquerque's regional architecture. In later decades, as modernistic architectural styles became the vogue, and regional styles were criticized as inherently "dishonest," Meem continued to design and build pueblo-style structures. [12]

Boosters staged the First America fair in the 1930s around an Indian pueblo facade. The pageant attempted to re-create the history of the town from its Indian origins, through Spanish and American periods, to the contemporary era of hopeful prosperity. The set remained a false front, however. Unlike Tucson, which marketed its Mexican and Old West heritage as palpably real, Albuquerque always seemed to wink at the rough traditions. The city's boosters, posing for a picture in front of the First America set, appeared in garish cowboy costumes, replete with Groucho-type moustaches and beards. The poses were comically fake. [13]

During the 250-year anniversary celebration in 1956, the city commission asked men to grow beards "in order to make the city look the way it did 250 years ago." The commission also asked women to stop wearing makeup. As Wood remarked, "The enthusiasm was dampened not at all when a researcher discovered that the men of the early 1700s were clean-shaven and grew their hair long and that the women indulged in cosmetics." [14]

Tucson boosters offered their promotional vignettes as the real McCoy. Barbara Walters' interview of Joseph Wood Krutch at a working cattle ranch was presented as a "true" image of Tucson. Most of Albuquerque's promotions skirted even an attempt at verisimilitude. In 1948 the motion picture *Albuquerque* premiered: "Blazing Guns Made History Each Day . . . And Warm Lips Made Memories At Night in Albuquerque."[15] (No doubt warm lips can make memories at night, but for the sake of contrast, the female lead in *Arizona* in 1939 was a mule-skinning Jean Arthur in a decidedly unglamorous role.)

The pageant on July 4, 1956, recounted the history of Albuquerque—in an ostensibly more realistic fashion than Hollywood—with depictions ranging from "Indian life" to "WWII and atomic research" (although, as was typical in the 1950s, the impact of atomic research on the natural environment was ignored). The pageant displayed a Turnerian sense of history flowing in waves of successive settlement leading to the most recent boom, which was forecast as happily progressing, and distant from the rough beginning.[16]

Also in contrast to Tucson was the way boosters kept Albuquerque's Indian heritage at arm's length. Quaint building patterns and festivals accommodating tourist excursions were deemed suitable. But as evidenced by the Chamber of Commerce's promotions describing Pablo Abieta as "Albuquerque's adopted Indian citizen," the Indians were not considered blood relations to the Anglo city.[17] Albuquerque lay in "the heart of the Pueblo country" but made no pretense of being an "old pueblo" itself.

Suburban residents on the fringe of the city may have adopted pueblo-style architecture, but they most often described their lifestyle as rural. At times, residents protested annexation of mesa land, but protests were not based on an explicit preservationist argument until the 1970s. Much of the mesa was annexed while still vacant in the 1940s and 1950s, avoiding the confrontation with residents who might have offered a Krutch-like critique. The 1949 annexation brought more than 7,000 acres into the city—and no people.

As Albuquerque's urbanization continued through the 1950s, rural lifestyles in north and south fringe areas grew in popularity. Realtors became aware of the marketability of pastoral lifestyles in the early 1960s: "The demand for housing in the valley areas is increasing faster than elsewhere. . . . If you want the phone to ring off the wall, just run an ad saying 'horses allowed.' "[18] Despite this popularity, however, annexation protests never explicitly defended nature per se. In the vehement protest against the 1964 annexation, the Rural Property Owners Association attacked the city's move on the basis of a defense of liberty and freedom from arbitrary government: "An attempt is being made to usurp the constitutional rights and privileges of some 62,000 residents." [19]

What did residents find appealing in the rural lifestyle outside the city limits? The East Mountain Survey in 1973 found residents in the Sandia foothills and mountains to be adamant in their desire to preserve the rural character of their lifestyle: "Over and over residents reiterated this desire. One third of the population has moved to the area during the past four years. They moved to escape from city noise, crowds, and pollution, and fear that the city will follow them to the mountains." The residents ranked the reasons for maintaining their pastoral lifestyle: 88 percent sought to escape city noise; 88.5 percent wanted fewer neighbors; 91 percent cited fresher air; 50 percent kept animals; 36.3 percent wanted lower taxes; 14 percent resided in family or childhood homes.[20] Nature lovers, political libertarians, or both? Concern over taxes ranked surprisingly low.

The 1973 survey may or may not indicate the opinions of residents in 1963. What is clear in the survey and in earlier accounts is a fear that the quality of life would degrade as the city continued to grow. Even city planners acknowledged the degrading conditions in Albuquerque in 1962, phrasing their call for action in urban renewal terms. The culprits were "growth, time and obsolescence." [21] This awareness resulted in renewal efforts within the city, and in the Project 1970 plan that attempted to bring the entire county within the city limits. The rationale for the annexation plan was to increase the effectiveness of planning efforts.

Despite the city's planning efforts, residents' uneasiness about growth increased to the point that political leaders finally noticed the angst. In 1964, City Commission Chairman Westfall commented on residents' perception of growth: "For the past year and a half or so a number of people have become keenly and greatly concerned over our little condition of 'sprawlitis.' " [22]

In 1966, the argument over development of Old Town Plaza drew a preservationist critique, but in this case directed toward a cultural artifact—the plaza. A cultural element of Albuquerque's uniqueness was being lost, not "nature." In 1950, local columnist and author Irene Fisher romantically described what Old Town represented: "That which Old Albuquerque has to offer is what New Mexico itself gives to those who seek it out—a way of life in which many persons from varied cultures live side by side in peace and friendliness." Fisher's romanticism also appeared in her dismissal of the area's poverty: "Here poverty is no disgrace; on the contrary, the 'rico' is looked on with suspicion, and must prove himself as a person before he is admitted into the casual, somewhat light-hearted group whose watchword is 'mañana.' "[23] Of course, poverty is no disgrace, but neither is it "light-hearted." Nonetheless, a letter to the editor in 1966 advocated preserving the plaza as a genuine cultural island within a "neon-lighted world."[24]

By 1968, the city's growth presented a "frightening picture" to some residents. The planning department projected that by the year 2000 the city's population would be 500,000, the county's population would be 1,000,000, and most frightening of all, the county would have to accommodate 700,000 automobiles.[25] Pastoral settings remained in some locales, but by the 1970s, new residents had to look farther afield to find these rural amenities.

The satellite communities of Paradise Hills and Rio Rancho flourished in the 1970s as a new wave of residents, including many retirees seeking "a pleasanter, less congested life," migrated to Albuquerque.[26] The mountains remained on the horizon, and golf courses interrupted the monotony of housing; implicitly, the natural environment was part of this Sun Belt way of life. The traditional Hispanic culture also was part of the "pleasanter" life in the older villages of Tijeras, Bernalillo, Corrales, and Placitas, which had also become retirement meccas.[27]

The concern over environmental degradation in its most general urban sense became explicit in 1972. Herb Smith, director of the planning department, described the uneasiness within the community over continuing growth: "I can nail the environmental situation in Albuquerque down to one word. And that word is capacity." The planning department, reflecting a national trend, had shifted its focus toward defining the limits of size and growth rather than forecasting future development so that the city infrastructure could accommodate the "new thousands."[28] Explicit concern over the community's health also appeared in the proliferation of studies and surveys by the city and county planning departments in the early 1970s. The concerted effort to catalogue existing conditions and attitudes is reminiscent of the surveys that Diocletian conducted within the declining Roman Empire: in order to stop the decline you must first know where you are—and how bad it is. The East Mountain Survey has already been mentioned. In addition, there was the Vacant Land Survey in 1972, which determined that 14,035 "useable acres" existed within the city limits.[29]

Another concern was air pollution. Planners proposed an air pollution control ordinance to the city commission in 1962, seeking to nip the smog problem in the bud, but the Chamber of Commerce opposed the ordinance, fearing that "an over-zealous air pollution control ordinance will serve to restrain industrial growth."[30] At that time it was still possible to deny the urgency of the problem. By 1968, however, air pollution had grown too noticeable to ignore, and the Environmental Health Department began keeping monthly records on pollution levels. In December 1971, the city experienced its first "pollution alert," in which "motorists were advised to drive only if necessary, and trash burning and fireplace fires were prohibited."[31]

The concerns about the consequences of sprawl brought the city to a fundamental juncture in the early 1970s. At one point a federal official accused the city of pursuing a no-growth policy. In August 1973, Manny Sanchez, regional director for the Department of Housing and Urban Development (HUD) in Albuquerque, said, "The City of Albuquerque is apparently determined that no new annexation should occur nor will city utilities be extended beyond existing municipal boundaries. The desired effect, of course, is to prevent over-extension of the city's ability to provide municipal services and force the utilization of 'passed-over' land within the existing city limits."[32]

But old habits die hard. City planners fired back that "no growth" was definitely not the city's policy, pointing to the annexation of 2,121 acres since January 1972. Nonetheless, the city was faced with a "financial dilemma, if not crisis," trying to determine the allocation of resources toward "maintaining and upgrading older parts of the city or providing limited service to new developments."[33]

By the late 1960s, environmental awareness had become more obvious and open, and resistance to growth from an environmental critique had surfaced. The Grass Roots Committee at the University of New Mexico served as a focal point for the "liberal-reform" movements that first championed environmental protection. These liberals were the most outspoken champions of environmentalism, but business and political leaders also grew more sensitive to the issue.[34] In 1969, a proposed paper mill was nixed by the city commission because of the mill's exorbitant water needs and the threat of river pollution. The mill plan was also opposed by the executive board of the Albuquerque Citizens Committee and the Chamber of Commerce.[35]

Another environmental issue in 1971 was the construction of a crest road in the Sandia Mountains. As part of a campaign to halt road construction, activists circulated petitions and staged a small "plant-in" of trees in the path of the bulldozers on the road site. In the end, the project died because the Forest Service cut funding, but the protest had served the purpose of rallying forces for environmental protection.

The issue of protecting the scenic qualities of Albuquerque's environment and establishing open spaces on the fringes of residential areas became a popular and unifying theme in local politics.[36] In May 1971, the City of Albuquerque, with the cooperation of the Rio Grande Council of Governments, began acquiring land in the foothills of the Sandia Mountains.[37] Later that summer, city leaders proposed a general obligation bond for $500,000 to acquire land for "open space." By July, the focus had shifted to the proposed development of the five dead volcanos on the western horizon. A "Save the Volcanos" committee formed, led by Mrs. George Eisenberg, who fretted publicly: "I'm so deathly afraid someone is going to plop an ugly restaurant on top of them or put up an industrial park or load them up with towers and lights."[38]

The open-space idea was thoroughly ingrained in city policy by 1975 when the city adopted the Comprehensive Plan. One-third of the plan was devoted to the acquisition of "major open space." The plan described the "functions" of open space as including the "satisfaction of psychological needs for space. . . . Relief from the urban environment is provided by large open spaces within or near the urban area, and the urban area itself can be made more liveable and aesthetically pleasing by including open space as an important part of the built environment."[39]

The concern over urban sprawl came after the city had grown to about eighty-six square miles, stretching from the volcanos in the west to the foothills of the Sandia Mountains in the east. Observers described the city as a swelling amoeba devouring the countryside: "Albuquerque seemed less like a rugged community thriving in the midst of natural splendor and more like a gigantic living organism expanding and adjusting its structure according to some daily perceived natural process."[40] At this stage, resistance to growth became noticeable to historians. The amoeba image led "naturally" to grassroots political action in defense of "the huge blue sky, the sharp peaks of the Sandia Mountains and the broad shallow ribbon of the Rio Grande."[41]

Resistance to the expansion of Albuquerque had always been motivated at least partially by an awareness of nature. The mountains, river, sagebrush, and sunshine are too omnipresent to ignore. But an explicit valuation of nature did not become part of the debate over growth until well after World War II. This transformation occurred later in Albuquerque, more closely mirroring national trends, due to the lack of a clear voice making the environmental argument in the 1950s.

A simple reason exists for the lack of an early preservationist critique in Albuquerque such as Joseph Wood Krutch provided in Tucson. In New Mexico, the people most inclined to offer such a viewpoint lived sixty miles to the north of Albuquerque in Santa Fe. Despite Santa Fe's status as state capital and 1990s boomtown, its image is still that of a cultural mecca for those drawn to New Mexico's natural and cultural attractions.

V. B. Price describes the mutual suspicion between the two cities in City at the End of the World: "Residents of Santa Fe delight in bashing Albuquerque's working-class aura and industrial ambience. And Albuquerqueans happily admit to finding Santa Fe pretty, but unbearably chichi and small-town."[42] Price acknowledges that the true character of each city often fails to match their images—both in ways positive and negative— but nonetheless, Santa Fe continues to enjoy a national reputation as "a Southwestern version of Beverly Hills, the 'in' city of the 1990s, a secret haven in which to hide far from the madding world—a sort of romantic, American cultural oasis complete with cowboys, Indians, señoritas, and a 'style' all its own that clothiers, interior decorators, and perfume manufacturers can rely on to make them a fortune."[43]

Santa Fe itself exemplifies contested development based on an environmental critique embodied in a slow-growth effort to preserve the natural and cultural identity of the community.[44] This opposition to development coincided with the general rise in environmental awareness most likely to be recognized by urban and western historians. Albuquerque also witnessed a rise in environmentalism, as discussed earlier, but in New Mexico, Santa Fe appeared the more likely headquarters for preservationists.

The acceptability of desert-landscaped lawns in Tucson has no direct corollary in Albuquerque. If sagebrush mesa appears within the city, it is most likely on a vacant lot. Albuquerque does, however, possess many examples of Santa Fe–style architecture, which remains an indigenous form of "built environment" meant to reflect native conformity to the resources and requirements of the natural environment. The blockish, stucco, flat-roofed buildings have always indicated at least an implicit environmental awareness.

Albuquerqueans often defended their lifestyle, culture, political idealism, and sense of community against threatening aspects of urbanization, but it was not until the early 1970s that opponents of the city's expansion added an explicit defense of nature to the antigrowth critique. In the 1970s, city government mandated "open space" on the fringe of the city as a necessary element of the "built environment," an argument that Frederick Law Olmstead had begun making a century earlier. In his effort to establish Central Park in New York City, Olmstead had faced resistance from residents who saw no need to expend time and energy to establish a nature preserve in the midst of the city. To these residents, the city was opposed to nature—not in a sense of antipathy but, rather, counterposition.

The same sense of urbanness describes Albuquerque through most of its history. From the days of the Spanish presidio, Albuquerque had always been certain of its future as a city—more certain than Tucson. Even the "spiritual" sense of the community, as perceived by V. B. Price, had more to do with human culture than nature. Not until the 1970s did it occur to residents, explicitly, that nature required preservation.

10 ALBUQUERQUE EPILOGUE

■ ■ ■ ■ ■ ■ ■ ■ ■ ■ ■ ■ ■ ■ ■

Thin Reeds and Buffers

Developers and boosters pushing Albuquerque's growth in the 1970s and 1980s continued to offer zealously conceived plans and schemes. Successes (as defined by the developers) were ballyhooed, failures decried. Giving great cheer to the pro-growth partnership was the appearance in 1982 of *Megatrends*, by John Naisbitt, which listed Albuquerque as one of "ten new cities of great opportunity."[1] But bad press also appeared in the 1980s describing the city as shabby and shopworn, echoing the local naysayers who had warned, and continued to warn, of the negative effects of uncontrolled growth. Tom Wolfe deflated boosterish promotions of Albuquerque in *The Right Stuff* when he described the city as "remarkably short on charm."[2] More serious criticisms than a lack of charm appeared in national journals cataloguing such shortcomings as high suicide and divorce rates.[3] Naturally, boosters found such criticism vexing.

Specific proposals for development met varied levels of success and acceptance. The Disney plan announced in 1969 to create a "winter recreational complex" around the Sandia peaks failed despite strong support by the Chamber of Commerce and city leaders.[4] The renewed effort to build an international airport on the West Mesa also failed, although construction on the site of the old airport resulted in the modernization and expansion of services envisioned by boosters.

The traditional bedrock form of development—housing subdivisions—continued to appear on Albuquerque's fringe, primarily on the West Mesa. A "cartel" of developers announced plans in 1987 to construct a huge new community on the West Mesa, of such girth it would double the city's population and size.[5] The plan ran afoul of groundwater concerns and doubts about the city's ability to provide services and infrastructure, and so stalled in the planning stage. In the meantime, however, seven separate West Mesa subdivisions continued to attract new residents.[6]

The Petroglyph National Monument provides an example of a "development" that appealed to both pro-growth forces and preservationists. The great tourist potential of the monument convinced boosters and developers to support setting aside 7,369 acres of the volcanic escarpment on the west bank of the Rio Grande's channel for the monument.[7] The relatively limited area to be preserved left much West Mesa land free for continuing subdivision. On the other hand, preservation of the petroglyphs assured residents that sprawl would fall short of utterly destroying their cultural icons, even as houses began to "lap at the base" of the monument.[8]

Boosters also pointed to the success of the Civic Plaza, which had resulted from the urban renewal programs of the 1970s. The downtown plaza sparkles on summer Saturday nights during cultural events sponsored by the city. But critics of the pro-growth partnership point to the sterile architecture of the plaza and the artificial quality of the "commercial cultural" events: renewal left the city's core a workday center of business and government and only occasionally, and tenuously, the cultural center of the community.[9]

Promotions of burgeoning growth enjoyed bipartisan political support in Albuquerque in the 1980s just as they did in the 1950s. City elections remain nonpartisan, although Republicans may appear to be more generally boosterish in their support of growth, and Democrats may claim a more sensitive appreciation of issues of historic and natural preservation. But the dichotomy breaks down almost immediately. In 1974, Harry Kinney, a "Republican old-guard growth proponent," defeated the "environmental planner" candidate for mayor.[10] The next year, however,

Mayor Kinney signed the Comprehensive Plan, one-third of which advocated the preservation of open space, to be accomplished, if necessary, through public acquisition of land.

Professional planners redoubled their efforts to rationalize Albuquerque's growth in the 1970s and 1980s. The 1975 Comprehensive Plan serves as a watershed of sorts, both culminating an early phase of planning begun in the 1960s and beginning a new series of planning efforts stretching into the 1980s. Specific plans, including (to a questionable degree) public input, appeared in 1978, 1987, and 1989.[11] The Southwest Area Plan (SWAP) appeared in the late 1980s after three years of study by the Metropolitan Planning Department. The plan sought to rationalize the development of 115 square miles in the southwest valley. Planners predicted the area to have a population of 115,000 residents by the year 2010.[12] As can be expected, such a plan, no matter how reasonably or sensitively proffered, generated plenty of protest. It has been my intention to demonstrate that such protest was not something new on the political horizon but deeply rooted within the community.

Political resistance in Albuquerque focused on plans such as SWAP as well as annexation moves by the city. The ploy of rival incorporation resurfaced when planners announced SWAP, and South Valley residents rekindled their effort to form a separate municipality. Organizers projected the new city, Las Playas del Valle (a less prosaic name than the 1960s' "South Albuquerque") to be the fourth largest in the state.[13] As of the summer of 1994, the issue of incorporation of the South Valley rested with the New Mexico Court of Appeals in Santa Fe.

The grandiose West Mesa proposal by the "cartel" generated protest on environmental and political grounds. "Rural" opponents specifically referred to their desire to stay outside the city limits. Three times between 1953 and 1973, county residents refused to approve the consolidation of city and county governments, and "studies" of the issue in 1983 and 1990 were quickly shelved.[14]

Political discourse continued to dominate the language of protest and provided the methodology used by protesters. Legal suits proliferated in a standard form of grassroots political activism. One target of court action was the Montano Road bridge project in the 1980s. Opponents of the bridge, who claimed the project was designed to stimulate development rather than simply accommodate existing residential densities, challenged Albuquerque's annexation of a small parcel of land necessary for one end of the bridge. By voiding the annexation, opponents hoped to cancel the project; resistance has successfully stalled the project for over eight years. Nonetheless, traffic engineers still argue for the necessity of the Montano Road bridge.[15]

Ethnic resistance in Albuquerque continued to reflect Hispanics' traditionally broad participation in city politics. In a general cultural sense, a sensitivity toward indigenous cultures in Albuquerque created a movement to preserve historic buildings after the Alvarado and Franciscan hotels were demolished in 1969.[16] Preservation efforts also arose within neighborhoods such as Los Duranes, where restoration of the "little church" bespoke reverence for an earlier, simpler, time.[17]

Neighborhood associations proliferated in the 1980s to number more than 150. Whether politically partisan or apolitical, the neighborhood associations serve as an indicator of Albuquerque's "contextual fragmentation."[18] Ethnicity constitutes one of the common organizational motivations for the associations. The South Valley opposition constituted a less structured neighborhood resistance and evinced broad-based Hispanic participation in resistance. Traditional political complaints surfaced in the South Valley: concern over higher city taxes and unreliable city services. These traditional critiques appeared in an area predominantly Hispanic (approximately 70 percent), and were voiced by Hispanic residents.[19]

In a very real sense, ethnic and political resistance meld in Albuquerque to a greater degree than in Tucson. Opposition movements in Albuquerque commonly crossed ethnic lines. The Montano Road bridge project, for example, faced opposition across a broad spectrum of ethnicity and affluence, from the pastoral bosque communities along the river to the quintessentially suburban Rio Rancho.

The proliferation of environmentally based resistance in the 1970s and 1980s sprang from the precedents established in the 1950s and 1960s. Only by understanding the origins and contexts of the opposition movements can the later successes be fully understood. The South Valley incorporation movement is only one of the examples of continuing resistance, often discussed as if it were new, unexpected, or especially innovative.

Sensitivity to issues of lifestyle and environment became more explicit in the 1970s and 1980s. Environmentalism had become part of the political lexicon. Arguably, earlier critiques contained the same sensibilities, but the earlier, more purely political language of protest precluded expression of such concerns. Perhaps a poet's sensitivity is required to grasp this simple assertion. Price argues persuasively that a "spiritual" awareness related to Albuquerque's Indo-Hispanic origins describes the community. I am simply arguing that environmental awareness has always described the community but has only recently become explicitly voiced as a rationale for resistance.

The media increasingly gave voice to the issue of sprawling development, and the increasingly visible degradation of the environment (both built and natural) caused unvoiced qualms to evolve into vocal concerns. News broadcasts and Albuquerque's daily newspapers regularly express environmental sensitivity. And preservation has resulted—but, eerily, in a fashion similar to Joseph Wood Krutch's description of "partial solutions."

A variety of assaults on the environment—such as the destruction of the landmark Alvarado Hotel in 1969 (demolished by the Santa Fe Railroad to make room for a gravel parking lot), continued flooding in low-lying neighborhoods in the 1970s, and bulldozed mesa land in the 1980s—have all engendered city, state, and federal preservation movements in Albuquerque. The three most visible, successful results of environmental concern are the city's Rio Grande Nature Center, established in 1982; the Rio Grande Valley State Park, created in 1983; and the Petroglyph National Monument, established in 1990.

The Nature Center preserves a traditional bosque, or rural, setting within the city limits, only minutes from downtown. Irrigation ditches dating back centuries, if not millennia, are preserved amidst a riparian area rich in wildlife and vegetation.

Planning for the Rio Grande State Park began in 1969 when the Bureau of Reclamation announced plans to clear hundreds of acres of bosque vegetation in an effort to regularize the river channel and save water. Outrage over the plan eventually resulted in state legislation setting aside six thousand acres along twenty-five miles of the river.[20]

The Petroglyph National Monument also sprang from grassroots activism. For decades, activists sought to awaken the community to the danger that continued development posed to the Indian artifacts remaining on the volcanic escarpment on the west bank of the Rio Grande. Defacement of the petroglyphs dates back hundreds of years, but as suburban development neared the escarpment, vandalism and destruction of the artifacts increased. Finally, in 1990, Congress passed legislation creating the monument on 7,369 acres of the West Mesa, thus preserving more than 15,000 examples of the rock art.[21]

Preservation of open space provides perhaps the most remarkable example of environmental awareness in Albuquerque. Since 1971, when the city purchased the West Mesa volcanoes, voters in Albuquerque have repeatedly approved expenditures slated for the preservation of open space.[22] The 1975 Comprehensive Plan advocated wide use of open space for the "satisfaction of psychological needs for space," and even the 1988 revision of the comprehensive plan, composed at a time of economic distress, advocated continued efforts to preserve open space on the city's fringe.[23] As of 1989, the city controlled 21,285 acres of open space, the fifth-largest holding of open space by any U.S. city.[24]

Unfortunately, the impressive record of preservation accomplished in Albuquerque in the 1980s and 1990s remains only a partial solution. For example, development threatened the new petroglyph monument even as it was being created. As one city planner explained, the monument is "a shoestring that runs through a large developed area. . . . We're fighting for all the buffer we can get."[25]

Degradation of the natural and built environment in Albuquerque continues despite the efforts of preservationists and planners. Perhaps the rate has slowed, but damage continues to mount. Increased awareness and concern over air and water pollution intrudes on the community's peace of mind. For the first time, in 1989, simply the availability of water sufficient for the future growth and health of Albuquerque came into question.[26] As sprawl continues on the city's fringe, calls for in-fill resonate throughout the community, but as part of city policy, in-fill remains a thin rhetorical reed.[27]

Albuquerque is not alone in New Mexico in its confrontation with sprawling development. Since I raised the comparison with Santa Fe in the previous chapter, and offered the state capital as a more environmen-

FIG. 13 Santa Fe Village, Albuquerque, New Mexico. Just as urban sprawl in Tucson crowds the Saguaro National Monument, urban sprawl in Albuquerque, here in the form of the Santa Fe Village subdivision, crowds the Petroglyph National Monument. The monuments provide only a "partial solution" to the problem of preservation; both cacti and artifacts remain vulnerable to society's encroachment. (Photo by the author)

tally aware alternative to Albuquerque, it is perhaps appropriate to mention Santa Fe's current circumstances.

Rigorously controlled development in Santa Fe, designed to preserve the cultural and historical ethos of the city, resulted in an unparalleled boom in the 1980s. The resulting gentrification threatened the economic viability of local residents who could not afford to keep pace with rising property values. City elections now turn on the issue of growth. The issue is not "controlled growth" per se—that has always been Santa Fe's policy, since at least 1957 when the city adopted its "Historic Styles" zoning code.[28] Rather, the political argument swirls around the types of controls and whether rigid building regulations designed to preserve a touristy kitsch are appropriately applied to a community of working residents. In a manner unforeseen by city leaders in the 1950s, preservation of Santa Fe's "style" has become a political bugaboo in the 1990s, and tagged with the same label of elitism so often applied to environmentalism.

Preservation often runs afoul of "use." Environmental historians such as Richard White recognize the difficulty that multiple use poses to land-management decisions. The same difficulty applies to the built environment. Just as many working Utah residents resent the effort by environmentalists to lock up their state as a nature preserve, so do Santa Fe residents who are working for wages and struggling to stay financially afloat resent the effort by the more affluent to preserve a stylistically consistent Santa Fe. Not everyone in our economically variegated society can afford what many consider to be the luxury of historic and environmental preservation.

CONCLUSION

■　■　■　■　■　■　■　■　■　■　■　■　■　■　■

Both Halves of the Story

The habit of earlier historians to focus on the consensus behind development in the urban Southwest during the post–World War II boom required a corrective to balance the depiction of the process of urbanization. Taken together, the pro-growth and antigrowth stories depict the development of Tucson and Albuquerque more accurately than either can accomplish singly.

The temptation may arise to characterize each city as fitting into either a cooperative or contentious urban paradigm, but evidence far back into the historical record supports both models. Booster activities in Tucson and Albuquerque accompanied development from territorial days and earlier. Less obvious in the historical record is the resistance. In Tucson, for example, litigious opposition to development plans was present at the very instance of U.S. acquisition. As negotiations proceeded for the Gadsden Purchase in 1854, Tucson residents lodged a legal challenge with the Sonoran government over the Mexican government's latest development plan. Mexico's 1848 colonization law sought to secure the northern frontier by establishing "military colonies." Establishing the colonies entailed granting arable land to former soldiers, thus stimulating both development and security. Resistance to the colonization plan arose in Tucson when the Sonoran military commander granted land that was already under cultivation and arguably "owned" by Tucsonenses. These land disputes accompanied Tucson and Tucsonenses into the United States.[1]

The cooperative and contentious models for describing community ethos reflect approaches to urban history from the 1950s and 1960s. Stanley Elkins and Eric McKitrick describe a community ethos founded on the cooperative management of conflict in their 1954 article "A Meaning for Turner's Frontier: Democracy in the Old Northwest." This update of Frederick Jackson Turner's "participatory democracy" thesis foretold placid and orderly growth, a particularly fitting image for urbanization in the "consensus" 1950s.[2]

Robert Dykstra's *The Cattle Towns* challenges this cooperative paradigm. Dykstra suggests that community conflict was not only normal, but inevitable.[3] Other authors have applied this contentious urban paradigm to descriptions of the "urban crisis" of the 1960s and 1970s, but studies of the 1950s remain largely untouched by this contentious model. Curiously, many of the new western historians seem willing to accept the consensus view of the 1950s as a period of mute acquiescence to urbanization, even as the recent historiography of the decade broadens and deepens.

Resistance to urbanization proved to be persistent and multifaceted. No simple dichotomy describes monolithic opposition to growth. The resistance to urbanization was as multifaceted as the booster/politician/planner forces pushing for expanded development. The accurate depiction of the process of urbanization must include both groups, those for and against growth.

Tucson and Albuquerque mirror each other's urbanization process to such a degree that they perhaps indicate a trend for the entire Southwest. Resistance abounds. Manifestations of opposition to urban growth took the form of political conservatism, ethnic solidarity, and environmental awareness in both cities, although the mix of each varied.

In general, Albuquerque's city government pursued expansion with greater aggressiveness through the 1940s and 1950s and as a result engendered more vituperative resistance than Tucson witnessed. Tucson's city government struggled with resistance to growth but to a lesser degree than Albuquerque. The Arizona legislature never had to step into the fray, as New Mexico's legislature did, declaring a moratorium on further annexations until tempers had cooled. Perhaps it's ironic then that Albuquerque accomplished more in the way of open-space protection than Tucson. Urban sprawl stretches in both cities to the extent of mountain foothills. But in Albuquerque, city government repeatedly succeeded in using public money for the purpose of acquiring land to preserve open space on the fringe of the city. Open space on Tucson's fringe is found only in federal, state, and county parks, none of which came into existence solely through actions by the city government.

The post–World War II boom in the Southwest transformed Albuquerque and Tucson from small towns into big cities. Thousands of residents in both cities protested the changes occurring in their communities. Boosters, planners, and politicians were forced to maneuver around their resistance. That maneuvering resulted in the cities that exist today.

NOTES

INTRODUCTION   THE OTHER HALF OF THE STORY

1. "Sky's the Limit," *Time*, pp. 20–27.

2. Turner, *The Frontier in American History*; Billington, *America's Frontier Heritage*; Lamar, "Persistent Frontier"; McGerr, "Is There a Twentieth-Century West?"

3. Webb, *The Great Plains*; Worster, *Rivers of Empire*; Robbins, "Laying Siege to Western History."

4. Ridge, "The American West"; McGerr, "Is There a Twentieth-Century West?"

5. Meinig, *Southwest*.

6. Limerick, *Legacy of Conquest*; Devoto, "The West Against Itself"; Pomeroy, "Reorientation of Western History"; Nash, *The American West*.

7. In the 1960s, W. Eugene Hollon (*The Great American Desert*) and David Bingham ("Impact of Urbanization") identified a growing uneasiness about urbanization amidst an otherwise optimistic appraisal of development in the West generally and Arizona specifically. More recent historians of the urban West either dismiss the opposition to growth or describe it as insignificant at first, growing noteworthy only with the rise in environmental awareness in the late 1960s (e.g., Luckingham, *The Urban Southwest*; Abbott, *The New Urban America*; Wiley and Gottlieb, *Empires in the Sun*).

8. One otherwise rigorous study that slips into the habit of discounting resistance to development is Lotchin's *Fortress California 1910–1961*. On the other hand, Spencer Olin's analysis of Orange County, California ("Globalization and the Politics of Locality"; Kling, Olin, Poster, *Postsuburban California*) centers on "intraclass conflict" and the resistance of "local capital" groups to the changes within their communities. Olin's description of Orange County's development as a "fragmented region" places local resistance to international economic trends at the center of the story.

9. Bufkin, "From Mud Village to Modern Metropolis," pp. 82–88; Sonnichsen, *Tucson*, p. 283.

10. Rabinowitz, "Albuquerque: City at a Crossroads," p. 262.

11. Price, City, p. xiii.

12. Wood, "Transformation of Albuquerque, 1945–1972," p. v.

13. Simmons, *Albuquerque*, p. 375.

14. White, "Trashing the Trails," p. 37.

PART 1 TUCSON

1. U.S. Department of Commerce, *Census of Population, 1960*, Table 5. According to census statistics, the average population increase by decade from 1900 to 1950 in Albuquerque was 76.8 percent. In Phoenix it was 45.4 percent.

2. Sonnichsen, *Tucson*, pp. 98–99, 102–4, 136–41.

3. Pedersen, "The Townsite Is Now Secure," pp. 151–74.

4. Lockard, *This is Tucson*, p. 236.

5. City of Tucson Annexation Index (mimeograph), pp. 3–5. As Pedersen explains, Tucson's legal designation was "village" with the approval of its federal land patent in 1874. The "city" designation applied to Tucson after its incorporation in 1877. In a cultural sense, Tucson was still a "village," or perhaps a "town," long after its incorporation, and became recognizable as a "city" sometime during its expansion—exactly when is subject to debate. The issue is confused further by the designations of "urban" and "metropolitan" used by the Census Bureau at various times. Offering no explicit definition, I will describe Tucson as a "city" following its first annexation in 1905.

6. Harte, *Tucson*, pp. 129–30. Tucson Medical Center originated as a tuberculosis sanitorium in the 1920s (Grubb, *Portrait of Progress*).

7. Harte, *Tucson*, p. 163. For a discussion of the regional impact of federal spending, see Nash, *World War II and the West*.

8. Boorstin, *The Americans*, pp. 113–23.

9. Molotch, "The City as Growth Machine"; Gottdiener, *Social Production*; Mollenkopf, *The Contested City*.

10. See, for example, Boyte, *The Backyard Revolution*; Plotkin, "Enclave Consciousness and Neighborhood Activism"; Logan and Rabrenovic, "Neighborhood Associations"; John Emmeus Davis, *Contested Ground*; Mike Davis, *City of Quartz*.

CHAPTER 1 "THE OPTIMISTIC ASSUMPTION"

1. Elkin, "Twentieth-Century Urban Regimes," pp. 11–28. Elkin's description of the "privatist" regime appropriately identifies the unifying theme of boosterish governments—what I call their "optimistic assumption." Caution must be used, however, when applying a social-science model to historical studies: the generalizing nature of models tends to leave out, or marginalize, recalcitrant facts. In the case of "privatist" regimes, for instance, dissenting voices within the pro-growth partnership tend to fade into silence, resulting in a "consensus" view of growth in the 1950s. I am arguing against that characterization of the post–World War II boom.

2. Sources differ as to the founding date of the Chamber of Commerce. According to the "Tucson Chamber of Commerce Newsletter," February 20, 1962, the Chamber of Commerce was founded in 1904. In 1938, the Chamber of Commerce issued an announcement for its thirty-sixth annual meeting, placing the founding date in 1902. James Officer puts the founding date in 1896 (*Tucson, the Old Pueblo*). The confusion is due partly to the loss of the Chamber of Commerce's early records when the group's offices were destroyed by fire in 1925. Fortunately a copy of the "Twenty-Fifth Anniversary Banquet Program," 1921, survives in the Chamber of Commerce file at the Arizona Historical Society. The program describes the founding in 1896: "October 31, 1896, was the date on which five pioneer business men, interested in the development of Tucson, met and formulated an organization known as 'The Traders' National Protective Association.' " The name of the group was changed in 1897 to the Tucson Board of Trade. The "board" became the "chamber" in 1902.

3. For instance, the *Arizona Daily Star* opposed the incorporation of South Tucson in 1936. Businessmen south of the city formed a separate municipality in an effort to avoid the higher taxes that would follow annexation into the City of Tucson. (This aspect of Tucson's growth will be discussed in chapter 3). Mathews described these activists as pie-in-the-sky optimists who foolishly thought they could run a modern city "by voluntary or free services" provided by residents (*Arizona Daily Star*, August 9 and 11, 1936).

4. Specific information about the founders is lacking, in part due to the 1925 fire that destroyed the chamber's records. The adjective "energetic" comes from the Tucson Sunshine Climate Club's 1941 subscription campaign brochure. There were 420 members in 1928, and 904 members in 1948. Of the 904 members in 1948, 70 were women, and 45 possessed obviously Hispanic surnames ("1929 Election of Officers," "1949 Directors Nominations").

5. The monolithic view of boosters relies on their identity within a capitalist class. Spencer Olin properly recognized the oversimplification within this schema in "Intraclass Conflict and the Politics of a Fragmented Region" (in Kling, Olin, and Poster, *Postsuburban California*). Olin described variations even within the "intraclass" camps (local capital and national/international capital) so that undue lumping was avoided. Conversely, Mollenkopf described "growth coalitions" so as to accommodate various pro-growth interests, but then egregiously and erroneously lumped together southwestern opponents to growth: "Where the transformation of older cities like Boston and San Francisco heightened conflict over growth and required an expanded public sector to contain that conflict, no such challenge arose in the cities of the Southwest" (*The Contested City*, p. 216). Historians of the urban Southwest, including Bufkin and Sonnichsen, acknowledge that conflict arose in the cities of the Southwest in the late 1960s; I maintain it arose much earlier, partly because pro-growth interests themselves were more seriously fractured than has been previously acknowledged.

6. Sheridan, *Los Tucsonenses*, p. 96.

7. Of the 904 members of the Chamber of Commerce in 1948, 45 possessed obviously Hispanic surnames. Since no record was kept of the ethnic identity of members, this rough estimate, certainly too low (given the inaccuracy of census counts using surname identifiers), must suffice. Included among the Hispanic members were three Jacomes and two Ronstadts. C. B. Sedillo was a member representing the Alianza Hispano Americano, the most prominent of the *mutualistas*. Lopez Montero, the consul of Mexico, was also a member ("1949 Directors Nominations").

8. Sonnichsen, *Tucson*, pp. 202–3.

9. "Tucson Sunshine Climate Club, 1941," brochure.

10. Ibid.

11. Athearn, *The Mythic West*.

12. Ibid., p. 131.

13. Ibid., p. 149.

14. Jervey, "When the Banks Closed," pp. 127–52.

15. Ibid.

16. Lazaroff, *Sabino Canyon*, p. 98; Drachman, *This Is Not a Book*, p. 39.

17. Klein, "Selling the Desert."

18. Tucson Chamber of Commerce, "The Sunshine City," brochure.

19. Tucson Chamber of Commerce, "Facts for Prospective Residents of Tucson, 1956."

20. Ibid.

21. Tucson Chamber of Commerce, "The Answers to All Your Questions," 1962, 1964, 1968, 1971, 1974.

22. Tucson Chamber of Commerce, "Come to the Growing Southwest."

23. Ibid.

24. Nash, *World War II and the West*; Lotchin, *Fortress California*.

25. Tucson Chamber of Commerce, "Facts and Figures."

26. Ibid., p. 12.

27. Tucson Chamber of Commerce, "Tucson . . . a city." The brochure juxtaposed a wide array of Tucson's attributes: "climate, sun, room and low taxes."

28. Ibid.

29. Tucson boosters arrived late on the scene of industrial—in this case, high tech—recruitment. Lotchin described the effort of southern California boosters from the 1920s to develop a close working relationship between local government, business, and the California Institute of Technology in order to "create the kind of interface between these sectors that later came to characterize the arms industry in Southern California" (*Fortress California*, p. 98).

30. Tucson Chamber of Commerce, "Tomorrow is Today in Tucson."

31. Ibid.

32. "Legal Opinions," No. 337, November 19, 1954.

33. Cooper, *The O.P. Chronicle*.

34. Ibid., April 15, 1955.

35. Ibid., April 27, 1960. Kimball was Pima County's state senator from 1940 to 1955. He retired from the legislature in 1955 after failing to gain the Democratic nomination for governor (*Arizona Daily Star*, April 12, 1961).

36. *The O.P. Chronicle*, April 12, 1961.

37. "Urbanization of Tucson, 1940–1990," S. L. Schorr interview, February 21, 1992.

38. "Those Wide Open Spaces are Filling In," *Tucson Citizen*, October 19, 1970.

39. Ibid.

40. Bufkin gives a full account of the development of city planning and zoning in "From Mud Village to Modern Metropolis," pp. 80–84. For a

more general discussion of the rise of planning and zoning nationally, see Glaab and Brown, *A History of Urban America*, pp. 289–95, and Krueckeberg, *Introduction to Planning History*.

41. Johnson, *The Politics of Urban Planning*, p. 66.

42. Tucson Planning and Zoning Commission, "Regional Plan."

43. Krueckeberg, *Introduction to Planning History*, p. 301.

44. Bufkin, "Mud Village," p. 82.

45. Tucson Planning and Zoning Commission, "Regional Plan," p. 4.

46. Bufkin described the planners as most influential during the 1950s: "When the planner was really trusted and used by the politician was in the fifties. Today the planner is pretty much downplayed in terms of his role" ("Urbanization of Tucson," Don Bufkin interview, July 25, 1991).

47. Citizen's Committee on Municipal Blight, "Pueblo Center Redevelopment Project."

48. Davis became city manager in 1953, replacing Donald P. Wolfer. Wolfer was a professional manager, formerly the city manager of Albany, Georgia, and stated after being fired that the mayor was "attempting to undermine the city manager form of government both publicly and privately." Davis was fifteen years younger than Wolfer (in 1953, Davis was 29, and Wolfer was 44). Perhaps more sanguine to the realities of Tucson politics: Davis started his first city job as a Democrat, but switched his registration to Republican before accepting the manager's position. The mayor and council in 1953 were staunchly Republican. By 1960, Davis had moved on to become president of Tucson Gas, Electric Light and Power Company ("Don Hummel, unprocessed collection," Box 1; *Arizona Daily Star*, August 1, 1953).

49. "Legal Opinions," No. 197, December 11, 1953.

50. "Legal Opinions," No. 336, November 1954.

51. Emery, "A City in Action."

CHAPTER 2 "THE LAWS SERVE THE MAJORITY"

1. U.S. Department of Commerce, *Census of Population*, 1960, Table 5; City of Tucson Annexation Index, pp. 3–5.

2. Abbott, *The New Urban America*, pp. 17–28; Nash, *The American West*; Hays, *Beauty, Health, and Permanence*.

3. U.S. Department of Commerce, *Census of Population*, 1960, Tables 11, 12; Bufkin, "Mud Village," p. 84.

4. Tucson's expansion to the east and north encompassed mostly middle-class subdivisions. Ethnic neighborhoods, mostly Hispanic, remained in the barrios near the original townsite and the City of South Tucson. Zoning and annexation disputes in the 1950s were generally free of ethnic or racial over-

tones. As Sheridan explains in *Los Tucsonenses*, "enclavement" of Mexican residents resulted from socially motivated segregation, not politically or legally mandated segregation. The "benign" environment in Tucson for Mexicans resulted largely from the vibrant cultural life that existed within Mexican neighborhoods. But Mexicans were not restricted to these neighborhoods: "the 'barrioization' of the city's Mexican population was rarely the result of restrictive covenants, which did exclude Blacks, Orientals, and Native Americans from many Anglo neighborhoods" (Sheridan, p. 251). Also, affluent Mexicans were free to move out of the barrios: "Members of the Mexican elite could live where they chose" (p. 252).

5. For example, the city manager and city attorney referred to articles in defense of annexation by Bollens, "Fringe Area Conditions and Relations" and "City Annexation Programs and Policies," *Public Management*, March and April, 1950.

6. Bufkin, "Mud Village," p. 84.

7. Minutes of the Tucson City Council, meeting of December 3, 1953.

8. Minutes of the Tucson City Council, meeting of April 13, 1953.

9. Opponents of growth also were mostly ignored by historians, perhaps due to the fact that they left few records or testimonials. The available oral histories (for instance, the Arizona Historical Society's Oral History Project) record the recollections of boosters, developers, and planners, with little attention paid to the naysayers. More recent opponents of urbanization (such as the neighborhood associations proliferating in the 1960s) remain in Tucson, available for interviews, and have been the object of study by University of Arizona geographers and sociologists. Particularly, I will draw on urban geographer Sallie Marston's account later in this narrative.

10. Emmert, "Annexation Study," p. 53.

11. Ibid., p. 4. Emmert cites the reference to individualist suspicion of city police protection from a report by Joseph E. Chamberlin on annexations in Colorado Springs, sponsored by the Colorado Springs Chamber of Commerce, March 1950.

12. *Arizona Daily Star*, June 2, 1953, p. B1.

13. *Arizona Daily Star*, Dec. 16, 1952, p. A4.

14. Ray Leon, City of Tucson annexation coordinator, personal interview with the author, July 17, 1989.

15. *Arizona Daily Star*, June 2, 1953, p. B1; Roy Drachman, letter to the city council, Oct. 29, 1953; City of Tucson, *Annexations: 1905–1968*.

16. Pima County's effort to adopt countywide zoning is summarized in the *Arizona Daily Star*, Feb. 5, 1953, pp. A1, B1.

17. *Arizona Daily Star*, Feb. 26, 1953, p. A5.

18. *Arizona Daily Star*, Feb. 5, 1953, pp. A1, B1.

19. *Arizona Daily Star*, Feb. 26, 1953, p. A5.

20. *Arizona Daily Star*, Aug. 7, 1952, p. A1.

21. The court fight is summarized in the *Arizona Daily Star*, February 7, 1953, p. A1.

22. The campaign against local-option is summarized in the *Arizona Daily Star*, January 11, 1953, p. A1.

23. *Arizona Daily Star*, February 11, 1953, p. A1.

24. Ibid. Local-option polled 31 percent countywide in forty-five precincts in the fringe areas. Of these forty-five precincts, local-option polled over 50 percent in six, from 45 to 50 percent in five, from 40 to 45 percent in four, and from 35 to 40 percent in two, for a total of seventeen precincts with a minimum of 35 percent support for the local-option alternative.

25. Anecdotal evidence provides a clear sense of community identity in the Flowing Wells and Amphitheater areas (to be discussed later, in the context of annexation resistance), but no contemporary survey, poll, or study exists that would provide an insight into the specific attitudes and values that defined that community identity.

26. Current annexation laws require both the approval of the owners of 51 percent of the assessed valuation and the approval of 51 percent of the population.

27. The city's annexation policies and protests during the 1950s are described in the minutes of the Tucson City Council.

28. Minutes of the Tucson City Council, meeting of March 2, 1953.

29. *Arizona Daily Star*, April 15, 1953, p. A1; April 18, 1953, p. B14.

30. Emmert, "Annexation Study," pp. 3–4. Concern over garbage service appeared in a 1953 letter to the editor by Nathan O. Lynn: "El Encanto Estates was annexed. Owners woke up to the fact that the city refused to collect (garbage) unless the cans were waiting at the side of the street. To leave unsightly cans in front of their property or be compelled twice a week to carry them back and forth proved too much for many owners who reverted to paying a private collector." Lynn's letter reiterated the theme that taxes increased in annexed areas, but service declined (*Arizona Daily Star*, April 18, 1953, p. B14).

31. *Arizona Daily Star*, July 2, 1953, p. B1.

32. Minutes of the Tucson City Council, meeting of October 5, 1953. The anti-annexation petition itself is nonexistent; only the reference to it remains in the meeting minutes. The microfilm reel of annexation documents prior to 1968 contains only a sampling of records. "Working documents," among others, were not saved at the time of microfilming.

33. *Arizona Daily Star*, January 8, 1954, p. A2.

34. In 1954, Senate Bill 107—the "tin pipe" bill—forbade cities from competing with a private water company if the company in question was providing adequate service as certified by the state corporation commission. The bill also required cities to allow the courts to establish the fair market value of utilities when cities exercised their right of eminent domain. In 1955 the legislature reinforced the legal standing of private utilities by requiring cities to fork over court-mandated payments in a "timely" fashion. If cities were late or obstructionist, then they were forbidden from pursuing acquisition of the utilities for three years (Richards, *History of the Arizona State Legislature*, Vol. 12, 1953–1954, pp. 125–126; Vol. 13, 1955–1956, p. 130).

35. Minutes of the Tucson City Council, meeting of Nov. 15, 1954.

36. Ibid.

37. Minutes, meeting of April 26, 1956.

38. *Arizona Daily Star*, May 5, 1956, p. A7. Ethnically, South Tucson was predominantly Hispanic, but the businessmen and residents opposing the City of Tucson's annexation were mostly Anglo. This situation will be discussed in more detail in chapter 3.

39. Ibid.

40. *Tucson Citizen*, June 6, 1975, p. 33.

41. Minutes of the Tucson City Council, meeting of March 4, 1957.

42. Minutes, meeting of April 7, 1958. Tucson's archives contain no petitions or affidavits for these annexations. The "working papers" of these annexations were perhaps deemed peripheral and were not saved when documents were placed on microfilm. Or, as Tucson's annexation coordinator suggested in 1989, petitions may never have existed in the first place (Leon, personal interview).

43. Minutes, meeting of Dec. 5, 1955.

44. *Arizona Daily Star*, Jan. 7, 1956, p. A7.

45. Mayor Hummel made reference to a KOLD radio show in 1959: "The City is not given a fair chance on these programs—it seems to be slanted in favor of the anti-annexation element" (Hummel, "Annexation—North and East").

46. Ibid.

47. "100 Facts for 100 Years," Amphitheater Schools District; Melissa Franklin, public affairs director, Amphitheater Schools District, personal interview, June 28, 1994.

48. *Arizona Daily Star*, March 27, 1959, p. A1.

49. Ibid.

50. Hummel, "Annexation—North and East."

51. Hummel, "Annexation—South and West."

52. An early indication of the north side's independence appears in the countywide zoning vote: Flowing Wells approved the local-option alternative, and Amphitheater narrowly defeated it. Petitions supporting or opposing the annexations would help determine the weight of opinion on either side of the annexation question but, unfortunately, are nonexistent.

53. Leon, personal interview.

54. Hummel, "Annexation—South and West," letter from Jack Newman, March 19, 1960.

55. City of Tucson Annexation Index, p. 5.

56. Memorandum from the city manager to Tucson mayor and council, May 10, 1954 ("Annexations: 1905–1968").

CHAPTER 3 "THE WRONG SIDE OF THE TRACKS"

1. "Telephone Directory, March 1950, For Tucson."

2. City of Tucson, "A Workable Program," p. 2.

3. In Los Tucsonenses, Sheridan argues that the environment for Hispanics in Tucson was relatively benign because in addition to the persistent presence of a Mexican elite with strong ties to Sonora, there was a gradual increase in Anglo population rather than the flood of Anglos that entered Texas and California after U.S. acquisition.

4. Sheridan, Los Tucsonenses, p. 252. An example of the Hispanic presence in the business elite was Carlos Ronstadt's election as president of the exclusive Old Pueblo Club in 1946–1947 (Cooper, The O.P. Chronicle).

5. Harte, "A Feisty Town Grows Up," Tucson Citizen, June 6, 1975, p. 33.

6. The population of South Tucson in 1940 was 1,066. As late as 1950, South Tucson's population was officially recorded as 7,004, of which 6,192 were "white," 223 "negro," and 589 "other." The committee organizing the incorporation movement in South Tucson included Mrs. McCormick, J. M. Glass, Sam R. Knipnis, O. A. Ellis, and Roy Baker (Arizona Daily Star, Aug. 11, 1936, p. 1). Harte identified the founders as "the owners of two tourist courts who did not want to be subjected to Tucson's building codes, and . . . liquor dealers who felt that the city's business licensing fees were too steep" (Tucson Citizen, June 6, 1974, p. 33).

7. Sheridan, Los Tucsonenses, p. 121.

8. Arizona Daily Star, Aug. 9, 1936, p. 8; Aug. 11, 1936, p. 1. Governmental records for South Tucson begin in 1940. Prior to the passage of the town's first ordinances in 1940, no paid employees worked for the town. The town's first attorney, Harry O. Juliani, who waged many legal battles on be-

half of South Tucson, volunteered his services (City of South Tucson, "Council Packets—Ordinances").

9. *Arizona Daily Star*, Oct. 29, 1937, p. 1.

10. According to Tucson phone and city directories, in 1939, McElroy operated Tucson Boot Works at 2104 South 6th Avenue, and later, McElroy's Tire Shop occupied the same address. But if you can't beat them, join them: McElroy later served on the South Tucson Town Council (City of South Tucson, "Council Packets—Ordinances").

11. *Arizona Daily Star*, Jan. 8, 1938, pp. 1, 8.

12. *Arizona Daily Star*, Jan. 9, 1938, p. 4.

13. *Arizona Daily Star*, Jan. 19, 1938, p. 1.

14. *Arizona Daily Star*, Jan. 20, 1938, p. 1; April 14, 1938, p. 1; Nov. 29, 1938, p. 1.

15. A single reference to Calhoun's suits appeared in *Arizona Daily Star*, Jan. 8, 1938, pp. 1, 8; but Calhoun's name was spelled "Colquhun." L. M. Calhoun operated Calhoun's Furniture Exchange at 1716 South 6th Avenue in 1939.

16. *Arizona Daily Star*, March 28, 1939, p. 1.

17. *Arizona Daily Star*, Oct. 11, 1939, p. 1.

18. *Arizona Daily Star*, July 23, 1940, p. 1. South Tucson passed its first three ordinances on September 26, 1940. The three ordinances set council meeting times, established a municipal court, and created town officials, including a marshal and tax collector (City of South Tucson, "Council Packets—Ordinances").

19. Emmert, "Annexation Study," pp. 48–49; Sonnichsen, *Tucson*, p. 258. South Tucson's finances were shaky from the start. In 1937, 20 percent of the town's revenues came from speeding tickets issued on South Sixth Avenue, commonly recognized by Tucsonans as a notorious speed trap. However, the South Tucson policemen who issued those tickets were required to furnish their own motorcycles. At one point, to help South Tucson avoid operating at a deficit, the town clerk forbore part of her salary (Harte, "A Feisty Town Grows Up").

20. Kimble, "South Tucson's No Different," *Tucson Citizen*, June 6, 1975, p. 33.

21. South Tucson's property tax was one-fourth that of the city in 1975 (Harte, "A Feisty Town Grows Up").

22. South Tucson's town council decided not to spend its "surplus cash" on the legal fees necessary to force the annexation (City of South Tucson, minutes of the South Tucson Town Council, meeting of April 27, 1949;

the "shang-haied" statement appeared in the *Arizona Daily Star*, March 13, 1956, p. A1).

23. Harte, "A Feisty Town Grows Up." No mention of Tucson's 1956 annexation appears in South Tucson Town Council meeting minutes, perhaps due to an ongoing county investigation into South Tucson's finances. The minutes for the May 14, 1956, meeting explain that "the County Attorney's Office has all available records."

24. Harte, "A Feisty Town Grows Up."

25. City of South Tucson, "Council Packets—Ordinances" and meeting minutes.

26. *Arizona Daily Star*, Dec. 14, 1954, p. A9.

27. *Arizona Daily Star*, May 29, 1956, pp. A1, D8.

28. Junior League of Tucson, "Beyond the Shadows." The Junior League misidentified Tucson's original settlers, who were in fact the Hohokam, as evidenced in archaeological sites throughout the valley.

29. Drachman, *This Is Not A Book*, p. 20.

30. Although the railroad tracks do indicate general settlement patterns in Tucson, the boundary was never legally or rigidly enforced. Barrio Adelanto and Barrio San Antonio were north and east of the tracks in 1940 (Sheridan, *Los Tucsonenses*, p. 238). Anglo flight did in fact take place from the fringes of barrio areas, but overall the ethnic character of neighborhoods south of downtown have always been, and remain, predominantly Hispanic (figs. 7 and 8 show Mexican American settlement patterns).

31. Drachman, *This Is Not A Book*, p. 239.

32. Sheridan, *Los Tucsonenses*, p. 244.

33. The City of Tucson's proposal "Need for Renewal" described "causal factors of blight" including improper platting; inadequate streets, sidewalks, and storm drains; inadequate control of land uses; poor construction or obsolescence; overcrowding; and "environmental deficiencies" such as noise, dust, and traffic (pp. 6–7). The proposal also described "social factors" that did not cause blight, but exacerbated it: low income; racial discrimination; high rental turnover, which promoted poor upkeep; and lack of education and training, which contributed to poor self-esteem.

34. City of Tucson, "A Workable Program," p. 2.

35. Sheridan, *Los Tucsonenses*, p. 126.

36. Citizen's Committee on Municipal Blight, "Pueblo Center Redevelopment Project," p. 9.

37. Mayor Hummel applied for federal funds under the 1954 act that provided for urban renewal loans administered by the Housing and Home Finance Agency (City of Tucson, "A Workable Program").

38. Anderson, *The Federal Bulldozer*.

39. The *Arizona Daily Star* reported in 1959 that the 400-acre project area had 5,000 people. "This figure represents 1,007 families of which 828 are Mexican or Anglo and 179 are Negro, Chinese or Indian." The overwhelming majority were Mexican, as can be seen in the maps of the barrio neighborhoods south of the central business district (figs. 7 and 8).

40. Schorr had been an attorney in New York before moving with his family to Tucson in 1957. He had developed a subdivision in the Tucson Mountain foothills and also served on the Pima County Planning and Zoning Commission. After being appointed assistant city manager, Schorr resigned from the Planning and Zoning Commission and the ethics committee of the Society of Planning Officials (S. L. Schorr interview, "Urbanization of Tucson, 1940–1990"; *Arizona Daily Star*, April 6, 1961, p. A11; May 19, 1961, p. A11.)

41. S. L. Schorr interview.

42. City of Tucson, "A Workable Program," pp. 26–27.

43. Ibid.; Sheridan, *Los Tucsonenses*, p. 168.

44. *Arizona Daily Star*, Jan. 15, 1960, p. C12.

45. *Arizona Daily Star*, Feb. 14, 1961, p. A4.

46. *Arizona Daily Star*, May 8, 1958, p. B1.

47. *Arizona Daily Star*, May 19, 1961, p. A11.

48. The renewal plan originally included nearly 400 acres, at a cost of $16.5 million. Tucson's share would be $1,150,000. *Arizona Daily Star*, April 12, 1961, p. C4.

49. Lazaroff, "Tucson's Canyon Oasis," *Arizona Highways*, April 1993.

50. *Arizona Daily Star*, Aug. 6, 1958, p. A1.

51. S. L. Schorr interview. Also, while presenting Tucson's redevelopment project at a meeting in California, Assistant City Manager Vincent Lung reported: "One gentleman from Orange County, California which, like Arizona, has a conservative political philosophy, thought that in view of our history, we have done a tremendous job to get to the present stage" (Citizen's Committee on Municipal Blight, "Pueblo Center Redevelopment Project," p. iii).

52. In 1959, Mayor Hummel assured Tucsonans that the "heritage of the past won't be lost, and some of the flavor of the Old Southwest retained" (*Arizona Daily Star*, May 15, 1959, p. B1). In 1961, the Historical Society announced its list of fifty-nine historic sites in Tucson, including nine sites within the redevelopment area ("Historical Sites Committee, 1960–61").

53. *Arizona Daily Star*, Nov. 10, 1961, p. A3.

54. A report commissioned by the city in 1969 summarized Tucson's low-cost housing resources in light of continuing urban renewal plans: "It is

estimated that future renewal plans will destroy 3,185 dwelling units and dislocate 10,000 to 12,000 persons over a ten-year period. . . . Existing housing resources in Tucson are minimal when compared with this projected need for relocation. If all the planned units of public housing were completed they would not be sufficient to accommodate even the present waiting list for public housing, and the existing 362 public housing units (up from 160 in 1957) do not represent a major relocation resource" ("Housing and Relocation").

55. In Sallie Marston's forthcoming book *Good Fences, Good Neighbors*, Bertha Valenzuela and John McNair, neighborhood activists in the 1970s and 1980s, trace the start of their community activism to an increasing political awareness in the 1960s.

56. *Arizona Daily Star*, Jan. 19, 1962, p. A1; Feb. 23, p. B3; March 14, p. A6; March 30, p. B1; April 25, 1962, p. A1.

57. *Arizona Daily Star*, April 4, 1962, p. B1.

58. *The Mullin-Kille Tucson Arizona City Directory*, 1962.

59. *Arizona Daily Star*, April 25, 1962, p. A1.

60. *Arizona Daily Star*, May 8, 1962, p. A1; May 22, 1962, p. A1.

61. Citizen's Committee on Municipal Blight, "Pueblo Center Redevelopment Project" pp. 4–5.

62. Sonnichsen, *Tucson*, p. 295.

63. Ibid., p. 287.

64. *Arizona Daily Star*, Oct. 8, 1967, p. D6.

65. Ibid.

66. Henry, "Old Barrio," pp. E1, E5. The "historico" name applied to Barrio Libre and "El Hoyo" ("Barrio Historico," 1972).

67. Marston, *Good Fences, Good Neighbors*.

68. Ibid.

69. Don Bufkin interview, "Urbanization of Tucson, 1940–1990."

CHAPTER 4 "BOTTOMLESS TOWERS"

1. Heald and Heald, "Tucson: Gracious Living in the Sun," p. 12.

2. Hays, *Beauty, Health and Permanence*, pp. 52–55. Also see, for example, Nash, *Wilderness and the American Mind*; Fox, *The American Conservation Movement*; and Foresta, *The National Parks and Their Keepers*.

3. For examples of the defense of nature for its own sake, see Stone, *Should Trees Have Standing?* and Singer, *Animal Liberation*.

4. *Arizona Daily Star*, Oct. 4, 1956, p. C5.

5. *Arizona Daily Star*, Oct. 2, 1971, p. A10.

6. "Mean as Hell," Southwind Music (BMI).

7. Carr, *The Desert Speaks*, quoted in Sonnichsen, *Tucson*, p. 300.

8. Tucson Chamber of Commerce, "The Answers to All Your Questions," 1962.

9. Hays, *Beauty, Health and Permanence*, pp. 23–24.

10. Tucson Chamber of Commerce, "Desert Vegetation Near Tucson" and "Come to the Growing Southwest." For the increasing valuation of the desert, see Hollon, *The Great American Desert*, and Limerick, *Desert Passages*.

11. Tucson Chamber of Commerce, "Tucson . . . A City."

12. Telephone Directory for Tucson, March 1950.

13. Tucson Chamber of Commerce, "Tucson Progress."

14. Hughes Aircraft Company, "Careers in the Sun."

15. Devoto, "The West Against Itself," pp. 1–12; Stegner, *The Uneasy Chair*, pp. 301–3.

16. Sonnichsen, *Tucson*, pp. 258, 265.

17. National Cancer Institute, *U.S. Cancer Mortality Rates and Trends, 1950–1979*, pp. 364, 394, 423, 429, 435, 465, 491, 499. For rates of skin cancer in New Mexico, see the National Institutes of Health's *Seer Report: Cancer Incidence and Mortality in the United States*.

18. Tucson Chamber of Commerce, "Healthful Tucson."

19. Ibid.

20. Tucson Chamber of Commerce, "Saguaro National Monument."

21. Tucson Sunshine Climate Club, "Sunshine News," December 1950.

22. Tucson Chamber of Commerce, "The Guest Informant."

23. Old Tucson Development Company, "The Classic Country."

24. Tucson Chamber of Commerce, "Private Schools."

25. Tucson Chamber of Commerce, "The Guest Informant."

26. The "pollen survey" for 1955 appeared without comment in the Chamber of Commerce's "Healthful Tucson," in 1956. Pollen counts for sixteen varieties of plants were listed, from a low of "19" for shadscale and a high of "1335" for bermuda grass.

27. Tucson Chamber of Commerce, "The Answers to All Your Questions."

28. The board of supervisors also required residents to trim bermuda grass before it went to seed (*Arizona Daily Star*, Feb. 7, 1985, p. A8).

29. Mees, "Tucson Air Pollution."

30. Tucson Planning and Zoning Commission, "Regional Plan," p. 1.

31. "Need for Renewal," p. 4.

32. Emmert, "Annexation Study," p. 3.

33. According to Frieden, the factors that encouraged lateral urban

development were lack of a strong central city core, relatively short travel times to and from the fringe areas, and the availability of cheap vacant land nearby ("Locational Preferences"). Factors that discouraged in-fill were neighborhood opposition to higher-density housing, and developers' reluctance to build low-density housing except for ultra-luxury homes (Johnston, Schwartz, and Tracy, "Growth Phasing").

34. "Tucson Chamber of Commerce Newsletter," Oct. 1, 1961.

35. Tucson Chamber of Commerce, "Tucson Progress," December 1968, January 1969.

36. "Goals for the Community," p. 2.

37. Ibid., p. 32.

38. "The Tucson Visual Environment," pp. 51–52. Radbill's study "Measuring the Quality of the Urban Landscape" recorded residents' reaction to Tucson's "visual environment" as well as other factors in the landscape.

39. *Arizona Daily Star*, July 6, 1969, p. C1.

40. Although no poll or survey exists from the 1950s or 1960s, plentiful anecdotal evidence supports the findings of a 1990 survey of 900 Tucson households in urban, suburban, and rural areas. "All three categories of respondents favored a move to a more rural (lower density) setting if forced to move. All strongly preferred detached single-family housing . . . yards or outdoor space to do with as they please, and a view of desert or mountains. Advantages of location . . . for urban dwellers and the disadvantages of location for rural respondents seem to be relatively unimportant in influencing satisfaction with present housing or desires for new housing" (Wilkin and Iams, "Characteristics and Attitudes," p. 42).

41. Margolis, *Joseph Wood Krutch*.

42. Limerick, in *Desert Passages*, correctly identified Krutch's "cheerful faith in the limited usefulness of desert property" in the early 1950s (p. 141), but then incorrectly dismissed Krutch's understanding of the issues surrounding urbanization in the desert: "the complicated problems of regulating the development of private property, or modifying the conventions of profit-centered land use, or of limiting the demands and aspirations of American consumers were by this time [early 1960s] beyond Krutch's reach" (p. 147). In fact, Krutch understood full well the character and agenda of the forces directing development in Tucson.

43. Krutch, *More Lives Than One*, p. 307.

44. Krutch, "Man's Mark on the Desert," *If You Don't Mind My Saying So*, pp. 361–67.

45. *Arizona Daily Star*, Oct. 4, 1956, p. C5.

46. Minutes of the Tucson City Council, meeting of December 5, 1955.

47. Krutch, *If You Don't Mind My Saying So*, p. 364.

48. Krutch, *More Lives Than One*, p. 360. Limerick misinterpreted Krutch's recognition of his own political marginality: "His public stance as a refined and cultivated gentleman of sensibility placed him a far distance from the trade centers, banks, real estate offices, and chambers of commerce that were directing the future of American settlement in the desert" (*Desert Passages*, p. 147). In Tucson there was never much distance between the boosters and preservationists since tourist promotions required undisturbed desert near the city. Krutch's "partial solution" (described in chapter 4) indicates his recognition of the political realities in Tucson. The question was not whether to preserve the desert, but rather how much desert to preserve, and where, when, and how.

49. *Arizona Daily Star*, Oct. 4, 1956, p. C5.

50. Ibid., p. A10.

51. Krutch, *If You Don't Mind My Saying So*, pp. 362, 365.

52. Ibid., p. 365.

53. Sonnichsen, *Tucson*, p. 300.

54. Krutch, *More Lives Than One*, p. 350.

55. J. W. Murphey papers, Arizona Historical Society. For example, "It is desired that roads built shall follow and cling to these washes or other depressions of natural drainage as closely as possible." And, "The hills are covered with cacti . . . and have restrictions against their removal except for construction purposes. Catalina Foothills Estates owns over 5,000 acres in the district and has determined to keep it clear of all objectionable commercial enterprises."

56. Kreutz, "The High Life."

57. Ibid.

58. Sonnichsen, *Tucson*, p. 217.

59. Kreutz, "The High Life."

60. Ibid.

CHAPTER 5   MONKEY WRENCHES AND MOUNTAIN LIONS

1. *Arizona Daily Star*, Jan. 8, 1965, p. B12.

2. Sonnichsen, *Tucson*, p. 284.

3. *Arizona Daily Star*, April 29, 1986, p. C1.

4. *Arizona Daily Star*, Oct. 18, 1973, p. B1.

5. Sonnichsen, *Tucson*, p. 282.

6. Ibid., p. 293.

7. Ibid.

8. Marston, *Good Fences, Good Neighbors.*

9. Sonnichsen, *Tucson,* p. 283.

10. *Arizona Daily Star,* Nov. 3, 1976, p. A1; Jan. 1, 1977, p. A1.

11. *Arizona Daily Star,* May 12, 1989, p. B7.

12. *Arizona Daily Star,* Nov. 14, 1989, p. B1.

13. Marston, *Good Fences, Good Neighbors.*

14. Sonnichsen, *Tucson,* p. 294.

15. *Arizona Daily Star,* May 11, 1974, p. B1.

16. *Arizona Daily Star,* Jan. 31, 1981, p. A1; Sonnichsen, *Tucson,* p. 294.

17. *Arizona Daily Star,* Oct. 12, 1978, p. A1; Oct. 11, 1980, p. A1.

18. Sonnichsen, *Tucson,* pp. 287–88, 293.

19. *Arizona Daily Star,* Sept. 12, 1974, p. A2.

20. Sonnichsen, *Tucson,* pp. 287–88.

21. Ibid.

22. Ibid., pp. 288–91.

23. *Arizona Daily Star,* June 9, 1979, p. A1.

24. *Arizona Daily Star,* May 15, 1981, p. B1.

25. *Arizona Daily Star,* Mar. 7, 1975, p. B1; Dec. 26, 1975, p. A1.

26. *Arizona Daily Star,* Sept. 19, 1973, p. A2.

27. *The Monkey Wrench Gang* was published in 1975.

28. *Arizona Daily Star,* May 9, 1994, p. A1.

PART 2 ALBUQUERQUE

1. Fitzpatrick and Caplin, *Albuquerque,* p. 69.

2. Ibid., p. 107.

3. Oppenheimer, "Historical Background," p. 33.

4. Fitzpatrick and Caplin, *Albuquerque,* p. 8.

5. Ibid., p. 20.

6. Gottberg, *Frommer's,* p. 2; Christensen and Sikes, *Tucson,* p. 3.

CHAPTER 6 "STEP LIVELY"

1. Oppenheimer, "Historical Background," p. 36.

2. Fitzpatrick and Caplin, *Albuquerque,* p. 41.

3. "University Heights," 1906, Center for Southwest Research (CSR).

4. Fitzpatrick and Caplin, *Albuquerque,* p. 43.

5. *Albuquerque Daily Citizen,* Dec. 13, 1890, quoted in Fitzpatrick and Caplin, *Albuquerque,* p. 3.

6. Commercial Club, "Compliments of the Educators," CSR.

7. Commercial Club, "Why Albuquerque," CSR.

8. Albuquerque Chamber of Commerce, untitled item 27, MSS 112, CSR.

9. "Step Lively," CSR.

10. "Albuquerque, 1925," CSR.

11. "Albuquerque: The Heart of the Well Country," Special Collections, University of Arizona Library.

12. Fitzpatrick and Caplin, *Albuquerque*, p. 144.

13. *Albuquerque Magazine*, 1939, CSR.

14. "Market Study of New Mexico," CSR.

15. "Pictorial Albuquerque," CSR.

16. Pyle, "Why Albuquerque?" p. 17.

17. Chamber of Commerce, "Only as a Community Prospers," CSR.

18. Wood, "Transformation of Albuquerque," p. 571.

19. *Albuquerque Journal*, April 23, 1950, pp. 1, 14.

20. *Albuquerque Journal*, July 19, 1948, p. 4; July 19, 1953, p. 4.

21. "Albuquerque . . . City of Flowers," CSR.

22. Wood, "Transformation of Albuquerque," p. 572.

23. *Albuquerque Journal*, Nov. 18, 1951, p. 2.

24. Albuquerque Chamber of Commerce, "See New Mexico," CSR.

25. "Albuquerque News Letter," April 26, 1963, Coronado MSS, CSR.

26. "America's Most Dynamic City," CSR.

27. *Albuquerque Journal*, Sept. 7, 1958, p. 6.

28. *Albuquerque Journal*, Nov. 9, 1968, p. A6.

29. "Albuquerque News Letter," Jan. 17, 1964, CSR.

30. Wood, "Transformation of Albuquerque," p. 49.

31. Minutes of the Albuquerque City Commission, Aug. 6, 1946, p. 4.

32. Nash, *American West*, pp. 213–14.

33. Albuquerque Planning Department, "Annexations, 1958," CSR.

34. *Albuquerque Journal*, Feb. 18, 1947, pp. 1, 3.

35. U.S. Department of Commerce, *Boundary and Annexation Study*, 1970–1973, p. 47.

36. Fitzpatrick and Caplin, *Albuquerque*, p. 108.

37. Wood, "Transformation of Albuquerque," p. 178.

38. Ibid., pp. 150–51.

39. Fitzpatrick and Caplin, *Albuquerque*, pp. 157, 159, 178.

40. *Albuquerque Journal*, July 2, 1972, p. G2.

41. *Albuquerque Journal*, May 17, 1963, p. A2.

42. Wood, "Transformation of Albuquerque," p. 326.

43. Ibid., p. 78.

44. Ibid., pp. 257, 260. Also, in 1963 the Chamber of Commerce established the Albuquerque Industrial Development Corporation, "a publicly-held, broad-based community organization for the purpose of buying, building and financing buildings and other services for industries which would like to move to Albuquerque, and existing firms that would like to expand" ("Albuquerque News Letter," CSR).

45. Wood, "Transformation of Albuquerque," pp. 257, 260.

46. *Albuquerque Journal*, Nov. 15, 1967, p. A4.

47. Wood, "Transformation of Albuquerque," p. 572.

48. Ibid., p. 513.

49. Ibid., p. 167.

50. *Albuquerque Journal*, Feb. 22, 1952, p. 1.

51. *Albuquerque Journal*, Feb. 26, 1947, p. 1; May 30, 1948, p. 1. Also, the Chamber of Commerce sponsored "Freedom Versus Communism" courses in 1963 ("Albuquerque News Letter," Oct. 4, 1963, CSR).

52. *Albuquerque Journal*, Aug. 19, 1953, p. 18; Feb. 7, 1958, p. A1; Sept. 17, 1959, p. A1.

53. *Albuquerque Journal*, Oct. 19, 1961, p. A2.

CHAPTER 7 "LAND, LOTS OF LAND"

1. Fitzpatrick and Caplin, *Albuquerque*, p. 131.

2. Pyle, "Why Albuquerque?" p. 17.

3. *Albuquerque Journal*, Dec. 31, 1946, p. 1.

4. Ibid.

5. The 1939 law amended the annexation statutes of 1884 and 1935, and appeared in the 1942 compilation of New Mexico statutes. At times the *Albuquerque Journal* referred to it as the "1942 annexation law."

6. *Laws of the State of New Mexico*, 1939, pp. 500–502.

7. Ibid., p. 502.

8. *Albuquerque Journal*, Feb. 18, 1947, pp. 1, 3.

9. Ibid.

10. Minutes of the Albuquerque City Commission, April 16, 1946, p. 10.

11. Minutes of the Albuquerque City Commission, May 7, 1946, p. 13.

12. *Albuquerque Journal*, Feb. 18, 1947, p. 1, 3. Montoya baited the Chamber of Commerce in the newspaper by comparing their support for annexation and their opposition to the "closed shop." According to Montoya, the Chamber of Commerce supported "democracy" if it would further their anti-union drive, but opposed "democracy" in annexation disputes.

13. Ibid.

14. *Albuquerque Journal*, March 14, 1947, pp. 1, 3.

15. *Laws of the State of New Mexico*, 1947, p. 505.

16. *Albuquerque Journal*, Feb. 19, 1947, p. 1.

17. Minutes of the Albuquerque City Commission, May 29, 1948, p. 1.

18. Minutes of the Albuquerque City Commission, June 25 through Sept. 9, 1947.

19. Minutes, March 11, 1947, pp. 1–4.

20. Minutes, June 1, 1948, pp. 1–3. (Although protest petitions were also filed in Tucson, they were lost during the process of microfilming; thus the historical "voice" of the resistance in Tucson was silenced.)

21. Minutes, June 15, 1948, pp. 2–4.

22. *Albuquerque Journal*, Aug. 14, 1948, pp. 1, 2.

23. *Albuquerque Journal*, June 29, 1949, pp. 1, 4.

24. Ibid.

25. Minutes of the Albuquerque City Commission, July 20, 1948; *Albuquerque Journal*, July 21, 1948, p. 1.

26. Minutes, Aug. 3, 1948, pp. 1–4.

27. Minutes, Aug. 24, 1948, p. 9.

28. *Albuquerque Journal*, Jan. 5, 1949, p. 1.

29. Minutes of the Albuquerque City Commission, Jan. 4, 1949, p. 6.

30. Minutes, Jan. 17, 1949, pp. 1–2; Jan. 18, 1949, pp. 2–4.

31. *Albuquerque Journal*, Jan. 30, 1949, pp. 1–2.

32. *Albuquerque Journal*, April 13, 1949, p. 1.

33. *Albuquerque Journal*, July 1, 1949, p. 1.

34. Ibid.

35. Ibid.

36. Minutes of the Albuquerque City Commission, Jan. 10, 1950, p. 11.

37. Minutes, Nov. 22, 1949, pp. 2–4; *Albuquerque Journal*, Nov. 23, 1949, pp. 1, 3.

38. L. J. Lippett to the city commission, minutes of the Albuquerque City Commission, Jan. 17, 1950, pp. 6–7.

39. Minutes, Albuquerque City Commission, Jan. 24, 1950, pp. 8–10.

40. The legal opinion itself is not included in the meeting minutes, only the reference to it. The city attorney's office has no record of it.

41. *Albuquerque Journal*, Jan. 25, 1950, pp. 1, 11.

42. Wood, "Transformation of Albuquerque," p. 113.

43. *Albuquerque Journal*, July 30, 1953, p. 1.

44. Wood, "Transformation of Albuquerque," p. 133.

45. *Albuquerque Journal*, April 7, 1954, p. 1; May 1, 1955, p. 1.

46. *Albuquerque Journal*, Oct. 19, 1957, p. 1; April 9, 1958, p. 1.

47. *Albuquerque Journal*, Oct. 7, 1959, p. 1.
48. Wood, "Transformation of Albuquerque," p. 239.
49. *Albuquerque Journal*, Nov. 13, 1960, p. A1.
50. *Albuquerque Journal*, Nov. 17, 1965, pp. A1–2.
51. *Albuquerque Journal*, April 7, 1960, pp. A1–2.
52. Ibid.
53. Ibid.
54. Minutes of the Albuquerque City Commission, April 19, 1960, pp. 22–24.
55. *Albuquerque Journal*, April 19, 1960, p. A2.
56. *Albuquerque Journal*, April 20, 1960, pp. A1–2.
57. *Albuquerque Journal*, April 21, 1960, pp. A2.
58. Minutes of the Albuquerque City Commission, April 26, 1960, p. 2.
59. Minutes, Sept. 18, 1961, p. 1.
60. Minutes, Sept. 27, 1960, pp. 11–13; *Albuquerque Journal*, Sept. 28, 1960, p. A2.
61. *Albuquerque Journal*, Sept. 28, 1960, p. A2.
62. *Albuquerque Journal*, Sept. 20, 1961, p. A1.
63. *Albuquerque Journal*, Sept. 22, 1963, p. A4.
64. *Albuquerque Journal*, July 17, 1964, p. A21.
65. Memorandum from City Attorney Donald B. Moses to the city commission, Nov. 8, 1946; minutes, Nov. 19, 1946, p. 9.
66. Minutes, Jan. 28, 1964, n.p.
67. *Albuquerque Journal*, Sept. 22, 1963, p. A4.
68. Wood, "Transformation of Albuquerque," p. 466.
69. *Albuquerque Journal*, June 24, 1964, pp. A1–2.
70. Ibid.
71. Ibid. No references to the protest or ensuing legal decisions appear in minutes of the city commission meetings.
72. *Albuquerque Journal*, July 17, 1964, pp. A1, A21.
73. *Albuquerque Journal*, Sept. 23, 1964, p. A2. Again, no reference to the controversy appears in city commission meeting minutes.
74. *Albuquerque Journal*, Oct. 8, 1964, pp. A1, A6.
75. *Albuquerque Journal*, Jan. 6, 1965, pp. A1–2.
76. *Albuquerque Journal*, Feb. 14, 1965, pp. A1, A11.
77. Paskin, "Annexations Now Made Without Furious Uproar," p. A4.
78. *Albuquerque Journal*, June 19, 1966, p. A4. No mention of Trigg's statement appears in meeting minutes.
79. *Albuquerque Journal*, Nov. 15, 1967, p. A4.

80. *Albuquerque Journal*, Jan. 30, 1962, p. B2.

81. Wood, "Transformation of Albuquerque," pp. 572–73.

CHAPTER 8 "THE ENCHILADA FLOOR"

1. Wood, "Transformation of Albuquerque," pp. 36, 51, 64, 96; census statistics.

2. Littlewood and Allen, "Joseph M. Montoya," p. 2; Swadesh, "The Alianza Movement."

3. "Roster of State Officials," *Laws of the State of New Mexico*, 1939.

4. Littlewood and Allen, "Joseph M. Montoya," pp. 3–4.

5. Fergusson, *Albuquerque*, p. 13.

6. Bergman, "Fate of Architectural Theory."

7. *Albuquerque Journal*, May 17, 1963, p. A2.

8. *Albuquerque Journal*, March 7, 1947, p. 13.

9. Wood, "Transformation of Albuquerque," p. 308.

10. *Albuquerque Journal*, April 4, 1959, pp. 1–2.

11. *Albuquerque Journal*, April 25, 1959, p. 2.

12. *Albuquerque Journal*, April 4, 1959, p. 1.

13. *Albuquerque Journal*, April 25, 1959, p. 2.

14. *Albuquerque Journal*, May 3, 1959, pp. 1–2.

15. Wood, "Transformation of Albuquerque," pp. 308–10.

16. Hoffman murdered his wife, then turned the gun on himself. *Albuquerque Journal*, Oct. 14, 1959, p. 1.

17. Wood, "Transformation of Albuquerque," p. 237.

18. The downtown area remained predominantly Hispanic due to the relatively constant immigration of Spanish Americans from rural New Mexico, and Mexican nationals (City of Albuquerque Planning Department, "Central Area Study," p. 21).

19. *Albuquerque Journal*, Nov. 17, 1965, pp. A1–2.

20. Minutes of the Albuquerque City Commission, Aug. 26, 1947, p. 11.

21. Wood, "Transformation of Albuquerque," p. 260.

22. Ibid., p. 349.

23. *Albuquerque Journal*, Sept. 15, 1965, pp. A1, A15.

24. Ibid.

25. Ibid.

26. *Albuquerque Journal*, April 24, 1970, p. A6; Jan. 3, 1971, p. A1.

27. *Albuquerque Journal*, Jan. 3, 1971, pp. A1, A6.

28. Wood, "Transformation of Albuquerque," p. 277.

29. Klein, "Downtown Planning Process," p. 10.

30. City of Albuquerque Planning Department, "Central Business District Study," p. 21.

31. *Albuquerque Journal*, Aug. 20, 1961, p. A4.

32. *Albuquerque Journal*, Dec. 2, 1960, p. 1; Dec. 12, 1960, pp. A1, A7.

33. *Albuquerque Journal*, Aug. 20, 1961, p. A4.

34. Ibid.

35. *Albuquerque Journal*, June 11, 1962, p. A1.

36. Ibid.

37. Wood, "Transformation of Albuquerque," p. 278.

38. *Albuquerque Journal*, Aug. 7, 1962, p. A1; Albuquerque Planning Department, "Central Area Study," pp. 21–22.

39. *Albuquerque Journal*, Sept. 12, 1965, p. C1.

40. *Albuquerque Journal*, Jan. 1, 1964, p. A1.

41. Klein, "Downtown Planning Process," p. 20.

42. *Albuquerque Journal*, Feb. 13, 1964, pp. A1, A7.

43. Ibid.

44. Albuquerque Planning Department, "Central Area Study," p. 37.

45. Ibid., p. 31.

46. The eight objectives for the central area were: 1. " . . . communication center;" 2. ". . . major center of attraction for tourists;" 3. ". . . attractive high density residential development;" 4. ". . . employment and labor center;" 5. ". . . civic and cultural center;" 6. ". . . regional recreation center;" 7. ". . . a special type of regional institutional center (hospitals, research, etc.);" 8. ". . . a vigorous commercial and business center" (Albuquerque Planning Department, "Central Area Study," p. 5).

47. *Albuquerque Journal*, Sept. 12, 1965, p. C1.

48. *Albuquerque Journal*, April 6, 1966, pp. A1–2.

49. Klein, "Downtown Planning Process," p. 84.

50. Wood, "Transformation of Albuquerque," p. 284; *Albuquerque Journal*, Aug. 9, 1966, p. A1.

51. *Albuquerque Journal*, Sept. 9, 1966, pp. A4–5.

52. Ibid.

53. Ibid., p. A5.

54. *Albuquerque Journal*, May 7, 1967, p. A4.

55. Buddecke, "Who Plans the Planning?" p. A4.

56. Klein, "Downtown Planning Process," p. 37.

57. *Albuquerque Journal*, Oct. 19, 1968, pp. A1, A4.

58. *Albuquerque Journal*, Feb. 2, 1969, p. A1.

59. Ibid.

60. *Albuquerque Journal*, April 6, 1969, p. A6.

61. Wood, "Transformation of Albuquerque," p. 288.

62. Ibid., p. 289.

63. *Albuquerque Journal*, May 6, 1971, p. A8.

64. Minutes of the Albuquerque City Commission, Dec. 16, 1970; August 24, 1975.

CHAPTER 9 "SPRAWLITIS"

1. Pyle, "Why Albuquerque?" p. 17.

2. Fergusson, *Albuquerque*, p. 1.

3. MSS 112, Center for Southwest Research.

4. MSS 112, Center for Southwest Research.

5. Minutes of the Albuquerque City Commission, Jan. 6, 1965.

6. Minutes, Dec. 17, 1963.

7. Minutes, Dec. 30, 1963.

8. Albuquerque receives about eight inches of rain per year. Tucson receives almost eleven inches per year. (*Frommer's*, p. 2; Lockard, *This is Tucson*, p. 236).

9. Fitzpatrick and Caplin, *Albuquerque*, p. 72.

10. *Albuquerque Journal*, Nov. 5, 1947, p. 1; Sept. 26, 1952, p. 1; July 25, 1953, p. 1; July 30, 1953, p. 1; summarized in Wood, "Transformation of Albuquerque," p. 132.

11. Fitzpatrick and Caplin, *Albuquerque*, p. 45.

12. Ibid., p. 65; Meem defended the pueblo style against "modernists" who condemned any "style" as "ignorant, sterile, untruthful—in fact, immoral" (Bergman, "Fate of Architectural Theory," pp. 301–2).

13. Fitzpatrick and Caplin, *Albuquerque*, pp. 80–81.

14. Wood, "Transformation of Albuquerque," p. 221.

15. *Albuquerque Journal*, Feb. 2, 1948, p. 10.

16. Wood, "Transformation of Albuquerque," p. 221.

17. Fitzpatrick and Caplin, *Albuquerque*, p. 105.

18. *Albuquerque Journal*, May 17, 1963, p. A2.

19. *Albuquerque Journal*, June 24, 1964, pp. A1–2.

20. Albuquerque/Bernalillo County Planning Department, "East Mountain Area District Plan," pp. 3, 6.

21. *Albuquerque Journal*, Jan. 30, 1962, p. B2.

22. *Albuquerque Journal*, Jan. 1, 1964, p. A1.

23. Fisher, "Old Albuquerque," 1950, p. 14.

24. *Albuquerque Journal*, Sept. 6, 1966, p. A5.

25. *Albuquerque Journal*, Jan. 26, 1968, p. A6.

26. Wood, "Transformation of Albuquerque," p. 314.

27. Ibid., p. 326.

28. *Albuquerque Journal*, Feb. 27, 1972, pp. A1, A14.

29. Albuquerque/Bernalillo County Planning Department, "Vacant Land Study," p. 1.

30. "Albuquerque News Letter," Dec. 7, 1962.

31. McNamara, *Social Report for Metropolitan Albuquerque*, pp. 85–86.

32. *Albuquerque Journal*, Aug. 24, 1973, p. D1.

33. Briggs, "Residential Infill Development," p. 4.

34. Wood, "Transformation of Albuquerque," p. 344.

35. *Albuquerque Journal*, Sept. 6, 1969, p. A1.

36. Wood, "Transformation of Albuquerque," pp. 515–16.

37. *Albuquerque Journal*, May 30, 1971, p. A2.

38. *Albuquerque Journal*, July 27, 1971, p. A1.

39. Albuquerque/Bernalillo County, "Plan for Major Open Space," p. 2.

40. Wood, "Transformation of Albuquerque," p. 531.

41. Ibid., p. 556.

42. Price, City, p. 42.

43. Ibid., p. 43.

44. Ibid.

CHAPTER 10 THIN REEDS AND BUFFERS

1. Naisbitt, *Megatrends*, p. 223. Naisbitt also named Tucson as one of the ten cities of "great opportunity."

2. Wolfe, *The Right Stuff*, p. 88.

3. The most damning indictment of Albuquerque appeared in the "City Stress Index," *Psychology Today.*

4. Price, City, pp. 85–86.

5. *Albuquerque Journal*, April 30, 1987, pp. A1, A7.

6. Price, City, pp. 19–20, 95.

7. Ibid., p. 94.

8. *Albuquerque Journal*, July 11, 1987, p. A4.

9. Price, City, p. 115.

10. Ibid., p. 18.

11. Ibid., p. 55.

12. Albuquerque/Bernalillo County Planning Department, "Southwest Area Plan," p. ii.

13. Price chronicles the South Valley incorporation movement without any reference to the 1960s "South Albuquerque" activism (City, pp. 20, 128).

14. Ibid., p. 126.

15. *Albuquerque Journal*, March 22, 1986, p. B1; interview with David Parks, Traffic Control Department, July 26, 1994.

16. Price, City, p. 54.

17. Dewitt, *Historic Albuquerque Today*, p. 50.

18. Price, City, pp. 119–20.

19. Ibid., p. 128.

20. Ibid., pp. 83–84.

21. Ibid., p. 94.

22. Ibid., p. 96.

23. Albuquerque/Bernalillo County Planning Department, "Plan for Major Open Space," p. 2.

24. City of Albuquerque, Open Space Advisory Board report; *Newsweek*, Feb. 6, 1989, p. 49.

25. *Albuquerque Journal*, June 29, 1990, p. E1.

26. *Albuquerque Journal*, Feb. 20, 1989, pp. A1, A7; Albuquerque/Bernalillo County Health Department, "Groundwater Protection Policy Action Plan."

27. Price, City, pp. 130–31.

28. Ibid., p. 49.

CONCLUSION   BOTH HALVES OF THE STORY

1. Sheridan, *Los Tucsonenses*, pp. 26–29.

2. Elkins and McKitrick, "A Meaning for Turner's Frontier," p. 321.

3. Dykstra, *The Cattle Towns*.

BIBLIOGRAPHY

Abbott, Carl. *The New Urban America: Growth and Politics in Sunbelt Cities.* Chapel Hill: University of North Carolina Press, 1981.

"Action Albuquerque." Center for Southwest Research, Zimmerman Library, University of New Mexico.

Albuquerque, City of. City commission meeting minutes.

———. Open Space Advisory Board annual report, 1989.

Albuquerque Planning Department. "Albuquerque Central Area Study, 1965." Municipal Development Library.

———. "Albuquerque Central Business District Study: Land Uses, 1957." Municipal Development Library.

———. "Annexations to the City of Albuquerque, New Mexico, 1958." "Annexation Index," Coronado MSS. Center for Southwest Research, Zimmerman Library, University of New Mexico.

———. "Downtown Plan, 1970." Municipal Development Library.

Albuquerque/Bernalillo County Health Department. "Groundwater Protection Policy Action Plan," May/June 1990.

Albuquerque/Bernalillo County Planning Department. "Comprehensive Plan," 1975. Municipal Development Library.

———. "East Mountain Area District Plan: Part 1: Citizen Attitude Survey,"

1973. Center for Southwest Research, Zimmerman Library, University of New Mexico.

———. "Plan for Major Open Space." "Comprehensive Plan" 1975.

———. "Southwest Area Plan." Municipal Development Library.

———. "Vacant Land Study," 1972. Municipal Development Library.

Albuquerque Daily Citizen. 1890.

"Albuquerque: The Heart of the Well Country." Special Collections, University of Arizona Library.

Albuquerque Journal. 1946–1990.

"The Albuquerque Magazine." Summer 1939. MS 112, Box I, Item 87. Center for Southwest Research, Zimmerman Library, University of New Mexico.

"Albuquerque, New Mexico: The City of Flowers in the Heart of the Well Country." MS 112, Box I, uncataloged. Center for Southwest Research, Zimmerman Library, University of New Mexico.

"Albuquerque News Letter." Coronado Collection, "Action Albuquerque." Center for Southwest Research, Zimmerman Library, University of New Mexico.

"Albuquerque, 1925." MS 112, Box I, Item 49. Center for Southwest Research, Zimmerman Library, University of New Mexico.

Albuquerque Tribune. 1990.

"America's Most Dynamic City." MS 112, Box I, uncataloged. Center for Southwest Research, Zimmerman Library, University of New Mexico.

Anderson, Martin. *The Federal Bulldozer.* New York: McGraw Hill, 1964.

Arizona Daily Star (Tucson). 1936–1994.

Arizona Historical Society, Tucson. "Historic Sites Committee, 1960–61."

Athearn, Robert G. *The Mythic West in Twentieth-Century America.* Lawrence: University of Kansas Press, 1986.

"Barrio Historico." College of Architecture, University of Arizona, 1972. Special Collections, University of Arizona.

Bergman, Edna Heatherington. "The Fate of Architectural Theory in Albuquerque." Master's thesis in architecture, University of New Mexico, 1978.

Bernard, Richard M., and Bradley R. Rice. *Sunbelt Cities: Politics and Growth Since World War II.* Austin: University of Texas Press, 1983.

"Beyond the Shadows." The Junior League of Tucson, Inc. Special Collections, University of Arizona Library.

Billington, Ray Allen. *America's Frontier Heritage.* New York: Holt, Rinehart, and Winston, 1966.

Bingham, David A. "The Impact of Urbanization in Arizona." In Wingfield.

Bollens, John C. "Fringe Area Conditions and Relations." *Public Management* 32 (March 1950): 50–54.

———. "City Annexation Programs and Policies." *Public Management* 32 (April 1950): 76–79.

Boorstin, Daniel J. *The Americans: The National Experience.* New York: Random House, 1965.

Boyte, Harry. *The Backyard Revolution.* Philadelphia: Temple University Press, 1980.

Briggs, Bruce Alan. "Residential Infill Development in the City of Albuquerque." Master's thesis in architecture, University of New Mexico, 1974.

Buddecke, Martha. "Who Plans the Planning?" *Albuquerque Journal,* June 16, 1968, p. A4.

Bufkin, Don. "From Mud Village to Modern Metropolis: The Urbanization of Tucson." *Journal of Arizona History* 22 (spring 1981): 63–98.

"Careers in the Sun . . . You're an Individual." Hughes Aircraft Company. Special Collections, University of Arizona Library.

Carr, William H. *The Desert Speaks: The Founding, Building, and Objectives of the Arizona-Sonora Desert Museum.* Tucson, Ariz.: Arizona-Sonora Desert Museum, 1957.

Carter, Paul. *Another Part of the Fifties.* New York: Columbia University Press, 1983.

Christensen, Anne, and Diane Sikes. *Tucson.* Phoenix, Ariz.: Valley Publishing Co., 1984.

"City Stress Index." *Psychology Today* (Nov. 1988): 52–58.

"The Classic Country, Tucson and Southern Arizona." Old Tucson Development Company, 1972. Special Collections, University of Arizona Library.

"Compliments of the Educators of Albuquerque." MS 112, Box I, Item 3. Center for Southwest Research, Zimmerman Library, University of New Mexico.

Cooper, James F. *The O. P. Chronicle: A 75-Year History of the Old Pueblo Club.* Tucson, Ariz.: Old Pueblo Club, 1983.

Cronon, William, George Miles, and Jay Gitlin, eds. *Under an Open Sky: Rethinking America's Western Past.* New York: W. W. Norton and Company, 1992.

Davis, John Emmeus. *Contested Ground: Collective Action and the Urban Neighborhood.* Ithaca, N.Y.: Cornell University Press, 1991.

Davis, Mike. *City of Quartz.* New York: Vintage Books, 1990.

Devoto, Bernard. "The West Against Itself." *Harper's Magazine* 194 (Jan. 1947): 1–12.

Dewitt, Susan, Mary Davis, and Rachel Abrams. *Historic Albuquerque Today: An Overview Survey of Historic Buildings and Districts.* Albuquerque: Historic Landmarks Survey of Albuquerque, 1978.

Drachman, Roy P. *This Is Not A Book, Just Memories.* Published privately, n.d. [1980].

Dykstra, Robert. *The Cattle Towns.* New York: Alfred Knopf, 1968.

Elkin, Stephen. "Twentieth-Century Urban Regimes." *Journal of Urban Affairs* 7 (1985): 11–28.

Elkins, Stanley, and Eric McKitrick. "A Meaning for Turner's Frontier: Democracy in the Old Northwest." *Political Science Quarterly* 69 (Sept. 1954): 321.

Emery, Fred. "A City in Action, 1951–1955: Four Years of Progress." Special Collections, University of Arizona Library.

Emmert, Eloise McCoy. "An Annexation Study of Tucson, Arizona." Master's thesis, University of Arizona, 1951.

Fergusson, Erna. *Albuquerque.* Albuquerque, N.Mex.: Merle Armitage Editions, 1947.

Fisher, Irene. "Old Albuquerque: Past and Present." 1950. MS 112, Item 101. Center for Southwest Research, Zimmerman Library, University of New Mexico.

Fishman, Robert. *Bourgeois Utopia: The Rise and Fall of Suburbia.* New York: Basic Books, 1987.

Fitzpatrick, George, and Harvey Caplin. *Albuquerque: 100 Years in Pictures, 1875–1975.* Albuquerque, N.Mex.: Calvin Horn Publisher, Inc., 1975.

Foresta, Ronald. *The National Parks and Their Keepers.* Baltimore, Md.: Johns Hopkins and Resources for the Future, 1983.

Fox, Stephen R. *The American Conservation Movement: John Muir and His Legacy.* Madison: University of Wisconsin Press, 1985.

Frieden, Bernard J. "Locational References in the Urban Housing Market." *Journal of the American Institute of Planners* 27 (Nov. 1961): 316–24.

Glabb, Charles Nelson, and A. Theodore Brown, eds. *A History of Urban America.* New York: Macmillan, 1983.

Gottberg, John. *Frommer's Santa Fe, Taos, and Albuquerque.* New York: Simon and Schuster, Inc., 1989.

Gottdiener, M. *The Social Production of Urban Space.* Austin: University of Texas Press, 1985.

Grubb, Reba D. *Portrait of Progress: A Story of Tucson Medical Center.* Tucson, Ariz.: Raim, Inc., 1984.

Halberstam, David. *The Fifties.* New York: Villard Books, 1993.

Harte, John Bret. "A Feisty Town Grows Up." *Tucson Citizen,* June 6, 1975.

————. *Tucson, Portrait of a Desert Pueblo.* Woodland Hills, Calif.: Windsor Publications, 1980.

Hays, Samuel P. *Beauty, Health, and Permanence: Environmental Politics in the United States, 1955–1985.* New York: Cambridge University Press, 1987.

Heald, Weldon, and Phyllis Heald. "Tucson: Gracious Living in the Sun." *Arizona Highways* (Feb. 1958).

Henry, Bonnie. "Old Barrio, It's a Way of Life All But Vanished." *Arizona Daily Star,* Aug. 23, 1992, pp. E1, E5.

Hollon, W. Eugene. *The Great American Desert: Then and Now.* New York: Oxford University Press, 1966.

"Housing and Relocation: Tucson Community Renewal Program, 1969." New York: Greenleigh Associates, Inc. Special Collections.

Hummel, Don. "Annexation—North and East." Arizona Historical Society, Tucson.

————. "Annexation—South and West." Arizona Historical Society, Tucson.

————. Unprocessed MSS collection. Arizona Historical Society, Tucson.

Jackson, Kenneth. *Crabgrass Frontier: The Suburbanization of the United States.* New York: Oxford University Press, 1985.

Jervey, William H. "When the Banks Closed: Arizona's Bank Holiday of 1933." *Arizona and the West* (summer 1968): 127–52.

Johnson, William C. *The Politics of Urban Planning.* New York: Paragon House Publishers, 1989.

Johnston, R. A., S. I. Schwartz, and S. Tracy. "Growth Phasing and Resistance to Infill Development in Sacramento County." *Journal of the American Planning Association* 50 (Oct. 1984): 434–46.

Kimble, Mark. "South Tucson's No Different: It Needs More Money." *Tucson Citizen,* June 6, 1975.

Klein, David Walter. "The Downtown Planning Process: An Analysis of the Albuquerque Experience." Master's thesis in architecture, University of New Mexico, 1974.

Klein, Kerwin. "Selling the Desert." Master's thesis, University of Arizona, 1991.

Kling, Joseph M, and Prudence S. Posner, eds. *Dilemmas of Activism: Class, Community, and the Politics of Local Mobilization.* Philadelphia: Temple University Press, 1990.

Kling, Rob, Spencer Olin, and Mark Poster, eds. *Postsuburban California: The Transformation of Orange County since World War II.* Berkeley: University of California Press, 1991.

Kreutz, Douglas. "The High Life: Foothills Living Part of the American Dream." *Arizona Daily Star,* July 12, 1987.

Krueckeberg, Donald A. *Introduction to Planning History in the United States.* New Brunswick, N.J.: Center for Urban Policy Research, 1983.

Krutch, Joseph Wood. *More Lives Than One.* New York: William Sloane Associates, 1964.

———. *If You Don't Mind My Saying So.* New York: William Sloane Associates, 1964.

Lamar, Howard. "Persistent Frontier: The West in the Twentieth Century." *Western Historical Quarterly* 4 (Jan. 1973): 5–25.

Lazaroff, David. "Tucson's Canyon Oasis." *Arizona Highways* (April 1993): 5–12.

———. *Sabino Canyon: The Life of a Southwestern Oasis.* Tucson: University of Arizona Press, 1993.

Leon, Ray. Interview by author. Tucson, Arizona, July 17, 1989.

Limerick, Patricia Nelson. *Desert Passages: Encounters with the American Deserts.* Albuquerque: University of New Mexico Press, 1985.

———. *The Legacy of Conquest: The Unbroken Past of the American West.* New York: W. W. Norton & Co., 1988.

Limerick, Patricia Nelson, Clyde A. Milner III, and Charles E. Rankin, eds. *Trails: Toward a New Western History.* Lawrence: University Press of Kansas, 1991.

Littlewood, John, and Frederick Allen. "Joseph M. Montoya: Democratic Senator from New Mexico." Ralph Nader Congress Project. Washington, D.C.: Grossman Publishers, 1972.

Lockard, Peggy Hamilton. *This is Tucson.* Tucson, Ariz.: Pepper Publishing, 1983.

Logan, John, and Gordana Rabrenovic. "Neighborhood Associations: Their Issues, Their Allies, and Their Opponents." *Urban Affairs Quarterly* 26 (1990): 68–94.

Lotchin, Roger W. *Fortress California 1910–1961: From Warfare to Welfare.* New York: Oxford University Press, 1992.

Luckingham, Bradford. *The Urban Southwest: A Profile History of Albuquerque, El Paso, Phoenix, Tucson.* El Paso: Texas Western Press, 1982.

Lynch, Kevin. *The Image of the City.* Cambridge, Mass.: M.I.T. Press, 1960.

Margolis, John D. *Joseph Wood Krutch: A Writer's Life.* Knoxville: University of Tennessee Press, 1980.

"A Market Study of New Mexico." MS 112, Box I, Item 86. Center for Southwest Research, Zimmerman Library, University of New Mexico.

Marston Sallie. *Good Fences, Good Neighbors.* Tucson: University of Arizona Press, forthcoming.

McGerr, Michael E. "Is There a Twentieth-Century West?" In Cronon, Miles, and Gitlin, 239–56.

McNamara, Patrick H. *A Social Report for Metropolitan Albuquerque.* Studies in Urban Affairs, No. 16. Albuquerque Urban Observatory, 1973.

"Mean as Hell." Recording. Southwind Music (BMI).

Mees, Quentin M. "Tucson Air Pollution, 1959–1964." Engineering Experiment Station Series Report #17. College of Engineering, University of Arizona.

Meinig, D. W. *Southwest: Three Peoples in Geographical Change, 1600–1970.* New York: Oxford University Press, 1971.

Mollenkopf, John H. *The Contested City.* Princeton, N.J.: Princeton University Press, 1983.

Molotch, Harvey. "The City as Growth Machine." *American Journal of Sociology* 82 (1976): 309–30.

Mullin-Kille Tucson Arizona City Directory, 1962. Tucson: Mullin-Kille of Arizona.

Murphey, J. W. Papers. Arizona Historical Society, Tucson.

Naisbitt, John. *Megatrends: Ten New Directions Transforming Our Lives.* New York: Warner Books, 1982.

Nash, Gerald. *World War II and the West: Reshaping the Economy.* Lincoln: University of Nebraska Press, 1990.

————. *The American West in the Twentieth Century: A Short History of an Urban Oasis.* Albuquerque: University of New Mexico Press, 1973.

Nash, Roderick. *Wilderness and the American Mind.* 3d ed. New Haven: Yale University Press, 1982.

National Cancer Institute. *U.S. Cancer Mortality Rates and Trends, 1950–1979.*

Washington, D.C.: National Cancer Institute/Environmental Protection Agency Agreement on Environmental Carcinogenesis, 1983.

"Need for Renewal, A Part of the Community Renewal Program of the City of Tucson, Az. November 1968." Special Collections, University of Arizona Library.

New Mexico. *Laws of the State of New Mexico, 1939.*

———. *Laws of the State of New Mexico, 1947.*

O'Connor, Carol. *A Sort of Utopia: Scarsdale, 1881–1981.* Albany: State University of New York Press, 1984.

Officer, James E., ed. *Tucson, The Old Pueblo: A Chronology.* Tucson, Ariz.: Tucson-Pima County Historical Commission, 1979.

Olin, Spencer. "Globalization and the Politics of Locality." *Western Historical Quarterly* (May 1991).

"Only as a Community Prospers. . . ." MS 112, Box II, "Chamber of Commerce." Center for Southwest Research, Zimmerman Library, University of New Mexico.

Oppenheimer, Alan J. "The Historical Background of Albuquerque, New Mexico." Albuquerque Planning Department, June 1962. Reprinted April 1969, Urban Development Institute of the University of Albuquerque. Center for Southwest Research, Zimmerman Library, University of New Mexico.

Pedersen, Gilbert J. "The Townsite is Now Secure." *Journal of Arizona History* 11 (autumn 1970): 151–74.

"Pictorial Albuquerque." MS 112, Box I, Item 89. Center for Southwest Research, Zimmerman Library, University of New Mexico.

Plotkin, Sidney. "Enclave Consciousness and Neighborhood Activism." In Kling and Posner.

Pomeroy, Earl. "Toward a Reorientation of Western History: Continuity and Environment." *Mississippi Valley Historical Review* 41 (March 1955): 579–600.

Price, V. B. *A City at the End of the World.* Albuquerque: University of New Mexico Press, 1992.

Pyle, Ernie. "Why Albuquerque?" *New Mexico Magazine* 20 (Jan. 1942): 17.

Rabinowitz, Howard N. "Albuquerque: City at a Crossroads." In Bernard and Rice.

Radbill, Martin N. "Measuring the Quality of the Urban Landscape in the Tucson, Arizona, Central Business District." Master's thesis in geography, University of Arizona, 1968.

Richards, J. Morris. *History of the Arizona State Legislature*, Vol. 12, 1953—1954, Vol. 13, 1955—1956. Phoenix, Ariz.: Arizona Legislative Council: Arizona Department of Library, Archive and Public Records, 1990. Microform at University of Arizona Main Library in "State Documents."

Ridge, Martin. "The American West: From Frontier to Region." *New Mexico Historical Review* 64 (April 1989): 125—41

Robbins, William G. "Laying Siege to Western History." In Limerick, Milner, and Rankin.

Rosaldo, Renato, Gustav Seligmann, and Robert Calvert, eds. *Chicano: The Beginning of Bronze Power*. New York: William Morrow, 1974.

"See New Mexico From Albuquerque." MS 112, Box, uncataloged. Center for Southwest Research, Zimmerman Library, University of New Mexico.

Sheridan, Thomas. *Los Tucsonenses: 1854—1941*. Tucson: University of Arizona Press, 1986.

Simmons, Marc. *Albuquerque: A Narrative History*. Albuquerque: University of New Mexico Press, 1982.

Singer, Peter. *Animal Liberation: A New Ethics for Our Treatment of Animals*. New York: New York Review and Random House, 1975.

"Sky's the Limit." *Time*. September 6, 1993.

Sonnichsen, C. L. *Tucson: The Life and Times of an American City*. 1975. Reprint, Norman: University of Oklahoma Press, 1982.

South Tucson, City of. "Council Packets—Ordinances." City clerk's depository.

Stegner, Wallace. *The Uneasy Chair: A Biography of Bernard Devoto*. Garden City, N.Y.: Doubleday & Company, Inc., 1974.

"Step Lively, the Albuquerque Way." MS 112, Box I, Item 28. Center for Southwest Research, Zimmerman Library, University of New Mexico.

Stone, Christopher. *Should Trees Have Standing? Toward Legal Rights for Natural Objects*. New York: Avon Books, 1975.

"Telephone Directory, March 1950, for Tucson." Mountain States Telephone and Telegraph Company, 1950.

Tucson, City of. Minutes of city council meetings. Microfilm, reels 32—35.
———. "Annexations: 1905—1968." Microfilm.
———. "Annexation Index." Mimeograph.
———. "Goals for the Community." Tucson Community Goals Committee, 1966. Special Collections, University of Arizona Library.
———. "Legal Opinions, City of Tucson," 1952—1955. Special Collections, University of Arizona Library.

————. "The Pueblo Center Redevelopment Project." Citizen's Committee on Municipal Blight, 1965. Special Collections, University of Arizona Library.

————. "The Regional Plan." Tucson Planning and Zoning Commission, 1945. Special Collections, University of Arizona Library.

————. "A Workable Program for Urban Renewal, 1957." Special Collections, University of Arizona Library.

Tucson Chamber of Commerce. "The Answers to All Your Questions about Tucson, Arizona." Special Collections, University of Arizona Library.

————. "A City of Diversified Interests," 1950. Special Collections, University of Arizona Library.

————. "Come to the Growing Southwest to Tucson for Industry and A Way of Life." 1952. Special Collections, University of Arizona.

————. "Desert Vegetation Near Tucson, Arizona." 1940. Special Collections, University of Arizona Library.

————. "Facts and Figures: A General Survey of Tucson and Pima County, Arizona." 1945–1956. Special Collections, University of Arizona Library.

————. "Facts for Prospective Residents of Tucson, 1956." Special Collections, University of Arizona Library.

————. "The Guest Informant, 1952–1953." Special Collections, University of Arizona Library.

————. "Healthful Tucson . . . The Sunshine City, Where Health and Recreation Go Hand in Hand." 1956. Special Collections, University of Arizona Library.

————. "Manufacturing Industry List." 1958. Special Collections, University of Arizona Library.

————. "1929 Election of Officers." Arizona Historical Society, Tucson.

————. "1949 Directors Nominations." Arizona Historical Society, Tucson.

————. "Private Schools of Tucson, Arizona." 1952. Special Collections, University of Arizona Library.

————. "The Saguaro National Monument." 1933. Special Collections, University of Arizona Library.

————. "The Sunshine City, Tucson, Arizona: Accommodations." Special Collections, University of Arizona Library.

————. "Tomorrow is Today in Tucson." 1954. Special Collections, University of Arizona Library.

————. "The Truth About Water in Tucson." 1953. Special Collections, University of Arizona Library.

————. "Tucson . . . a city, an opportunity, a way of life." 1958. Special Collections, University of Arizona Library.

————. "Tucson Chamber of Commerce Annual Dinner." 1951. Special Collections, University of Arizona Library.

————. "Tucson Chamber of Commerce Newsletter." 1962. Special Collections, University of Arizona Library.

————. "Tucson Progress." Special Collections, University of Arizona Library.

————. "Twenty-Fifth Anniversary Banquet Program," 1921. Arizona Historical Society, Tucson.

Tucson Citizen. 1974–75.

Tucson Sunshine Climate Club. "Subscription Campaign, 1941." Special Collections, University of Arizona Library.

————. "Sunshine News: Monthly Bulletin of the Tucson Sunshine Climate Club." 1950. Special Collections, University of Arizona Library.

————. "Tucson Sunshine Climate Club, 1941." Special Collections, University of Arizona Library.

"The Tucson Visual Environment." Special Collections, University of Arizona Library.

Turner, Frederick Jackson. *The Frontier in American History.* Edited by Wilbur Jacobs. Tucson: University of Arizona Press, 1986.

"University Heights, Albuquerque, New Mexico." 1906. MS 112, Box I, Item 13. Center for Southwest Research, Zimmerman Library, University of New Mexico.

"Urbanization of Tucson, 1940–1990." Oral History Project. Arizona Historical Society, Tucson.

U.S. Department of Commerce, Bureau of the Census. *Boundary and Annexation Study, 1970–1973.* Washington, D.C., 1975.

————. *Census of the Population, 1950,* Vol. 1.

————. *Census of the Population, 1960,* Vol. 1.

U.S. Department of Health and Human Services. *Seer Report: Cancer Incidence and Mortality in the United States, 1973–1981.* Washington, D.C.: National Institutes of Health, 1984.

Webb, Walter Prescott. *The Great Plains.* Lincoln: University of Nebraska Press, 1931.

White, Richard. "Trashing the Trails." In Limerick, Milner, and Rankin.

"Why Albuquerque, New Mexico, Will Make You Well." MS 112, Box I, Item

22. Center for Southwest Research, Zimmerman Library, University of New Mexico.

Wiley, Peter, and Robert Gottlieb. *Empires in the Sun: The Rise of the New American West*. Tucson: University of Arizona Press, 1982.

Wilken, D. C., and D. R. Iams. "Characteristics and Attitudes of Pima County Residents Related to Urban Expansion Into Rural Areas." *Landscape Journal* 9 (spring 1990): 42–46.

Wingfield, Clyde J. *Urbanization in the Southwest*. El Paso: Texas Western Press, 1968.

Wolfe, Tom. *The Right Stuff*. New York: Farrar, Straus, and Giroux, 1979.

Wood, Robert Turner. "The Transformation of Albuquerque, 1945–1972." Ph.D. diss., University of New Mexico, 1980.

Worster, Donald. *Rivers of Empire: Water, Aridity, and the Growth of the American West*. New York: Pantheon Books, 1985.

INDEX

Arizona Municipal League, 43
  See also Tucson, annexation laws,
  "tin–pipe bill"
Arizona-Sonora Desert Museum, 72,
  82
Arizona Supreme Court, 55–56
Arledge, Judge R. F. Deacon, 116
Army Corps of Engineers, 20
Asta, Ron. *See* Pima County, board of
  supervisors
Athearn, Robert, 19
Atkinson, W. W. *See* Albuquerque,
  city commissioners
Atrisco land grant, 125, 134–135
  board of trustees, 135
Atsha, Janet, 102

Baca, Rudy, 137
Barber, Mary. *See* annexations, Tuc-
  son, Freedom Homes
Baughman, Morris F., 41–42
Bel-Aire (proposed village), 118–
  119, 121, 123
Bellamah, Dale. *See* developers, in
  Albuquerque
Benitez, Frank. *See* City of South
  Tucson, mayors
Bennett, Dick. *See* Albuquerque, city
  planning commission
Bernalillo County Commission,
  118, 125
  Gerald Cornelius, 128
Bernalillo County Courthouse, 97
Bimson, Walter R., 106
Boorstin, Daniel, 14, 18, 26
"bottomless towers," 79
Broome, C. C. *See* Albuquerque,
  Chamber of Commerce
Buchanan, Harry L. *See* Tucson, city
  attorneys

Buddecke, Martha, 143
Bufkin, Don, 7, 14, 68, 71
Burr-Brown Industrial Research
  Company, 87
Butterfield route (proposed free-
  way), 90

Calhoun, L. M., 56
Candelaria, Jack, 145
Canning, Gordon. *See* Tucson;
  neighborhoods, subdivisions;
  Ocotillo Park
Caplin, Harvey, 109
Carmichael, Ken, 111
Central Area Study. *See* Albuquerque,
  planning department, studies
Central Arizona Project, 77
Central Business District Study: Land
  Uses, 1957. *See* Albuquerque, planning department, studies
Chavez, Denis, 133
City of South Tucson
  city attorney: Harry O. Juliani,
    55
  city clerk: Elizabeth Martiny,
    57
  city council, 55–56
  mayors
    Benitez, Frank, 58
    Gonzales, Pat, 58
    Knipnis, Sam, 53
  1978 lawsuit, 90–91
"consensus history," 15, 39, 47,
  107, 113, 167
conservatism, 8, 168
  in Albuquerque, 107, 109, 140,
    142
  in Tucson, 8, 31, 49, 62–63, 65
Cordova, John. *See* Albuquerque,
  city sanitarian

Flying V Ranch. *See* Shields family
freeways
    in Albuquerque, 104
    in Tucson, 71, 89–90, 104

Gadsden Purchase, 167
Garland, A. P. *See* Albuquerque,
    building inspection team
Gates Lear Jet, 87
Godfrey, Arthur, 75
Goldsmith, John. *See* Volunteers in
    Service to America
Goldwater, Barry, 4, 63, 65
Gonzales, Pat. *See* City of South Tuc-
    son, mayors
Gordon, Larry. *See* Albuquerque,
    building inspection team
Grass Roots Committee. *See* Univer-
    sity of New Mexico
"The Great American Desert," 74
Great Society, 14, 61, 65, 68
    See also Model Cities
Guthrie, R. R. *See* Tucson, right-of-
    way agent

Hannett, A. T., 115–116, 119
Hawkins, Warren, 143
Hays, Samuel, 71–72
Hedges, J. W., 117
Heights Businessmen's Association,
    107
Henry, Bonnie, 68
Hensley, George, 126–127
    See also Rural Property Owners
    Association
Hispanics
    in Albuquerque city government,
    162
    in New Mexico state govern-
    ment, 132–133

in Tucson city government, 50–
    51
See also Albuquerque, population,
    Hispanic; Sheridan, Thomas, *Los
    Tucsonenses*
Hoffman, Sam. *See* developers, in
    Albuquerque
Hoffman City (Snow Vista), 124,
    135
Hontas, James. *See* Albuquerque,
    Citizen Improvement Committee
Hughes Aircraft Company, 6, 14,
    74, 87
    and trichloroethylene pollution,
    92
Hummel, Don. *See* Tucson, mayors

IBM, 87
individualism
    in Albuquerque, 113, 141, 148
    in Krutch's critique, 80
    in Tucson, 37–38, 56–57
    in the culture of the West, 4

Jacome family, 51
Joesler, Josias, 83
Johnstone, Don. *See* Albuquerque,
    water board

Kennedy, John F., 62, 64
Killgloom Gazette, 100
Kimball, William F., 25
Kinney, Harry. *See* Albuquerque, city
    mayors
Kirtland Air Force Base, 6, 95
Klein, Kerwin, "Selling the Desert,"
    76
Knipnis, Sam. *See* City of South Tuc-
    son, mayors
Kreutz, Douglas, 85

New Mexico Supreme Court, 115
new western history, 7, 9
New York Times, 75
North Albuquerque Association,
107
North Barelas Community Development Association. *See* Albuquerque, neighborhood associations

Oden, Clyde, 103
Office for Economic Opportunity,
143
Old Albuquerque Society Hall, 116,
118
Old Pueblo, 21, 50–51, 64, 66, 68,
133
Old Pueblo Club, 25
Old Town. *See* Albuquerque, Old
Town
Old Tucson (theme park and movie
set), 74
Old Tucson Development Company,
76
"Old West," traditions and marketing, 21–22, 73, 151
Olmstead, Frederic Law, 158
Oro Valley, Arizona, 57, 90

Padillas, Blaise, 137
Paleck, B., 89
Paradise Hills, New Mexico, 105,
154
"partial solutions." *See* Krutch, Joseph Wood
Peace Corps Training Center, 137
Petroglyph National Monument,
160–163
Phelps-Dodge Mining Company, 26
Phoenix, Arizona, 48, 55, 71, 92,
149

air pollution, 92
as model of sprawl, 92
Pima Association of Governments,
90
Pima Canyon, 88
Pima County
  Air Quality Control District, 92
  board of supervisors, 22, 40, 46,
    55, 77, 88–89
    Asta, Ron, and "Astacrats,"
      88
    Yetman, David, 89
  Parks Advisory Committee, 72
  planning and zoning commission, 26–27, 40, 81
pollution, 7, 77, 92, 155, 156, 164
  in Albuquerque
    air pollution, 155
    air and water pollution, 164
    and proposed paper mill,
      156
  in Tucson
    air pollution, 77
    American Atomics Co. and
      tritium emissions, 92
    pollen counts, 77
    trichloroethylene, 92
Pomeroy, Earl, 6
Price, V. B., *City at the End of the World,*
  7, 134, 157–158, 163
Project 1970-Plus. *See* Albuquerque,
  annexation plan, 1964
Property Owners Protective Association (POPA), 120, 136
Pyle, Ernie, 101–102, 110, 148

Rabinowitz, Howard, 7–8
Redd, C. K. (Budd), 141
Rio Grande Council of Governments, 156

South Tucson Chamber of Commerce, 58
South Tucson Lions Club, 58
Southern Pacific Railroad, 5, 11, 41
Southwest Sun Country Association, 103
"Southwest Sun Cast," 149
Southwest Valley Booster Club, 122–123
Sprague, Mrs. T. D. *See* Tucson NAACP
Steinfeld, Albert, and Company, 20
Sunshine Climate Club. *See* Tucson, Sunshine Climate Club
Szerlip, Sidney, 38

Thurman, Albert R., Superior Court judge (Nogales), 55
Tingley, Clyde. *See* Albuquerque, city commissioners
topography, 9, 11, 12–13 (fig. 1), 37, 45, 78, 96 (fig. 10), 165 (fig. 13)
  basin and range, 4, 72, 77, 149
  mesas, 104, 106, 134, 150, 156, 159, 164
  mountains, 3, 11, 23, 70, 72, 83, 110, 149
Torres, Mrs. Elva B. *See* Tucson, Committee to Save La Placita
tourism, 3, 6
  in Albuquerque, 102–103, 151, 160
    Old Town Plaza, 105, 142–143
    "Southwest Sun Cast," 149
  in Santa Fe, 165–166
  in Tucson, 14, 72, 92
    and the barrios, 21
    during 1920s, 19, 70

and marketing western images, 21, 73–75
Treet, Martin A., 115
Trigg, Ralph. *See* Albuquerque, city commissioners
tuberculosis sanatoriums, 6, 14, 100
Tucson
  annexation coordination, Ray Leon, 47
  annexation laws, 41, 43, 55
    Ordinance 1532, 43
    "tin–pipe bill," 43
  annexations, 11, 37, 41–48, 81
    Amphitheater, 45–46
    Country Club Manor, 42
    Desert Highland, 42
    Flowing Wells, 45–46
    Freedom Homes, 45
    North Campbell, 41
    Southside, 44, 46
    Winterhaven, 45
  assistant city manager
    S. Lenwood Schorr, 26, 61, 63–64
  Bank Holiday of 1933, 20
  barrios, 21, 28, 48, 49, 51, 73, 90
    Barrio Historico, 66, 68, 91
    El Rio, 59
    Rio Nuevo, 91
    Snob Hollow, 91
    as "blighted," 28, 51, 59–69, 91
  Board of Realtors, 37–39
  Chamber of Commerce, 15, 17, 19–20, 23–24, 37, 39, 101
    Al Coudron, 20
    Industrial Development Department, 22–23

ABOUT THE AUTHOR

MICHAEL F. LOGAN, an assistant professor of history at Oklahoma State University, Stillwater, received his Ph.D. in United States history from the University of Arizona in 1994. His interest in the intersection of environmental perceptions and urban lifestyles motivated the research that culminated in this book. Logan's interest in the urban West stems in part from having witnessed the growth of Tucson, Arizona, from a modest-sized city to a metropolis.

Logan is currently researching the environmental history of the Santa Cruz River, to be published by the University of Arizona Press.